HOW TO BE A SUCCESSFUL
TECHNICAL TRAINER

How to Be a Successful Technical Trainer

Core Skills for Instructor Certification

Terrance Keys

Andrew R. Zeff

McGraw-Hill
New York   San Francisco   Washington, D.C.
Auckland   Bogotá   Caracas   Lisbon   London
Madrid   Mexico City   Milan   Montreal   New Delhi
San Juan   Singapore   Sydney   Tokyo   Toronto

McGraw-Hill

A Division of The McGraw-Hill Companies

Copyright © 2000 by The McGraw-Hill Companies, Inc. All rights reserved. Printed in the United States of America. Except as permitted under the United States Copyright Act of 1976, no part of this publication may be reproduced or distributed in any form or by any means, or stored in a data base or retrieval system, without the prior written permission of the publisher.

1 2 3 4 5 6 7 8 9 0 DOC/DOC 0 5 4 3 2 1 0

ISBN 0-07-213033-4

The sponsoring editor for this book was John Read, the associate developmental editor was Franny Kelly, and the production manager was Clare Stanley. It was set in Century Schoolbook by D&G Limited, LLC.

Printed and bound by R. R. Donnelley & Sons Company.

McGraw-Hill books are available at special quantity discounts to use as premiums and sales promotions, or for use in corporate training programs. For more information, please write to the Director of Special Sales, Professional Publishing, McGraw-Hill, Two Penn Plaza, New York, NY 10121-2298. Or contact your local bookstore.

To my wife, Jennifer, for her ongoing support and encouragement throughout this project!

Terry

To my wife Eve, for her creative contributions and continuing support, and my daughter Savannah, who is my inspiration.

Andrew

CONTENTS

Contents

Contents

PREFACE

The world is changing so rapidly that it is difficult for business, industry and education to keep up with it. On-the-job training and life long learning have become a standard component in the work place and the need for competent trainers in the technical and professional development arenas has never been greater. This book is designed to assist anyone who desires (or is required) to teach others by covering the skills that are necessary for success in this profession.

Improving your teaching or training skills can be accomplished in a variety of ways. Feedback from colleagues or students provides a trainer with invaluable feedback, yet being proactive about your training skills is critical to becoming a good or even better trainer. This can be accomplished by understanding and implementing the training standards discussed in this book.

The training industry standards have been established by the International Board of Standards for Training, Performance and Instruction. They are called the ibstpi standards (listed next.)

14 Instructor Competencies of the ibstpi Standards

1. Analyze course materials and learner information.
2. Assure preparation of the instructional site.
3. Establish and maintain instructor credibility.
4. Manage the learning environment.
5. Demonstrate effective communication skills.
6. Demonstrate effective presentation skills.
7. Demonstrate effective questioning skills and techniques.
8. Respond appropriately to learners' needs for clarification or feedback.
9. Provide positive reinforcement and motivational incentives.
10. Use instructional methods appropriately.
11. Use media effectively.
12. Evaluate learner performance.
13. Evaluate delivery of instruction.
14. Report evaluation information.

The structure of this book is based on the standards and each chapter focuses on one of them. This book is intended to provide a solid understanding of the specific skills and tasks that you must master in order to become proficient in each of these standards.

If you master these competencies, you will also be prepared to apply for the Certified Technical Trainer certification, a cross-industry credential for technical and professional development trainers. The CTT certification also fulfills some of the requirements in vendor specific certification as well. (Chapter 15 discusses this in greater depth.)

These standards are the basis for the CTT exam and scoring process. If you can understand and implement these standards successfully then you should be able to be successfully complete the CTT certification requirements. This book will to prepare you for the CTT certification by walking you through these standards or competencies. You need to be able to

1. Learn and understand the 14 competencies for the CTT computer-based knowledge exam.

2. Learn how you can implement the competencies into your training so that you can demonstrate them in an actual instructional performance (a 20-minute videotape must be submitted).

This book will serve as an ongoing reference guide throughout your career as a trainer. We strongly believe that the ibstpi standards are THE training benchmarks and therefore are a wonderful framework for all good training. This applies to all types of professional trainers . . . technical, professional development skills, mechanical and scientific.

If you think of "the standards," (as we will refer to them) as training benchmarks then it makes sense that as you implement them or strive to excel in these areas your training skills will improve, and therefore your success as a trainer. In examining the standards we give you training tips, situational examples and practical advise, all with the goal of making this book a good resource for trainers. We believe that if you successfully practice the standards you will be a successful trainer and if you are a successful trainer chances are you implement all of the ibstpi standards already.

ACKNOWLEDGMENTS

A couple of people deserve acknowledgement for their significant contributions to this work. Thanks to Andrew Zeff for working with me as a co-author on this project and contributing his experience and expertise. Thanks to Jeff Thompson for his assistance with artwork and for modeling for several of the pictures. A special thanks to Gail Kipp, for her technical review of the work as it relates to the CTT certification and for all of her moral support throughout the project.

I also greatly appreciate the dedication and efforts of the staff at McGraw-Hill (specifically Francis Kelly, Jennifer Perillo, & Regina Brooks) and thank them for their willingness to work through any roadblocks that arose and to see this work to completion.

I also appreciate the contributions and feedback from Judith Lauter (The Chauncey Group) and Jewel Bishop (Novell).

Thanks! Terry

Andrew would also like to thank Eve Lempert for all of her advice and support in the writing and editing process.

HOW TO BE A SUCCESSFUL
TECHNICAL TRAINER

Analyzing Course Materials and Learner Information

Introduction

By the end of this chapter, you will be able to perform the following tasks:

- Analyze course information and learners' backgrounds
  - Identify course objectives
  - Discover the learner's experience, background, and motives for attending the course

- Adjust the course based on information
  - Course objectives
  - Schedule
  - Instructional methods

Competency 1 of the ibstpi[1] Standards centers on the trainer's ability to analyze the course materials and to evaluate the learners, then make appropriate adjustments to the class based on this information. Preparation is a theme that will repeat itself frequently throughout this book. To be an effective trainer, you must take the time to properly prepare for each course that you teach. This competency deals exclusively with preparing for your students' various backgrounds, skill levels, and experiences.

Preparation includes checking and reviewing many aspects of a class that are interrelated. One of the most significant factors is an intimate knowledge of the course materials and the audience for which they are designed. In a perfect world, all of the students in the class will have the appropriate prerequisite knowledge and will learn at the same rate. The training room is rarely a perfect world, however. Students will have diverse backgrounds, levels of knowledge, and reasons for attending the class. In order to teach effectively, you must understand these differences and prepare for them. The more preparation that you do before the class begins, the less confusion and stress there will be during the course. Therefore, you must find out as much about the students as possible before the class begins so that you are prepared to address their individual needs and determine what modifications you might have to make to the course material in order to accommodate the learners.

This chapter will identify a number of factors that might affect the success of your course. Keep these points in mind as you continue through this book. You will discover that all of the competencies are inter-

---

[1]International Board of Standards for Training, Performance and Instruction

related, and mastering all of them is necessary in order to be a competent trainer.

Reviewing Course Materials

The first step in preparing for a course is to develop a strong mastery of the skills and concepts that are covered. This book assumes that you have already completed this step and that you are an expert in the subject area that you teach. If you have not completed this step, you will not be able to train others—and you must master the required skills before continuing. Given this assumption, your role as the trainer is to effectively teach the skills to the students.

Course Objectives

Every course that is taught should have a clear set of objectives that determines the content, activities, and assessment tools that are included in the course. Objectives should be measurable skills that can be assessed. For example, if you are teaching a course on Internet search skills, one objective might be that by the end of the class, students will be able to access a particular search engine and set up parameters that search for a specific phrase, including appropriate capitalization. Another objective might be that the students will be able to look up the current weather for a given city. Notice that each objective starts with the phrase, "The students will be able to . . ." Each of these objectives is measurable and requires the students to learn specific skills. Clear and measurable objectives are a necessity for every course.

When preparing to teach a course, you should review the course objectives and see how the activities that are built into the course assist the students with achieving the objectives. Each module of the course should have a specific relationship to the course objectives. The learning activities that the students work through must fit into this relationship.

NOTE: *Everything you do throughout a course should be related to achieving the course objectives.*

The trainer's role in the development of the course will depend on the purpose and origin of the material. You can teach two types of courses: prepackaged courses, which others develop, or courses that you develop yourself. Most courses that are part of a technical certification will most likely be developed by instructional designers or be based on a specific list of skills that must be mastered. You will be expected to adhere closely to the structure and content included in the course.

NOTE: *You must follow the instructional design of a prepackaged course in order to maintain its integrity and to meet the instructional objectives.*

We do not mean that you cannot make certain adjustments based on your audience. Types of adjustments will be discussed in depth throughout this book. If you design the course yourself, then you are free to modify the course in any way necessary in order to adapt to the user's needs. The point is that you must always consider the objectives of the course, any certification requirements with which the course is associated, and the needs of the students. Balancing these factors is what makes training a challenging and exciting profession.

Throughout this book, you will learn a variety of instructional methods and activities that can be incorporated into your training program. At this point, we will only discuss course modifications that are based on the information that you gather prior to the course. Chapter 4, "Managing the Learning Environment," will cover more strategies for handling situations that arise throughout the training session, and Chapter 10, "Using Instructional Methods Appropriately," will address a variety of methods that you can use. When determining which strategy is best, your primary responsibility is to assist the students with meeting the objectives of the course.

Analyzing the Learners

To understand your students, you will find it helpful to gather as much information as possible about them. If you are teaching an intermediate or advanced training session that requires a base level of knowledge and some of your students do not have that knowledge, you have an extremely difficult situation. Your best plan is to solicit as much information as possible about each student. This information will also be useful when we look at the other ibstpi competencies. For example, understanding the students and relating the course examples to their experiences is a good method for establishing and maintaining your credibility (refer to Chapter 3, "Establishing and Maintaining Instructor Credibility"). Figure 1-1 illustrates the diverse backgrounds that are possible in each class.

Gathering the Information

Collecting information about each student is often a challenge and can require a significant time commitment. If time allows, you can send pre-training participant surveys to each student to gather this information. Try to coordinate your efforts with anyone who handles the registration process

Figure 1-1
Types of learners

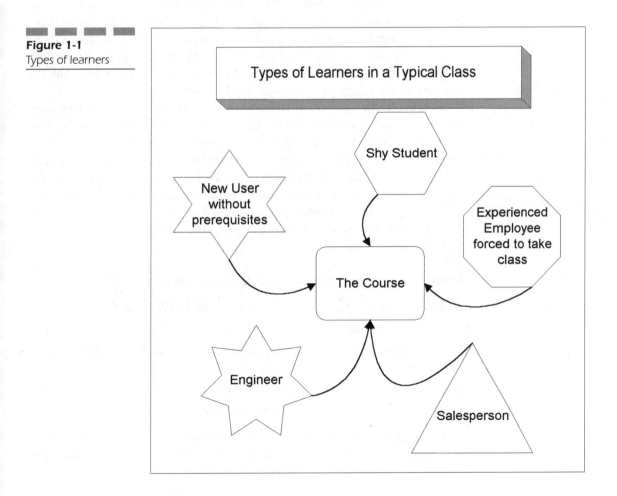

for your courses. If you can incorporate your pre-course survey into the registration form, you will have a much higher number of responses than when you send the survey separately. You will always have students who do not provide you with the information that you request. Accept this fact, and use the information that you are able to gather to assist you with your preparation.

NOTE: *If a participant does not respond to the pre-course survey, you cannot assume that he or she has the prerequisites for the course. You should assume and plan for the worst, and you will be pleasantly surprised at best.*

Another method that you can try, if the course is being delivered to a specific group or organization, is to contact the employer of the group. This technique might not give you specific information about each student, but it will enable you to learn about the characteristics of the group as a whole. Contacting the employer also provides a good chance to confirm that the group is aware of any prerequisites for the course.

You cannot always survey the students before they arrive. In this case, you should provide information with the course registration material that will enable participants to better determine whether a particular course is appropriate for them. You can accomplish this task by providing a self-assessment test that they can take before registering for a course. Consider an example of teaching a course on one of the programs in the Microsoft Office suite. If the students need to know how to navigate the Windows environment, you could include the following self-assessment questions with the course description:

Basic Windows Knowledge Self-Assessment

- What is one method for starting a program in Windows 95?
- How do you select an icon with the mouse?
- What is the difference between single-clicking and double-clicking the left mouse button?
- How do you minimize a program window?
- How do you maximize a program window?

You would include instructions with this self-assessment, indicating that you expect the students to have mastered these skills before the class begins. Self-assessments are not a foolproof method for ensuring that the students will meet the requirements of the course, but they will help minimize the problems.

Keep in mind that you will not always be able to gather all of the information that you need prior to class. Your initial presentation at the start of the training session is the ideal time to collect any of the information that you were unable to gather prior to the class. In Chapter 4, we will discuss initial presentation strategies in depth.

Types of Information

While ideally you would like to know as much information as possible about each student, the following items are most useful:

- Job responsibilities
- Background
- Skill level
- Reason(s) for attending the course

You should ask each student to list his or her job responsibilities and any specific projects that he or she is or will be involved in that might benefit from the material taught in the course. You want to learn as much as possible about what the students currently do.

The students' backgrounds related to the topic of the course are also useful information and will complement the knowledge that you gather concerning their jobs. You want to discover what the challenges will be for each student. Try to determine whether they are familiar with the environment in which you will be working (Windows 95, Macintosh, and so on) and with the topic (spreadsheets, professional development, and so on).

The students' skill levels refer to how competent they are with the topic. This factor is most important when the course covers intermediate or advanced material but is relevant whenever there is a base level of knowledge required to succeed in the course. This question might include a list of specific skills or proficiencies with a place for the student to rate his or her level of comfort. If there are prerequisites for this course, clearly stating them in this section might prevent under-prepared students from registering for the course.

The reason a student is taking the course will give you insight into his or her level of interest and motivation for learning the material. This information might also assist you with identifying any potential problem students who do not want to be there. We address the topic of responding appropriately to various types of students in Chapter 4.

If you can gather this information about each of your students, you will start the class with a strong sense of their strengths and weaknesses and will be well prepared to address their individual needs.

Evaluation of Information

Once you have gathered the information, you need to evaluate it in relation to the course that you are teaching. In this section, we will discuss the types of information that you can gather and discuss possible adjustments that you might need to make in order to accommodate your students.

By gathering information about each student's job responsibilities, background, skill level, and reason for attending, you can develop a profile of the type of students that will be in your class. While it is dangerous to automatically stereotype students based on their backgrounds, it is useful to make some generalizations about different types of students. You should not automatically assume that students will behave in a certain way, but you can be prepared for any behavior if you think about the types of people that you might have in your classes. Having made this statement, make sure that you assess the validity of these generalizations before you act on them.

Job Responsibilities

A student's job responsibilities will have a significant impact on what he or she hopes to gain from the class. This knowledge will enable you to use examples and exercises that are directly related to the student's job, which will assist him or her with relating to the information and internalizing the knowledge. This technique is especially helpful when the course covers complex and involved tasks.

NOTE: *Students will "stick with it" and strive to master the material if they can see the direct application of the information to their work.*

Identifying the students' job responsibilities will also enable you to emphasize the functions and features that are most useful to them. Consider the following scenario:

> You are teaching a course on word processing to a group of technical editors and another course (same subject) to a group from the sales department. You have to decide which software features you should address. The technical editors might be interested in the options for tracking changes to a document, which will enable them to easily identify modifications between versions of a document. The sales department might frequently be sending mass mailings to potential customers and would be interested in the merge features.

Identifying the students' needs and interests ahead of time is the only way to ensure that you can address these needs and that the course is appropriate for the students.

Background

Each student's background will affect his or her frame of reference, which determines how well he or she will relate to and understand associations that you make between the material you are covering and similar topics. For example, cases exist where children cannot determine the time from a clock with hands because they are only used to seeing digital clocks. If your topic includes examples with clocks, those students might miss the point of the exercise completely because of this weakness. Some analogies are related to a particular generation, and being aware of this fact can have a significant impact on your course. Therefore, when looking at the students' backgrounds, you should try to identify their frames of reference. Consider the following scenario:

> You are teaching students how to use a new e-mail system. You decide to ask them questions about their experience with the operating system and the prior e-mail programs. If you know that their previous experience is with a text-based e-mail system and that they are not familiar with Windows, then you know that they should understand the concept of e-mail but might have difficulty with the graphical environment. If you discover that they are proficient with Windows but have never heard of e-mail, then your training focus will be quite different.

The approximate age of the students can also be useful information. A student's age by itself is not a determining factor when analyzing a student's abilities and skill sets, but the average age of your class might help you decide on appropriate examples and analogies that you will use during instruction. You also might find it helpful to identify a group's level of comfort with the technology that you are teaching. Consider the fact that current high school students have never known a time in their lives when computers were not commonplace. The use of cellular phones, pagers, and Automatic Teller Machines (ATMs) is second nature to most younger people, while in many homes without children, the Video Cassette Recorders (VCRs) are still blinking "12:00." In technical courses that have prerequisites, this issue should not exist; however, if you are teaching an introduction to computers class to young adults and another course (same topic) to senior citizens, your pace and examples would be considerably different.

Another area of background information that will reveal a lot about the students is the type of field in which they work. Consider the stereotype that people often make about engineers or "techies." People who have these occupations are often extremely technical, detail-oriented people who want the information that they need in order to do their work without any extra "fluff." They often have a strong technology background and pick up new concepts quickly. They will want to know why something needs to be done a certain way and will expect you to be able to answer their questions. They are used to talking in technical terms and are not overwhelmed by them. While this stereotype does not apply to everyone who is an engineer, these traits fit many of them.

NOTE: *If you know that you will be teaching a group such as this one, you should ask them for examples of the things that they want to learn so that you are prepared for their particular questions.*

Learn as much as possible about the background of your students. This information should factor into your thinking when you plan a lesson.

Skill Levels

Knowing the skill level of each student related specifically to the topic of the course is the most important information that you should gather. This knowledge helps you make appropriate modifications to the lesson, including your selection of examples and exercises.

If you discover that you have students who are under-prepared for the lesson, you will have to determine the appropriate course of action. If prerequisites exist for the course and a student has not met these requirements, the best thing you can do for the student and for the rest of the class —and for you—is to recommend for the student to take another more appropriate class to prepare for this one. This technique prevents the student's weaknesses from becoming a detriment to the rest of the class's progress and does not set up the student to fail. If this option is not possible, you will need to inform the student that he or she does not meet the prerequisites. Warn them that the course must progress at a certain rate in order to cover all of the materials and that they might need to do extra work outside of class in order to succeed.

You will also have students in your classes who already know some of the material. They might need the course for certification or to learn the new options in the latest version of the software. These students also need to understand that the pace of the class is based on the objectives and that you might spend time on information with which they are already familiar. Try to provide them with extra information to satisfy their needs while you cover the material for the rest of the class.

We will discuss more of these strategies in Chapter 4. The key point is that by identifying the students' skill levels ahead of time, you can prepare for whatever situation arises.

Reason(s) for Attending Training

The information that you gather in these areas can significantly impact a student's rate of progress in the course. The student's reason(s) for attending the course will most likely determine his or her attitude. The following list includes many of the reasons why a person might attend a course:

- To acquire a new skill for his or her current job
- To enhance skills for future opportunities
- For the joy of learning
- To fulfill a requirement for certification
- To learn about new features of a software application
- To meet the demands of his or her employer

Each of these reasons can determine the student's motivation and receptiveness to learning. All students fit into two categories: those who want to be there, and those who do not. If they want to be in the class, they will be more open-minded than those who are forced to attend. Your job will be to show each student how the material is relevant to them and describe ways in which the information will assist them with their work.

Adjusting the Course

Once you have gathered and analyzed information about the students, you have to decide which modifications are appropriate. Every course should include the following components (among others):

- Course objectives
- Course schedule
- Instructional methods
- Examples

You can make many modifications to a course in order to address individual students' needs, and throughout this book we will address many modifications that you can make to each component of a course.

Course Objectives

The course objectives are the specific tasks or knowledge that you expect the students to master by the completion of the course. Figure 1-2 illustrates several examples of course objectives.

If the course is part of a certification process or is "prepackaged," you should not change the course objectives without consulting the instructional designer of the course first. If you have developed the course to address a client's need, then you should consult the client in the develop-

Figure 1-2
Course objectives

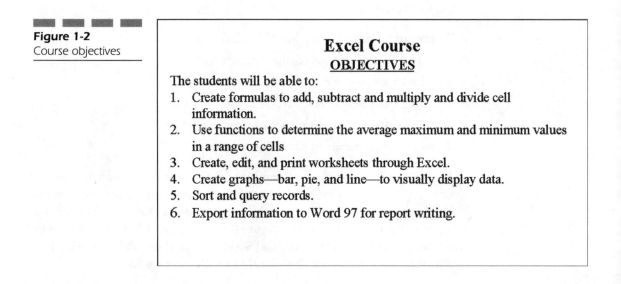

Excel Course
OBJECTIVES

The students will be able to:
1. Create formulas to add, subtract and multiply and divide cell information.
2. Use functions to determine the average maximum and minimum values in a range of cells
3. Create, edit, and print worksheets through Excel.
4. Create graphs—bar, pie, and line—to visually display data.
5. Sort and query records.
6. Export information to Word 97 for report writing.

ment of the objectives. If you discover that it is not possible for specific students to meet the objectives because of a lack of prerequisite knowledge, then those students need training to meet the prerequisites before attending the class.

NOTE: *The objectives are the one component of the course that you should not change without prior consent from the vendor, certification group, or employer.*

We do not mean that you cannot add additional objectives in order to address the learners' needs and interests. You just need to be careful that you do not remove any required objectives.

Course Schedule

The course schedule is the road map that you and your students will follow throughout the course. You can often modify the course schedule to address a group's strengths and weaknesses. Each class might vary in the time that is needed to complete a specific component of a course, and you can modify the pace accordingly.

NOTE: *Be careful that you do not remove required material from the schedule to make more time for other topics.*

You should base the pace of the class on the average students so that you address the needs of the majority of the class. If you discover that the students do need more time on a specific topic, you will have to evaluate the content and determine whether you can omit any optional material. You might have to try to create opportunities for students who are behind by offering assistance during breaks or at the end of the day. As long as you are careful about maintaining the integrity of the course, based on the objectives, certification requirements, and expectations of the students, adjustments to the schedule and course length are the best ways to accommodate the need for additional instruction.

Instructional Methods

We will discuss in depth the appropriate use of instructional methods in Chapter 10, "Using Instructional Methods Appropriately." An effective instructor always has several methods ready for teaching a topic that will address each student's needs. You can use a variety of methods to teach a particular topic, and your audience will help determine the most appropriate technique. Recall the stereotype of engineers and techies that we discussed previously in this chapter. This type of group might be more receptive to short lectures on the details, with handouts to read later if needed, and exercises that they work through independently (rather than having instructor-led, step-by-step demonstrations that they must sit through, followed by group work). Your goal is to select a learner-centered instructional method that best suits the needs of the particular audience.

Examples

We already discussed the fact that the examples you use in your presentations and exercises should be related to the students, so that they can see the direct application to their work. By analyzing your students' backgrounds, this task will be easy.

As you read the rest of this book and study each of the competencies, you will learn a variety of methods for engaging the students and meeting their individual needs. By analyzing the students, you can determine the appropriate modification(s). Always keep the needs of each of your students in mind and use this information to create the best possible learning environment for your students.

SUMMARY ■■ ■ ■ ■ ■ ■ ■ ■

One of the greatest challenges of the instructor is to address the needs of the individuals in his or her classes. You must always remember that each student is unique and brings to class strengths and weaknesses that you must identify and for which you must prepare. The key to being prepared for this task is to gather as much information as possible about each student, then see how the course materials need to be modified in order to meet the particular group's needs. Preparation is a trainer's greatest asset. If you are prepared, you will be able to solve most issues that will arise during your classes. The first step to being prepared is to know the course materials and the audience.

QUESTIONS

There might be multiple correct answers for some questions. The answers are located at the end of the chapter.

1. When is it acceptable to change the course objectives?

    a. Never

    b. If you know that the students are under-prepared and cannot meet these objectives

    c. Only after consultation with the designer of the course

    d. Whenever you feel a change is appropriate

    e. None of the above

2. What information should you solicit regarding the students to aid in planning the course?

    a. Marital status

    b. Prior experience with the subject matter

    c. Gender

    d. Job responsibilities

    e. All of the above

3. What should you do if you discover that a student does not have the prerequisites for the course?

    a. Remove him or her from the class immediately.

    b. Tell the student that you will assist him or her as much as you can, but without the prerequisite knowledge, he or she might have difficulty completing the objectives of the course.

    c. Modify the pace of the course to accommodate the student's needs.

    d. Ignore them.

    e. None of the above

4. Which of the following is a good example of a course objective?

   a. The students will better understand spreadsheets by the end of the course.

   b. The students will be able to add a row of numbers by the end of the class.

   c. The students might be ready for the certification test by the end of the class.

   d. The instructor will create a positive learning environment where the students will learn as much as possible.

   e. All of the above

5. Why is it useful to know a student's job responsibilities?

   a. To be able to show the student why the material will be useful to him or her

   b. To determine appropriate examples for the lesson

   c. To understand why the student is attending the class

   d. To determine appropriate modifications to the material

   e. All of the above

6. What should you do if you discover that a student has already mastered the material in the course?

   a. Determine why the student is attending the course.

   b. Ask him or her to leave the course, because the student will intimidate the other students.

   c. Provide the student with extra material so that he or she can move on while others progress at the usual pace.

   d. Accelerate the course schedule to accommodate the student's needs.

   e. All of the above

7. What components of the course can you modify in order to address learners' differences?

   a. Examples

   b. Course objectives

   c. Course schedule

   d. Instructional methods

   e. All of the above

8. When is it appropriate to modify the instructional methods used in a course?

    a. Anytime
    b. As long as the modification does not eliminate a course objective
    c. In order to accommodate diverse student backgrounds
    d. To keep the course exciting
    e. Never

9. What are course objectives?

    a. The specific skills that you expect the students to master by the end of the course
    b. The goals that the instructor plans to accomplish during the course
    c. Items that you might teach in the course
    d. The course prerequisites
    e. All of the above

10. Which of the following are effective methods for gathering information about the learners?

    a. Asking the student's employer why he or she is attending
    b. Sending pre-training questionnaires to each of the students
    c. Not worrying about it
    d. Asking the students to fill out a self-assessment form
    e. All of the above

ANSWERS

1. c
2. b and d
3. b
4. b
5. e
6. a and c
7. a, c, and d
8. b, c, and d
9. a
10. a, b, and d

Assuring Preparation of the Instructional Site

Introduction

By the end of this chapter, you will be able to perform the following tasks:

- Assess the instructional site, including the following elements:
  - Logistical arrangements
  - Schedule
  - Food
  - Support

- Assess the physical environment, including the following components:
  - Room layout
  - Lighting
  - Equipment
  - Furniture

- Determine ways to optimize the environment and minimize the distractions

Many factors help determine the success of a lesson. One of the most important (but sometimes overlooked) factors is the instructional site. Competency 2 of the ibstpi Standards requires that the instructor "assure preparation of the instructional site." In other words, the instructor is responsible for evaluating the training facilities prior to the start of the class and for identifying any potential physical and logistical problems. The instructor must then be prepared to minimize the problems and be in control of the environment.

Being familiar with the training site gives an instructor peace of mind, because he or she knows the strengths and limitations of the particular environment and can prepare to use the strengths and minimize the weaknesses. This chapter examines strategies for becoming familiar with the instructional site and discusses steps to ensure a positive learning environment.

Evaluating the Logistical Arrangements

The instructor must make all logistical arrangements before the first student walks through the door. The beginning of the session is not the time to worry about whether the training manuals have arrived or to check whether you have ordered the refreshments. At the beginning of the class, the instructor must focus on building a positive and relaxed learning environment. If the instructor is dealing with last-minute problems, the students' first impression of the session and the instructor might be negative. Proper planning and preparation are important but are often-overlooked parts of training. Logistical issues include the following items, most of which seem obvious (which is why people often overlook them):

Logistical Issues

- Session times
- Food
- Transportation/parking
- Support
- Communications

To address each issue, ask the following questions in order to ensure that you cover everything:

Logistical Questions

- Have you reserved the room for the proper time(s)?
- Have you ordered refreshments?
- When and where will the refreshments arrive?
- What are the easiest directions to the training site?
- Is parking available, and what is the cost?
- Are there signs to direct students to the proper room?
- What type of support is available in case of any emergencies?
- Where are the restrooms?
- Are phones available for students to use?
- Where is the smoking area?
- Have you communicated all of the necessary information to the students before the class?

Session Times

You must clearly communicate the start and end times for the training session when the students register for class, and you must reiterate this information at the beginning of the course. You should also make it clear that the course will begin promptly and that students who cannot attend the entire session must verify with the instructor whether they can still benefit from the class without creating a distraction and inconvenience for the rest of the students. Nothing is more frustrating for students then waiting for the instructor to "catch up" a student who is tardy. You should also verify that the training room (and any other resources) will be available at the appropriate time. If the facility is not normally open during the scheduled time or if security needs to open the facilities, make sure that you have obtained the proper clearance or keys before the session.

Food

Never underestimate the power of food. Food is an important part of most people's days, and although not directly related to most technical training, the punctuality of breaks and lunch can make or break a training session. If you state at the beginning of the session that there will be a break at 10 A.M., lunch at noon, and a second break at 3 P.M., make sure that you have the food delivered on time and that the breaks occur as scheduled. If the food will arrive at the training room, be sure that the food does not arrive too soon. This situation creates the problem of trying to maintain the students' attention while the sight and smell of the food are distracting them. Unless the material is extremely exciting, the students will find it difficult to overcome the attraction of the food. I once attended a session in which a hot lunch arrived at the training room at 11:45 A.M., and the instructor did not break until 12:30 P.M. The students were not only angry about having to wait for the food (while smelling it for 45 minutes), but the food was cold by the time they were dismissed for lunch. The rest of the session did not go too well. If you have the option, have the breaks/lunch served in a separate room to avoid this distraction.

Transportation/Parking

If the students will be traveling to the training session, make sure that they have travel information ahead of time. You should provide maps that clearly state directions from a variety of starting points. Include information about public transportation, parking fees or passes, toll roads, and so on. If there are local events that might cause delays on certain routes, provide alternate directions. An example of this situation occurred recently when an event was scheduled to start at 7 P.M. at a location in the downtown section of a major city. A corporate run with more than 5,000 participants was scheduled to begin at 6 P.M., and the most common route to the site was closed. Luckily, the planner discovered this problem ahead of time and averted this potential disaster by sending notices to each participant, indicating alternate routes. If parking passes are necessary, try to have them sent to the students ahead of time so that they do not have to walk into the classroom, get the passes, and walk back to their cars. The goal is to prevent any surprises that could delay or inconvenience the students so that they can arrive on time and be ready for training.

Support

Who will be available to help if there is a problem with the network, if the food does not arrive on time, or if the manuals do not arrive at the proper location? Find out ahead of time whom to contact in case of various emergencies. Determine whether or not there will be immediate assistance to develop contingency plans if problems do arise.

Communications

In today's world of wireless communication, many students (such as system managers) will need to keep in touch with their office throughout the training session in case of emergencies. The instructor should verify what type of access is available to the students. Find out where the phones are, and if they are pay phones, warn the students that they will need money or a calling card. If there are computers in the class, can students remotely access their systems through them? Will analog phone lines be available for modem use? As the instructor, you should be prepared to answer students' questions regarding such concerns. You should also think about any rules that you should set regarding the use of this equipment. Although access is good, access can be a distraction from the lesson. You might want to stipulate ahead of time that students can only check e-mail during breaks.

Evaluating the Physical Environment

If at all possible, you should visit the room before the training session to assess the strengths and weaknesses of the layout and to determine whether you have any flexibility or options. Bring a checklist to make sure that you remember everything that you need to evaluate.

Room Evaluation Questions

- How is the furniture arranged?
- Can the furniture be moved?
- What are the lines of sight?
- How are the acoustics?
- Is there wheelchair access?
- Can the lighting be controlled?
- Where are the light switches?
- Where are the controls for any computer or audio-visual (A/V) equipment?
- Where are the printers?
- Where are the supplies for the printers, overhead projector, and so on?
- Are there telephones?
- Where are the breaks/lounges/restrooms in relation to the training room?
- Can the heating and air conditioning be controlled?
- Are there any unsafe conditions that need to be addressed?

By answering these questions, you will be able to determine how to create the best possible learning environment, given the space with which you have to work. Once you have evaluated the room, you have to determine how much flexibility you have. Can you rearrange the layout to better accommodate the modes of instruction that you plan to employ? If there are computers in the room, you are most likely stuck with the current layout. If this situation is the case, plan your lessons accordingly and determine ways to overcome the weaknesses of the room. If the room is conducive to only one instructional method, ask whether there are alternate rooms that you can use when needed. If you have the option to rearrange the room, consider the following layouts.

Room Layout

We discuss a variety of instructional methods in Chapter 10, and the choices that you make regarding the method(s) you plan to use in the course will determine the optimum room layout. A variety of ways exist to arrange the furniture in the room, and each has strengths and weaknesses depending on the teaching methods that you plan to use. If you have the ability to rearrange the room, organize it based on the type of interactions that will take place. Some of the more common layouts include the following:

- Rows
- U-shape
- Circle
- Clusters

Rows   Rows are useful when the instructor is presenting material to the students or when the students are working independently. Figure 2-1 shows a row layout. Group activities are often difficult with this arrangement, because it might not be possible to move chairs or tables to accommodate them. When setting up the rows, make sure that there is room at each end for students to enter and adequate space between the rows for students to enter and exit their seats without disturbing other students. If you are setting up computers or other equipment, make sure that the cables are not in danger of being accidentally pulled out. A power cord unplugged inadvertently or a monitor pulled off the table is an avoidable disruption. The students should also be able to see the instructor and any instructional material without having to peek over the monitors or around other students. One solution is to use desks that enable the monitor to be recessed below the surface. You can also set up rows perpendicular to the front of the room so that students can form groups, but this setup forces the students to turn in order to see the board. You have to weigh the strengths and weaknesses of each layout to determine which setup best suits your needs.

U-Shape   The U-shape arrangement, depicted in Figure 2-2, is conducive to both lectures and large group discussions. The instructor can lecture

Figure 2-1
Row layout

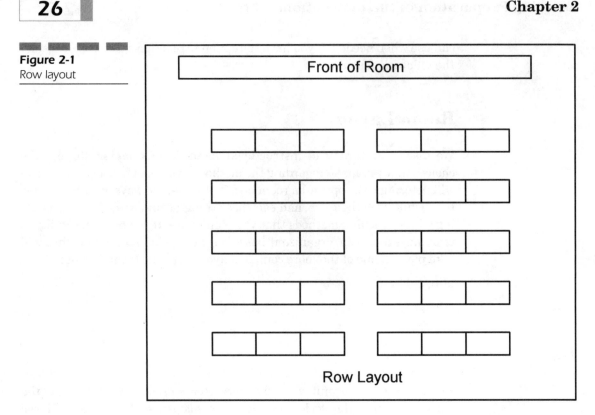

from the top of the U and walk inside the U-shape to interact with individual students or to hand out materials. Each student at the table can see everyone else, which helps during discussions. The down side of this arrangement is that it limits the number of students, because if the U-shape grows too large, students at one end might feel distanced from the lecture or discussion. This setup also increases the distance that the instructor must travel if he or she must work along the outside edge of the U-shape.

Circle   The circle layout, illustrated in Figure 2-3, is best for group discussions. Although the instructor can lecture in this setting, visuals are difficult because some of the students will have to turn in their seats to be able to see them. If the instructor stands in the middle of the circle, his or her back is always facing someone; if the instructor is outside the circle, then he or she is always standing behind a student. This layout, which is similar to the U-shape, works well only when there are a small number of students in the class. If you set up computers in a circle, it might limit the

Figure 2-2
U-shape layout

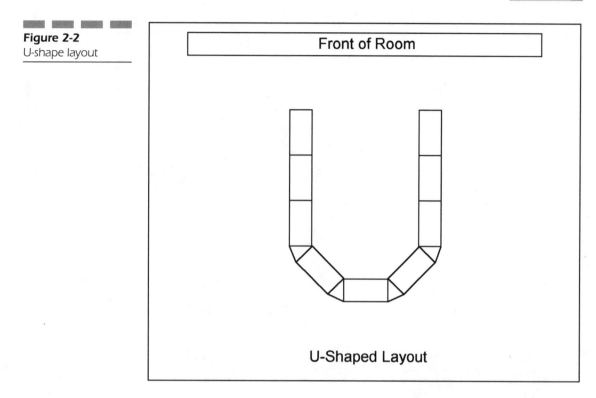

Front of Room

U-Shaped Layout

visibility among students but can provide the benefit of protecting the cables and power cords against mishaps.

Clusters   The cluster layout, or cluster, is most useful for small-group interactions or individual lab work. Figure 2-4 shows the cluster layout. The students at each cluster can work on projects without distractions, and the instructor can easily move from station to station and interact with each individual without disturbing the other students. You can often arrange computers or other lab equipment in this fashion to protect cables, and depending on the furniture, to provide private space for each student.

The most important factors in determining room layout are the size and dimensions of the room. The goal is to arrange the room so that each student can easily see and hear the instructor. If the room is long and narrow, with the instructor at one end, some students might have difficulty seeing anything projected on a screen or written on the board. If you do not have

Figure 2-3
Circle layout

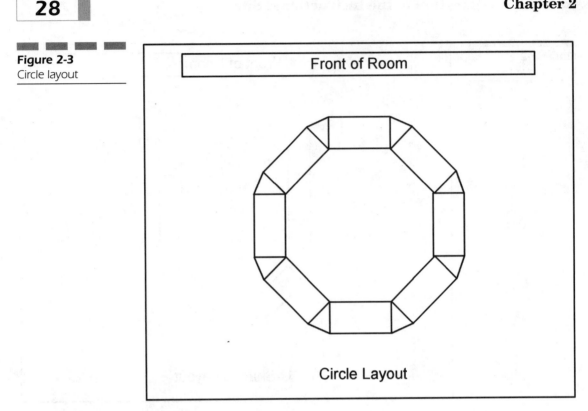

Circle Layout

the option to change the room, then you must make sure that your materials are large enough for all of the students to see. You should also check whether the students can hear you and other students easily and arrange for a microphone if they cannot. When there are seats that have an obstructed line of sight, block them off if possible so that students cannot use them.

Lighting

People often overlook the lighting options in a room when the room is constructed. Unless you have input into the design of the room, you have to work with whatever you have and determine how the environment will impact your instruction. Previously, to see something on an overhead projector or projection from a computer, you had to turn down the lights. If the room had staged lighting, however, where you could turn off just the lights over the projection screen, this problem did not exist. In most cases, however, you had to dim or turn off the lights in the entire room, and everyone

Figure 2-4
Cluster layout

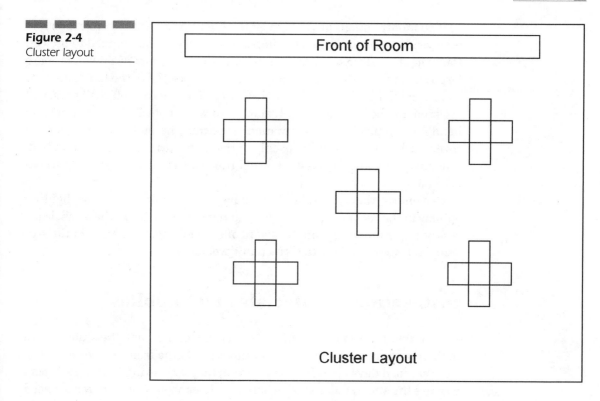

Cluster Layout

had to sit in the dark. This situation is deadly, and you should avoid it at all costs. Even in the most exciting classes, some students will find remaining awake difficult. This situation also creates a barrier between the instructor and the student, because it might be difficult to see students and evaluate their reactions to the lesson. The ideal learning environment enables the students to have adequate light for reading, taking notes, and remaining attentive—especially after lunch.

Over the last several years, the available options have improved. Bulbs are significantly brighter for overhead and *Liquid Crystal Display* (LCD) projectors, enabling students to view the screen without dimming the lights. If the equipment available to you still requires dimmed lights, be creative. Unscrew the bulbs near the projection screen, rather than turning off all of the lights. Just remember to screw the bulbs back in or tell the maintenance staff what you did. Otherwise, you might find a new bulb replacing the "defective" one each day. Another option is to shade the problem bulbs with dark paper.

If your only options are to turn off the lights or not use the projection system, you have to determine the importance of what you planned to project. Can you instead write on the white board or chalkboard? Can you prepare large posters ahead of time and work from an easel? Are the handouts that you use sufficient for most examples? If you have to turn off the lights, will the students be able to see well enough to write notes? If not, you need to hand out supplemental information regarding the material that you are covering. If you find that your only option is to turn the lights on and off, remember to warn the students each time so that the sudden brightness does not blind them.

Remember that you might not have much control over the lighting options in the room, but light level is an important factor in the overall success of the training session. Be aware of the lighting, keep track of the students' reactions, and try to correct any problems.

Instructional Materials and Supplies

Picture this situation: you arrive the morning of the class, the students are in their seats ready to go, and you cannot locate the training manuals that were shipped days ago. Unknown to you, they are sitting in the mail room because the staff did not know where to deliver them. If any materials need to be shipped to the location, if possible have them delivered to a specific person so you know how to track them down. Check with the person or mail room ahead of time to make them aware of the delivery, find out how the materials are then transported to the training room, and find out how long this process normally takes. At some organizations, transferring materials from the mail room to a classroom might take several days. Find out ahead of time and determine when you have to ship the materials accordingly. As a backup, always bring several copies of the handouts with you. Most cities have copy centers that you can use in an emergency. If you have a copy of the material on disk, it could accelerate the duplication process.

When you survey the room before class, make sure you find out where any necessary supplies are located. Delays caused by missing chalk, overhead pens, printer paper, and so on are inexcusable. They show a lack of preparation on the part of the instructor and can undermine credibility. You should also find out where replacement supplies, such as overhead bulbs and toner cartridges, are located. The students often pay a considerable amount (of money and time) to attend training sessions and expect everything to be prepared and well organized when they arrive.

Equipment

You must evaluate the equipment in the room during the pre-training visit to make sure that it is adequate for your needs. Make a list of the equipment that you plan to use, mark off each item that is already available at the site, and then plan how you will acquire whatever is missing. Some of the more common items that you might find in training rooms are listed as follows:

- Chalkboards
- White boards
- Easels
- Overhead projectors
- Computers
- LCD projectors
- Visualizers

Determine how to turn on each item (remote controls, power strips, hidden switches, and so on) so that you are not hunting for the switch at the beginning of class. Just because you see equipment in the room on the day you visit, do not assume that it will be there when you arrive to teach. Also, make sure that the equipment functions properly. Find out which equipment is dedicated to the room and what you must reserve. If you require any specialized equipment, find out whether anyone is available to set it up for you or if you need to take care of this matter yourself.

Computers

If you will use computers for training, they deserve special attention. You should check a number of items when evaluating the computers.

Computer Evaluation Questions
- How fast is the CPU?
- What operating system (and version) is installed?
- How much memory does the computer have?
- How much hard-drive space is available?
- Is a there a CD-ROM?
- Is there a ZIP drive?

- Is there a sound card with speakers?
- What software programs are available (and versions)?
- Are all of the options installed with each program (clip art, add-ins, fonts, and so on)?
- Are the computers networked?
- Is there a way to share files between the computers?
- Is a password required?
- At what resolution is the default?
- Can the display on one computer be shared with others?
- Is there Internet access?
- Is there anything specific to the program(s) that you will be using that is not covered in these previous questions?

When you evaluate the computers, you should test each of the tasks that you and your students will need to perform. Many training sites lock down the computers, preventing the users from performing certain functions in order to maintain the default setup. If you are teaching file management and cannot create directories or perform various file operations (copy, move, or delete), then the computers are useless. If you will be making changes, find out whether a quick way exists to rebuild the computers at the end of the class, and know the condition in which are you expected to leave the computers when you are finished. You must determine the status of the computers and who is responsible for them in order to guarantee that they are adequate for your needs and that they will be ready when the class begins.

Other Equipment

The brightness of LCD projectors has improved significantly over the past several years. The brightness of the light source is rated in ANSI lumens (the measure of brightness that a projection unit puts out, standardized by the American National Standards Institute). Recently, projectors have become available with ratings of 1400 ANSI lumens or higher, which enable the image to be clear and legible without turning down the lights. You should also determine the maximum resolution for the LCD projector. If you prepared your materials based on a resolution of 800-by-600 and the projector is only capable of 640-by-480, you have a problem.

A useful tool for demonstrating detailed tasks or small components is a visualizer, which is a camera that is suspended on an arm over a light source similar to an overhead projector. You can project the output from the camera through an LCD projector or other video output device. The camera, with zoom features, enables you to project small three-dimensional objects in great detail. If you place a penny on the device, you can zoom in to display the mint mark clearly. You can also use the visualizer as an overhead projector or to project pictures and other documents. This specialized device is becoming popular in many training environments. Chapter 11 will discuss these and other media options in-depth.

Furniture

The furniture is an important feature of the room. Evaluate the furniture by asking yourself the following questions. When you ask yourself these questions, think about the types of students that you will have in your class. Students who work at computers all day and who are touch typists might be distracted if they cannot adjust their chairs to the proper height or if the monitor is recessed in the desk, rather then at eye level. Although these issues might seem minor to some, they will cause major aggravation for others.

Furniture Evaluation Questions

- Can the furniture be rearranged?
- Is it ergonomically correct?
- Is it comfortable?
- Can the students see over the equipment?
- Will it accommodate students who have special needs (wheelchairs, left-handed students, visually impaired students, and so on)?
- Must the instructors be sitting or standing to use the instructor station?
- Would you be comfortable sitting in this seat all day?

If your students are uncomfortable, their attention span and concentration will suffer.

Environment Issues

When surveying the site, determine whether you can adjust the heating and air-conditioning systems. The room might be comfortable in the morning but feel like an oven after turning on the equipment, filling the room with people, and the sun shining through the windows. If you do not have access to the controls, find out who does or develop a contingency plan if possible.

Each of the categories that we just discussed combine to enhance or detract from the learning environment. You, as the instructor, must assess the situation before the class and take whatever actions are possible to create the optimum setting. Visiting the site before class is the best method to evaluate the site, but if this visitation is not possible, use a phone interview to evaluate the room with the questions we asked in each section.

Managing the Physical Environment

Once you have evaluated the physical environment, if modifications are required, find out what options you have and develop a plan for preparing the site. The following list summarizes the items to remember:

Checklist for Controlling the Physical Environment

- Determine the appropriate contacts for the following areas:
    - Reservations
    - Access to facilities
    - Technical support
    - Delivery of materials
    - Food preparation and delivery
- Decide on the optimum room layout based on the instructional methods to be employed, and rearrange the room accordingly.
- Order any necessary equipment.
- Ship instructional materials (if necessary).
- Send information to students including times, directions, parking, and other pertinent information.
- Research emergency options, such as copy centers.

Eliminating Distractions

One factor in preparing a positive educational environment is to eliminate as many distractions as possible. When instructors evaluate the instructional site, they must keep in mind anything that could distract the students from the lessons. For students who do not want to be in class in the first place, anything can become a distraction.

The Five Senses

To eliminate as many distractions as possible, address all five senses: sight, sound, smell, taste, and touch.

Sight What can the students see from their seats? If there are windows in the room, there should be blinds that you can close. If there are Venetian blinds, make sure that they are turned so that the students cannot see the people walking by or the other class that finished early. Many people debate about whether there should be a clock in the room. Knowing the time is useful, but clocks can also be a distraction—especially if they are analog and they tick. If there are signs or posters on the wall that are unrelated to the lesson, take them down. Close the doors, or crack them open, to eliminate the distractions that people walking by can cause.

Sound To what will the students be listening? You hope that the answer will be you and their peers; however, there are always other sounds to distract them. When you evaluate the room, you should turn on all of the equipment and then sit and listen. With the rapid increase in *Central Processing Unit* (CPU) power, there comes the need for bigger fans to keep the machines cool. A room full of computers can create quite a hum. A defective light bulb also can make an annoying noise. Try to identify the noises and eliminate the ones that you can control.

Smell The item relating most to the sense of smell is food. As we stated previously, food can be a significant distraction. If at all possible, have breaks and lunch in a separate room so that food is not in the classroom while you are trying to teach. You must also decide on your policy regarding food and drink in the classroom. Commonly, people start their day with coffee and want (or need) coffee first thing in the morning. If you are teaching on computers, you should set ground rules at the beginning of the class. This policy might already exist, depending on the location where you are teaching. If there are signs stating no food or drink, enforce the policy and adhere to it yourself; otherwise, you are setting a bad precedent and could jeopardize your credibility with the students.

A distraction relating to smell that is a little more difficult to deal with is perfume and cologne. Some people wear perfume and/or cologne regularly and think nothing of it. In some cultures, perfume and/or cologne is a way of life. Some people, however, are allergic to many scents and develop headaches or other symptoms when exposed to them. You, as the instructor, should not wear any perfume or cologne that could distract students or cause allergic reactions. If you have students in class who do, you will have to handle this situation based on your observations of other students' reactions. Again, this situation is extremely delicate, but the instructor has the responsibility to make sure that one student's actions do not negatively impact other students. On a related issue, have breath mints available in case they are necessary. One option is to have a bowl of peppermints, or other hard candy, available for the students and for you throughout the class.

Taste   The only concern that you should have with the sense of taste should be breaks and lunch. You, or whoever is responsible for registration, should make sure that any dietary needs, such as vegetarianism, are addressed. We cannot reiterate this point often enough. Food is an important factor in determining a student's state of mind.

Touch   You address the sense of touch when you evaluate the furniture and work surfaces. Are the chairs comfortable and adjustable? Are the desks, keyboards, and mice clean? Find out whom to call if someone spills something so that they can clean up the mess immediately. If the room is too warm or too cold, know how to adjust the thermostat. When you look at the room arrangement, do the fans from the computers or projector blow onto a student? If so, rearrange them to avoid this problem.

Technology Distractions

Technology can offer a variety of distractions for the students. Because many technical courses involve computers, they will be discussed specifically; but the same issues apply to all technology. When evaluating the learning environment, you need to determine which potential distractions exist and how you can minimize their effects.

The Instructor's Computer

The instructor's computer can be a significant tool in the learning process, or it can be a source of distraction. During the site evaluation, you should spend some time testing this computer. You need to check the video, audio, and network settings.

Video and Audio   The goal is to eliminate any visual or audio setting that could detract from the lesson. Check to see whether any default settings need to be changed in order to eliminate potential distractions. If there is a screen saver, make sure that it is turned off or that the activation time is long enough to accommodate your discussions. When you are lecturing, you should not have to worry about the "scrolling marquee" or "flying toasters" appearing because you talked too long without using the computer. These distractions interrupt not only your train of thought but also the students' concentration. Also, check to see whether there is a hotspot on the screen that will automatically turn the screen saver on when the mouse is moved to that location.

Make sure that the video resolution settings are the same as the computer on which you developed your training materials, or you might find that all of your slides do not fit on the screen. If you will be projecting any graphics in your lessons, check the color settings to ensure that the pictures will appear properly.

Sound effects are also a disruption, so make sure that you check the sound settings to see what options are selected. Check the volume on the speakers to make sure that the volume is not too loud (or too quiet). If you are using a computer that has a scheduling tool that has reminders, make sure that the reminders are turned off. You do not need to remind the class that lunchtime is approaching or is overdue.

Many programs now come with assistants or wizards to assist the user with performing certain tasks. Depending on the settings, they might appear automatically when you take specific actions or only when you request them. Tools such as these are quite useful when needed, but you should consider whether they add anything to the particular lesson. If you decide that they are just a distraction, turn them off.

The Network   With the current level of technology in most training environments, the computers will likely be connected to an intranet (and possibly, to the Internet). If this is the case, you need to know whether the applications are loaded locally (on the hard drive) or whether they reside on a server. The two concerns surrounding this issue are the speed of the network and what contingency plans you need to take if the network goes down. Will you notice a slowdown in the network at any point in the day? If so, you should plan the lessons accordingly and try to minimize the network access at peak usage times. You should also think carefully about whether you really want to depend on live Internet demonstrations being available when you need them. Delays caused by slow or lost connections can be a deadly distraction.

Computer Checklist   Make sure that you specifically check the following items:

- Screen savers or power savers
- Audio settings
- Calendar reminders
- Screen resolution
- Colors
- Assistants
- Network connections (access and speed)

Students' Computers

The instructor should also check the students' computers for the same distractions as well as a few other items. Because some students do not want to be in class, they might look for programs on the computer to play with, such as games, e-mail, or the Internet. You should decide ahead of time what your policy will be regarding the use of these programs. If you want to eliminate the distractions, then try to uninstall them. Otherwise, you need to determine a method for monitoring and discouraging their use.

Remember, when evaluating the computers, try to identify any potential distraction and see whether it can be eliminated. In some courses, the computer is an integral part of the curriculum, and if computers are unavailable, the lesson cannot continue. In other courses, the computer is just one of the tools that is available for conveying concepts. If possible, plan for the worst-case scenario. Most of the time, everything will work perfectly, but by being prepared for the worst and eliminating as many distractions as possible, you will create the best possible learning environment.

Covering All Bases

Now that you have assessed the learning environment and have worked out a plan for optimizing it, you need to follow through with the plan. If anyone else is responsible for portions of the preparation, follow up with them to make sure that everything will be ready on time. The day before the session, go through your checklist and verify that everything is ready. If someone installed software for you, test it to make sure that it works properly. Call each of the contacts that you have already established to make sure that everything (the room, computers, food, support, parking arrangements, and so on) is arranged as you planned. On the day of the training session, arrive early and give the site a final check. If you have covered all of the areas discussed in this chapter, the learning environment should be ready.

Backup Plans

Unfortunately, everything does not always go as planned. You might be teaching strategies for conducting research on the Web when the Internet access goes down. There might be a traffic jam, and most of the students arrive late. I once taught a class when a torrential downpour flooded the parking lot and many of the students' cars floated away. For some reason, I could not hold their attention with the intricacies of spreadsheet formulas. Despite your best planning, problems will arise that will need solutions. To prepare for the unexpected, create contingency plans that enable you to move on despite unforeseen problems.

Contingency planning can include the following tasks:

- Bringing extra equipment for backup purposes
- Having transparencies prepared in case the computer and/or LCD projector fail
- Preparing extra short and long hands-on exercises in case the class runs faster or slower then you anticipated
- Researching several sites on the Internet that will demonstrate the lesson in case one of the sites is down

- Bringing extras (handouts, disks, and so on)
- Preparing to teach a concept in several ways in order to address multiple learning styles

You will not always be able to fix every problem that occurs. The worst *will* happen sometime, and you might have to reschedule a class (I could not stop the flood), but by planning and good organization, you can be prepared for most problems that arise. By checking the site ahead of time and making sure that it is ready for the class, you not only reduce your stress but also create a positive environment and enhance your credibility in the eyes of the students.

Ongoing Evaluation

Preparing the classroom before the beginning of the session is just the first step in delivering a successful training session. You have gathered a great deal of information about the training site that you should share with your students. You also need to constantly assess the attitudes of the students and react to any situations that might occur. The planning and preparation will assist you with deciding which reactions are possible in the current setting.

Setting the Stage

At the beginning of the class, you should orient the students to the facilities and discuss any rules. Make sure that you address the following housekeeping details:

Overview of the Session

- Classroom policies (food, drink, e-mail, and so on)
- Restrooms and water fountains
- Message boards
- Telephones/cellular phone usage
- Break room
- Smoking regulations
- Fire exits
- Snacks

- Meals
- Contents of student kit, manuals, and so on
- Outline of the course

This orientation sets the stage for the rest of the course by conveying your plans to the students, and based on their responses, it gives you a chance to identify any potential concerns or problems.

During the Course

Throughout the course, you should continue to assess the students' verbal and nonverbal reactions to the physical environment and address any problems that might arise. In the scenario discussed previously, in which the food arrived at the room early, the instructor should have noted the lack of concentration and aggravation arising in the students. The instructor should have asked the students if they would like to break early (and then return early) or push on for the next 15 minutes and get through the lesson. There is no use pushing through a lesson just because your schedule states that you should, when you have lost your students' attention anyway. The students will not learn anything at this point.

Final Evaluation

The students should always have the opportunity to fill out an evaluation form at the end of the course, and one section of the evaluation should address the physical environment. The questions should cover the areas discussed, including the scheduling and logistics, physical layout, equipment, food, and the instructor's reactions to issues that arose during the session. These responses will assist the instructor with determining what did and did not work and will enable him or her to improve the course in the future.

SUMMARY

When designing a course, the instructor will determine the various modes of instruction. Armed with this information and an understanding of the requirements of the physical environment, you will be able to evaluate a training site effectively and create the best learning environment given the restraints with which you will have to work. The key to being successful is forethought and planning. You must give yourself adequate time to work through this process and to make sound logistical and environmental decisions based on each of the factors discussed in this chapter.

This chapter discusses the physical environment and all of the factors involved. The planning you do to organize and control the physical environment will have a significant impact on the learning environment. Always visit the site ahead of time (if possible) and plan how to minimize distractions that will detract from the lesson. Planning and preparing ahead of time will benefit you and the students throughout the lesson.

QUESTIONS

There might be multiple correct answers for some questions. The answers are located at the end of this chapter.

1. Ideally, when should you turn off the lights in a classroom?

   a. Always
   b. When using an overhead projector
   c. When using an LCD projector
   d. When the class is over and everyone has left
   e. During breaks

2. Which room layouts are well suited for lectures?

   a. Row
   b. U-shape
   c. Cluster
   d. Circle
   e. All of the above

3. Which room layouts are well suited for lab work?

   a. Row
   b. U-shape
   c. Cluster
   d. Circle
   e. All of the above

4. Which room layouts are best suited for large group discussions?

   a. Row
   b. U-shape
   c. Cluster
   d. Circle
   e. All of the above

5. When evaluating the training room, you should check which of the following items?

   a. Computers
   b. Lighting
   c. Heating
   d. Parking
   e. All of the above

6. Which senses are vulnerable to the most number of distractions in a training room?

   a. Sight
   b. Sound
   c. Smell
   d. Taste
   e. Touch

7. When should you first evaluate the physical environment?

   a. Never
   b. Before the day of the training session
   c. The morning of the training session
   d. After the training session

8. When a student complains about the physical environment, what should the instructor do?

   a. Tell the student to stop complaining.
   b. Question the student about the problem, and determine whether you can find a resolution.
   c. Make a note of the problem so that you can remember to prepare for it in the future.
   d. Ignore the student.

9. What are reasonable contingency plans if the LCD projector bulb breaks during class?

   a. Preparing overheads of each of the computer slides
   b. Canceling class
   c. Taking a break until you can locate another bulb and install it
   d. Switching to the chalkboard and referring students to their detailed handouts

10. Where is the best place to serve food?

    a. In the front of the classroom
    b. In the back of the classroom
    c. In an adjacent room
    d. Nowhere; food is not needed

11. What information should you always send to students before class?

    a. The classroom layout
    b. Directions
    c. The instructor's name
    d. Food options

12. Which of the following are examples of preventable distractions?

    a. The sound of the computer fans
    b. The screensaver activating every five minutes
    c. The sound of airplanes flying overhead
    d. The flickering of a faulty light bulb

13. Which room layout is least conducive to lectures?

    a. Rows
    b. U-shape
    c. Clusters
    d. Circles
    e. Any layout will work.

14. What problem(s) could occur if the video resolution on the instructor's station is different then the resolution on the computer on which you created the training material?

    a. There will not be any problems.
    b. The slides might not fit on the screen properly.
    c. The programs will not run.
    d. All of the above
    e. None of the above

15. What items should you check if the computers in the classroom are networked?

    a. What brand of computers are being used

    b. If the software is loaded locally or on the server

    c. If games are installed

    d. The network speed

    e. None of the above

16. When you are shipping your training materials, what should you do?

    a. Not worry about them; they will arrive on time

    b. Bring backup materials in case there is a problem with shipping.

    c. Mail them the day before training by using overnight delivery.

    d. Establish a contact at the training site to whom they can be delivered.

    e. None of the above

17. When do you evaluate the state of the instructional site?

    a. Before the training session

    b. During the training session

    c. After the training session

    d. All of the above

18. If your lesson is taking longer than expected, what should you do concerning the lunch break?

    a. Tell the students that you are delaying lunch because the lesson is more important than food.

    b. Stop the lesson at the scheduled time and skip some material.

    c. Ask the students if they would like to finish the lesson first or go to lunch on time.

    d. Skip lunch completely.

19. When evaluating the furniture, what should you examine?

    a. Comfort

    b. Color

    c. Determine whether the furniture is ergonomically correct.

    d. Weight

    e. None of the above

20. What is the best device to use in order to view three-dimensional objects?

   a. Overhead projector

   b. LCD projector

   c. Visualizer

   d. Easel

   e. Chalkboard

21. What are some of the negative traits of a cluster room layout?

   a. It is difficult to set up computers with this layout.

   b. It is not conducive to large group discussions.

   c. There is no privacy for any of the users.

   d. It is only conducive for lectures.

   e. There are no negative traits of a cluster room layout.

22. What items should be checked on the students' computers that might not be a concern on the instructor's computer?

   a. Screen saver settings

   b. Games

   c. Hard-drive space

   d. E-mail

   e. The version of the software

23. Which of the following items should you use to enable maximum lighting when projecting the computer image on a screen?

   a. Overhead projectors

   b. LCD projector

   c. Visualizer

   d. None of the above

   e. Any of the above

24. What is the purpose of having the students fill out an evaluation at the end of the course?

   a. To assess the appropriateness of the physical environment

   b. To make more work for the students and the instructor

   c. To determine the overall success of the course

   d. To learn how to improve the course for the future

25. What might be the rationale for requesting a second room to be available for part of the training?

    a. To cost the company more by renting more rooms

    b. To provide an alternative environment that would be more conducive to a particular instructional mode

    c. To give the students exercise when travelling between rooms

    d. To have a place to deliver food where it would not interfere with instruction

ANSWERS

  1. d

  2. a and b

  3. a and c

  4. b and d

  5. e

  6. a and b

  7. b

  8. b and c

  9. a and d

10. c

11. b and d

12. b and d

13. c

14. b

15. b and d

16. b and d

17. d

18. c

19. a and c

20. c

21. b

22. b and d

23. b

24. a, c, and d

25. b and d

Establishing and Maintaining Instructor Credibility

Introduction

By the end of this chapter, you will be able to perform the following tasks:

- Establish credibility
  - Knowledge
  - Experience
  - Appearance
  - Preparation

- Maintain credibility
  - Professionalism
  - Interaction with students

Competency 3 of the ibstpi Standards deals with the trainer's ability to establish and maintain credibility. In order to be an effective trainer, you must be able to create a positive and safe learning environment. Many of the skills that other competencies address (communication skills, presentation skills, listening skills, and feedback skills) are important components of this process and contribute to your ability to establish and maintain credibility with the students. You can be the most knowledgeable person in the world on the subject matter, but if the students do not respect or trust you, you will not be an effective trainer. For this reason, the *Certified Technical Trainer* (CTT) certification is so beneficial. The certification exam is based on the fact that subject-matter expertise and training competence are separate skills that individually need to be addressed in order to be an effective trainer. This chapter will cover some broad areas of personal conduct and actions that are necessary for establishing and maintaining credibility, which leads to a positive learning environment. If you keep these concepts in mind as you read the rest of the chapters, you will see how all of them interrelate.

Establishing Credibility

The time and care that you invest in preparing for each course will influence your credibility with the audience. We have mentioned preparation several times already throughout this book, and preparation will continue to be an important theme. Preparation includes much more than being a subject-matter expert—it also impacts everything you do before, during, and after the course in order to ensure a positive learning environment. Aside from being an expert in the subject, how prepared you are (or at least, how prepared you appear to be) will be the most significant factor in establishing and maintaining your credibility.

Subject-Matter Expertise

Having credibility means that others recognize that you are knowledgeable in a particular area and that you gained your knowledge through study of the theories and application in the real world. Consider the CTT certification. The reason why multiple-choice and video components exist is to ensure that you can apply the skills that comprise each competency, as well as answer the questions about them. If the video was not necessary, you could pass the exam by simply studying this book and knowing all of the right answers without ever standing in front of a class. The video component makes sure that you are more than book smart. This component is also crucial for the subject that you are teaching. You must know the theory, but you also need to be experienced in applying the theory to real-world situations.

In Chapter 1, "Analyzing Course Materials and Learner Information," we also discussed the fact that we assume that you are an expert on the topic that you are teaching. Being an expert means more than just having memorized the technical documentation (and, in the case of software, just memorizing where all of the menu items are located and what the shortcut keys are). Being an expert means that you have hands-on experience using the application in the workplace. If you lack this experience, you will not be able to address questions that students have regarding how they can apply this knowledge to their situations. Imagine the following scenario:

> An instructor, Mr. Smith, is teaching a course on how to create spreadsheets. The students are all professors, and they hope to be able to learn how to use the spreadsheet to calculate their grades. The instructor starts by setting up a simple spreadsheet that lists each student's name and their scores for three tests (refer to Figure 3-1).
>
> The instructor then shows them how to use a function to determine the average scores and how to use another function to convert the score to a letter grade. The instructor asks if there are any questions. The students are excited and start asking the following questions:

Figure 3-1
Grade sheet example

Test Grades for Math 101					
Students	Test 1	Test 2	Test 3	Average	Letter Grade
Doe, Jane	68	88	91		
Garcia, Jim	75	77	82		
Meyers, Gretchen	89	53	77		
Torres, Rita	92	86	89		

- "How do I drop the three lowest grades?"
- "How do I track homework grades when I only record whether or not they are turned in?"
- "How do I weight the midterm more than the quizzes?"

Although the instructor is an expert with the software and knows how to create formulas, more than 200 functions are available in some spreadsheet programs—and it is difficult to be an expert on all of them. Unless he has thought about these types of questions, it will be difficult for the instructor to determine these formulas while standing in front of the eager students.

In this scenario, the instructor's credibility is damaged because he does not know the answer immediately. He can try to explain to the students that when utilizing a spreadsheet, you rarely memorize all of the functions, only the ones that pertain to your field (accounting, statistics, and so on), and you will need to be able to research these functions when a particular question arises. While you are describing how it works in the "real world," the students want and expect an answer from you, the expert.

How can you be prepared for situations such as these? How can you gain this experience? You need to gain experience applying your knowledge in various situations. We do not mean that you have to become a teacher for a year, then an accountant, and then an engineer to discover all of the uses for a spreadsheet. Rather, you need to do some research on your intended audiences and discover how they will need to apply the knowledge that they learn in your course. In this example, the instructor should have asked the students ahead of time for the common elements of their grading systems so that he or she could prepare for the questions. Whenever I teach a course on spreadsheets to a group that has similar backgrounds, I ask them to give me sample spreadsheets ahead of time so that I can use them as examples during the class. I might have no idea what the solution in a particular formula would mean to an accountant, but I will be able to show them how to create it, which helps me build and maintain credibility.

If you know your topic, you can usually address problems and unexpected situations as the instructor in the following scenario did:

> An instructor was hired to teach an intermediate and advanced class in Microsoft Excel. The class was being held at a training site that she had used previously. She was familiar with the classroom and decided not to check it before this course. She arrived at 8:30 A.M. to get ready for the 9 A.M. start time and discovered that the room had recently been upgraded to version 5.0, which she had never seen before. She quickly surveyed the new version and discovered that there were only minor changes and several new options, but all of the basics were still the same. The class began at 9 A.M. and progressed smoothly. The course received rave reviews, and the students never knew that it was the first time that the instructor had ever seen that version of Excel.

Two morals to the story exist. First, you should always check out the training facilities before you teach a class so that you do not have any surprises like the trainer in this scenario (refer to Chapter 2, "Assuring Preparation of the Instructional Site"). The second moral is that if you really know your subject matter, you can work through most problems.

Another reason for gaining experience beyond knowing what the technical manual says is that things do not always work as expected or planned. If you have ever installed software on a computer, you realize that there are sometimes problems that the documentation does not cover. Having experienced the problem, you are better prepared to pass along hints and warnings to the students.

NOTE: *Know your subject matter and how to apply it to situations that interest your audience.*

Training Experience

Many people believe that if you know a subject inside and out, you can teach the subject. If this statement were true, then there would be no reason for CTT—and you would not be reading this book. Chapters 5 and 6, which cover communications and presentation skills, will address many of the skills that you will need to master in order to become an effective trainer. In addition to the specifics that we will mention there, you should always give yourself enough time to properly prepare to teach a class. This process should include observing other instructors teaching the topic, team teaching with an experienced instructor, and even videotaping your training session for later review. These activities will give you the experience that is necessary to become a confident and knowledgeable trainer. These characteristics are crucial for building a sense of confidence in the students, which will be a significant factor in establishing your credibility. We will discuss this topic in much greater depth in later chapters.

Credentials

Depending on where you teach, to be credible you might be required to hold certain certifications or degrees. For example, to teach in public high schools, you must obtain a teaching certification. If you do not have the certification, you cannot teach. To work in higher education, you are often required to hold a master's or Ph.D. in a particular field. Regardless of your experience and knowledge of the subject matter, your credibility might be questioned if you have not earned the appropriate degree.

In technical training, many groups offer certifications on particular software applications or manufacturing procedures. If a certification is available on the topic that you teach, you should obtain it in order to strengthen your credibility. Of course, you are already aware of this fact because you are reading this book. You may be working towards the CTT certification, which will validate that you are a competent technical trainer. Obtaining the appropriate certifications will ensure that you have a solid understanding of the topic.

Course Preparation

In case this point has not hit home yet, the preparation that you do for each course will significantly impact your credibility. Always follow the practices discussed in Chapters 1 and 2 to minimize the surprises during class. Preparation will also set your mind at ease, and you will be more relaxed. We will mention preparation in every chapter of this book.

Appearance

Your personal hygiene and the way that you dress can send a powerful message to the students about your attitude towards them and the material.

While different situations will dictate your dress code, your appearance should always be clean and neat. What message does the appearance of the instructor in Figure 3-2 send compared to Figure 3-3?

Figure 3-2
Appearance 1

Figure 3-3
Appearance 2

Personal Hygiene   Do not neglect the small details of personal hygiene. Before each training session, look in the mirror and make sure that you are presentable. We are not saying that you have to be a model to be an effective teacher, but we do mean that you should not have any personal hygiene issues that will distract or negatively affect the students. Remember to check the following items:

■ Your breath—Will the students know what you had for lunch?

■ Your teeth—See above . . .

■ Your hair—Does it look like you just rolled out of bed?

■ Your fingernails—Did you work in the garden or on the car this weekend?

■ Your eyes—Did you get enough sleep?

■ Your odor—Did you just return from the gym?

While this list might seem humorous, always be aware of the impact that these items will have on the students' reactions to you. You do not need anything to distract them from the task at hand.

Dress   Imagine that you are hired to teach a new e-mail program to a company. You will offer multiple sessions specifically designed to cover appropriate features for different groups within the company. You will have different sessions for the executive staff, middle management, and the production-line staff.

Does it matter what you wear? Should your dress be different for each group? The answer will depend on the culture at the specific organization, but you can make a few generalizations. The goal when choosing your attire is to make the students feel comfortable and at ease. Therefore, while maintaining a clean and professional look, you should try to match the clothing that the students wear.

In this scenario, you would most likely wear a suit for the executive staff, if that is what they wear. For the middle-management and production-line staff, you do not want to dress like the executive staff, because it might be intimidating. For the middle management, possibly select a blazer instead of the suit. If they dress more casually, follow their lead. For the production line, choose a casual outfit. Remove your jacket and/or tie. Do not, however, dress too casually—or else they will get the impression that you do not care about your appearance. Generally, stay away from jeans, shorts, or T-shirts. In Chapter 5, "Demonstrating Effective Communication Skills," we will discuss the nonverbal signals that your appearance sends in greater depth.

NOTE: *There is no right way to dress that will accommodate all audiences. The general rule is that your appearance should always be clean and neat, but your audience will determine your specific attire.*

The Course Introduction

Chapters 1 and 2 included many of the steps that you should follow in order to properly prepare for a course. If you follow the preparation mentioned there, you will be well on your way to establishing your credibility. The next chapter, "Managing the Learning Environment," will cover many issues that you should be aware of when instructing. You will learn that the first 15 minutes of the course can set the tone for the entire session. This statement holds true regarding your credibility, as well.

Part of the course introduction should include introducing yourself to the audience. Consider the following scenario and think about how you would react to this introduction:

The instructor starts the class with the following introduction:

"Welcome everyone! I will be your instructor today. Please call me Dr. Smith. If you haven't heard of me before, I have been using this application for the last 5 years and have been the primary contributor of suggestions for each new version. I have earned all of the certifications that cover this topic plus a number of others. I have also written numerous articles on the topic. Therefore, you can be assured that what I tell you is correct. I am here today to share my knowledge with you."

What would your reaction be? Some students might think that they are lucky to be in the presence of such greatness; however, I think that many others would be put off by his arrogance. This introduction certainly does not encourage anyone to question what the instructor says.

NOTE: *Remember, credibility does not equal superiority.*

You need to be able to convey your experience and expertise to the audience without appearing arrogant or superior. The following bullets include several options for achieving this goal:

- Prepare a brief biography stating your credentials and experience, and include this biography with the registration materials or with the training packet.
- Place a slide on the screen with a brief overview of your background that students can read while waiting for class to begin.
- Ask someone else to introduce you.

Any of these methods are better than the previous scenario. Let's look at another scenario and determine what the instructor should do.

An experienced trainer is asked at the last minute to fill in for a colleague who is sick. The trainer is an expert with the material and is a competent trainer; however, she has not seen the course outline before and has never taught the class. She starts the course with the following introduction.

> Hi, I'll be your instructor for this session. I want to let you know that the normal instructor for this course has just come down with a cold. I was asked last night to teach this course. I haven't taught it before, but do know the subject very well. Bear with me if I make a few mistakes, and we'll get through this together.

Was this introduction a good way to start the class? Does it instill confidence in the instructor's abilities? Do you think that the students are relieved that the course was not cancelled and that they found someone to teach it?

If I were a student, I would answer all of these questions with a resounding "no." The fact that the normal instructor is sick is not the students' problem; rather, it is the problem of the company that is offering the training sessions. The solution that the company has found is to have this trainer teach the course. The problem with this introduction is that it starts the class on a note of uncertainty. The students will be asking themselves if they are getting their money's worth because this trainer has never taught the course before, and they will be asking themselves whether they can trust the answers that the instructor gives them.

What would be the right way to start the class? First, the training company should cancel the course if the instructor is not competent. Therefore, assuming that the instructor is capable of teaching the course, she should start the course like she would any other—without excuses or explanations.

The key to establishing credibility is to project an air of confidence and enthusiasm, even if you are really scared to death. We will talk more about the initial presentation in Chapter 4.

Maintaining Credibility

A trainer's mannerisms are almost as important as his or her knowledge and training experience. While the first 15 minutes of the course set the tone for the rest of the class, you are always in the spotlight—and your actions and mannerisms are under constant scrutiny by the students. You must monitor your personal conduct throughout the training session, because it will have a significant effect on your credibility. Chapters 5 and 6 will cover specific communications and presentation skills that will assist you with presenting a positive message to the students. The general areas that we will focus on in this chapter are professionalism, interactions with learners, and awareness of diversity.

Professionalism

Your general attitude and behavior must always be professional, and you must require this standard of your students, as well. We do not mean that you cannot joke with them and have a fun, relaxed class, but you need to make sure that the environment is free of any behavior that could make a student feel uncomfortable. Do not immediately treat the students as if they are your best friends. Ask them how they would like to be addressed. Some people prefer being called Mr., Mrs., Ms., or Doctor, while others prefer their first name. If you do not know how to pronounce a name, ask the student. Treat your students with the respect and dignity that they deserve.

Another aspect of professionalism is to not disparage companies, groups, products, or anything by name. There might be someone in the class who has an affiliation with the item that you just put down. For example, if a trainer is teaching a class in Rochester, New York, then it would not be appropriate to comment negatively on Kodak, because just about everyone who lives in Rochester knows someone who works at Kodak. Even if your comment is in jest, you never can tell the reaction that people will have to a negative comment. You will notice that throughout this book, I never use names for people or companies in examples of the wrong way to do something. If I did, I am sure that I would offend someone.

Interacting with Learners

Each student in your class must feel that you give him or her as much attention and assistance as you give everyone else. If you praise and commend one student for a success, you should do the same for every other student. If you spend time with one group of students during the first break, you should seek out others during the next break. Quite naturally, you will enjoy interacting with certain students in your class more than others, but the students should never know this fact. Your treatment must be fair and equal for each student to feel comfortable taking risks, such as asking and answering questions, which could expose their weaknesses to the rest of the class.

You should also be conscious of the message, both verbal and nonverbal, that you send to students when you answer their questions. You do not want to be viewed as condescending or arrogant. Chapter 5 will discuss body language in depth. Every action or reaction can affect your credibility. You are in the spotlight and should be conscious of the messages that you are sending to the students.

Another aspect of interaction is how you deal with unexpected questions that arise during the course. We will deal with this topic in depth in future chapters, but your response will impact your credibility. Never make up an answer if you do not know it, and never purposefully give an incorrect answer. You also should not ignore questions that are not part of the course outline. Direct the students to the appropriate course or place to find the answer. Part of maintaining your credibility is assisting the students in any way possible, as long as it does not detract from meeting the objectives of the course.

We already discussed the issue of subject-matter expertise. If you are knowledgeable and have experience working with the subject matter, you should be able to identify learners' errors and assist them with finding the right answers.

Diversity

In your classes, you will meet people who have a variety of ethnic, religious, and cultural backgrounds. You must be accepting and supportive of each student's differences and needs. You should never show any bias toward or against a learner. Any indication of this type of action will instantly discredit you in the eyes of the class.

Intolerance or inappropriate comments often occur when telling jokes or stories. If you believe that there is any chance that something you say will offend a learner, do not make the comment. Find a different way to make your point. You also must make sure to not allow students to act inappropriately towards other students.

SUMMARY

In order to succeed with this competency, you must master the rest of the competencies. Your knowledge and experience with the topic, coupled with your interpersonal, communications, and training skills, all combine to determine the level of credibility that you establish with your students. You need to be able to address individual students' needs and be prepared for the surprises that occur during every training session. Every one of your actions will elicit a reaction from the students that will either improve or damage your credibility. If you are conscious of this fact and monitor the students' reactions, you will be successful in developing and maintaining your credibility.

QUESTIONS

There might be multiple correct answers for some questions. The answers are located at the end of the chapter.

1. Which of the following items contribute to an instructor's credibility?
   a. Knowledge
   b. Experience
   c. Appearance
   d. Preparation
   e. All of the above

2. What steps should the instructor take to prepare for a class that he or she has already taught many times?
   a. No further preparation is needed.
   b. Redesign the entire course to keep it exciting for the instructor.
   c. Evaluate the audience to determine specific examples and questions that they might have.
   d. Review the course outline to ensure that it is appropriate for the students' needs.
   e. None of the above

3. What is the appropriate dress for a trainer?

   a. Always wear a suit.
   b. Dress casually to put the students at ease. Being underdressed is better than being overdressed.
   c. It does not matter what you wear; it is your skills as a trainer that count.
   d. Your dress should match the standard dress of the students.
   e. None of the above

4. When it is acceptable to give a wrong answer to a student's question?

   a. Anytime, as long as the students do not catch you
   b. If you think the answer might be right
   c. Only if the question is apart from the subject matter and will not affect the outcome of the class
   d. Never
   e. None of the above

5. When is it appropriate to tell an off-color joke?

   a. Anytime
   b. Only after you ask the students if they would mind and if no one objects
   c. Towards the end of the class, once everyone is comfortable with each other
   d. Only if it helps to illustrate a point of the lesson
   e. Never

6. How should you interact with the students during breaks?

   a. Spend an equal amount of time with each of the students.
   b. Do not socialize with anyone during breaks; they need a break from the class.
   c. Only socialize with students who approach you. The other students just want to be left alone.
   d. Treat them as friends. Be open, joking, and friendly.
   e. None of the above

7. What level of experience with the subject matter is necessary in order to be an effective instructor?

   a. You must be a subject-matter expert.
   b. As long as you have memorized the material, you will be effective.
   c. You must have hands-on experience.

    d. You just need to know more than the students.

    e. None of the above

8. Which of the following actions would have the most negative impact on your credibility as an instructor?

    a. Making a mistake in front of the students

    b. Making up an answer to a question

    c. Misunderstanding a student's question

    d. Forgetting a student's name

    e. Keeping the class late

9. Which of the following methods are effective ways to introduce yourself to the students?

    a. Include a short biography in the course packet.

    b. Start the class by reading your resume and explaining all of your certifications and experience.

    c. Start with a brief greeting stating who you are and immediately begin the lesson.

    d. Ask someone else to introduce you.

    e. All of the above

10. What should be done to maintain credibility with the students?

    a. Always act professionally.

    b. Respect student diversity.

    c. Never tell jokes or make comments that might offend a particular group of people.

    d. Interact with the students equally.

    e. All of the above

ANSWERS

1. e

2. c and d

3. d

4. d

5. e
6. a
7. a and c
8. b
9. a, c, and d
10. e

Managing the Learning Environment

Introduction

By the end of this chapter, you will be able to perform the following tasks:

- Plan and deliver the course introduction
  - Introductions
  - Course expectations
  - Course schedule
  - Timeline

- Adapt your delivery to meet students' needs
  - Pace
  - Questions
  - Breaks

- Manage interactions
  - Involve learners
  - Instructor/student interactions
  - Student/student interactions
  - Group strategies

Competency 4 of the ibstpi Standards deals with the trainer's ability to manage the learning environment. Planning is the key to being able to manage the learning environment effectively. The previous chapters discussed analyzing the course materials, the learner information, and the instructional site. This chapter covers a variety of factors that enable the instructor to manage the learning environment effectively. Note that many of the skills discussed in the other competencies are required to master this competency. For example, good communication and presentation skills are essential to set the proper tone for the course. This chapter will discuss the skills that are specific to managing the learning environment; however, you must also master the other competencies in order to succeed at this competency. Remember that all of the competencies inter-relate. The skills in this competency begin with the creation of a course outline that includes contingency plans that you can employ to adapt to various student needs. We also discuss managing group dynamics and individual behavior problems. One goal of every lesson is to create an interactive learning environment. By properly managing the learning environment, the instructor can provide each student with the opportunity to learn and succeed.

Setting the Stage:
The Course Introduction

In Chapter 10, "Using Instructional Methods Appropriately," we will discuss a variety of standard instructional methods and their proper use. Using this information, the instructor must develop an outline for the course that includes appropriate presentation strategies and instructional methods. An important part of the outline that instructors often overlook is the course introduction. First impressions are hard to change, and this saying holds true in training sessions. The first 15 minutes of class can set the tone (either positive or negative) for the entire session. You should give careful thought to the items that need to be addressed and to questions that you should ask during the course introduction. Consider the following scenario and ask yourself if you would feel comfortable in this class:

> You are sitting in a training room with 10 other people, waiting for the training session on creating your own Web page to begin. The instructor enters the room, passes out the course material, and starts the class by saying the following: "Hi everyone! I know we are all busy people here and we have a lot of complicated stuff to learn and not a lot of time to do it, so let's jump right into the material. Everyone open your book to page three and follow me." The course begins.

What was wrong with this introduction?

The real question is, "What was right about it?" The instructor did not give the students any information about logistical issues, the course objectives, the schedule, or the prerequisites. The students do not know when the breaks or lunch will be (remember food from Chapter 2), who the instructor is, whom they are sitting next to, or whether they belong in this class. If students are nervous about the class when they arrive, this introduction will just augment the problem.

Managing the learning environment begins with a well-planned introduction that covers all necessary information about the course and that puts the students at ease (refer to Figure 4-1). You should include the following items in the introduction:

Course Introduction Checklist

- Introductions: instructor and student
- Physical and logistical issues (refer to Chapter 2)

Figure 4-1
Instructor welcoming
a class

- Course information (description, any prerequisites, objectives, and materials)
- Course schedule
- Course expectations and benefits

Introductions   The instructor should start the class with a cheerful and sincere welcome, as pictured in Figure 4-1. Even if this course is the tenth one that you have taught over the past 12 days, you still need to impart your enthusiasm for the material to the students. They have to believe that you want to be there and that you are ready to assist them. This attitude also plays a significant role in establishing your credibility (refer to Chapter 3) and sincerity. We discussed some of the items in the introduction checklist in prior chapters. The course introduction puts them all together.

Have the students introduce themselves. This introduction not only gives you a chance to learn their names, but it also starts to raise the comfort level in the class as the students begin to learn about each other. If the session lasts multiple days, the students will be spending a lot of time together, assisting each other and possibly working on projects together. When you ask them to introduce themselves, you have an opportunity to find out who they are and why they enrolled in the course.

I have attended training sessions in which the instructor asked people to share a secret about themselves. Most answers are humorous, and it sets a positive, fun tone for the class at the beginning. This technique is similar to beginning a speech by telling a joke. This activity will only work if you participate and if the questions do not embarrass anyone. Stay away from any personal questions regarding gender, age, race, or religion. If a student does not want to answer a question, move on to the next person. Take notes on the answers as each student introduces himself or herself. Keep track of their jobs so that you can relate your examples to areas with which they are familiar. You should learn their names as quickly as possible to add to their comfort level. Also note whether they are interested in any topic that you will not specifically address so that you can talk to them about the topic later. A critical component of effectively managing the learning environment is adapting instruction to meet the needs of the learners. This situation is your best chance to learn why students are attending the training class and to learn about any special needs that they will have, so take advantage of this situation.

Physical and Logistical Issues   The introduction is the time to familiarize everyone with the training facilities by using the information that you learned during the site visit. The section on setting the stage in Chapter 2 covers this topic in depth. Cover all of these issues at the beginning of the course. The introduction is your chance to verify that there are no environmental concerns that could distract the students.

Course Information   During the introduction, you should also review the course description, prerequisites, and objectives. You can tell the students exactly what the course will and will not cover. You do not want students thinking that they will learn something in particular and waiting eagerly for it throughout the course, only to discover at the end that you will not be covering the topic. An example occurred recently in a class on exploring the Internet. The goal of the course was to teach the students how to find information on the Web by using various search engines. Two of the students sat through the entire class and at the end asked when they would get their e-mail accounts. Unfortunately for them, the use of e-mail (and the creation of accounts) was covered in a separate course. The instructor could have prevented this problem if he or she had reviewed the course objectives at the beginning of class and asked students to state what they hoped to learn from the course.

Chapter 1 discusses students who might be under-prepared for the course. Remember that course prerequisites help make sure that students have the appropriate skills necessary to take a class. By reminding the students of these prerequisites at the beginning of the course, you are ensuring that the students are aware of what is expected of them. This explanation will help prevent problems caused by under-prepared students and will also reassure students who do have the necessary skills but think they need to know more than is required. You should request for any student who does not meet the course requirement to talk to you immediately. These students might discover that there is another course that is better suited to their skill set, or they might take the course but will need to do some additional work outside of class to keep up.

Course Schedule　The course schedule is the framework for the training session and gives you and your students a guide to follow. Hand out copies of the schedule to each student and post a copy of each day's schedule, including break times and lunch times, on the board. Students can use this material to check off each section as you complete it, and it will remind students how much material is left for the day. A clearly defined course schedule will assist you with managing time throughout the course.

Course Expectations　The course introduction is the time to discuss your expectations of the students and what the students can expect to learn from the course. Your introduction should include the topics in the course expectations checklist:

Course Expectations Checklist

- Attitude
- Questions
- Punctuality
- Attire
- Student expectations
- Mistakes
- Benefits

These items refer to the students' behavior while in the class. You want your students to have a positive and supportive attitude. They should relax and put aside any concerns or issues unrelated to the course. This situation is a chance to forget about upcoming deadlines at work or unfinished projects at home. They need to concentrate on the work at hand. If they do not understand something, they need to ask questions. You will do your best through verbal and nonverbal cues to determine their comprehension, but if they do not ask questions when they do not understand, you might not know that they need assistance. They also need to understand that some of them will start with a greater knowledge of the material than others, so they should be encouraged to assist each other and to not make those who have less experience feel uncomfortable.

This point is also a good time to remind the students when the class will start and when they can expect to finish. Once you announce a start time, make sure you stick to it unless extenuating circumstances arise. Having to wait for a student who is tardy is not fair to the students who arrive on time.

In Chapter 3, we discussed the issue of attire. Remember that unless you are training on location and rules are already in place, I recommend leaving attire up to the students. Just remind the students to dress so that they will be relaxed and comfortable. If any situations related to dress do arise, handle them on an individual basis.

You also need to address the expectations that the students should have for the course. State what they should expect in phrases such as, "When you finish today, you will be able to . . . " and "When you finish the course, you will be able to . . . " By conveying the goals of the course in this fashion, the students understand the specific skills with which they should leave the course. You should also tell them that they should expect to make mistakes, because mistakes are an essential part of learning. I heard a story about a computer-programming student who was extremely good at writing code. In fact, he rarely had to rewrite programs because they worked the first time. Although he was skilled at creating programs, he had significant problems troubleshooting others' programs and correcting errors, because he had little experience with code that did not work. The classroom is the place to make mistakes and determine how to correct them, and your students need to understand this fact.

During the introduction, we address the benefits of successfully completing the course to help motivate the students. Motivation is also an integral part of competency 8, and we will discuss this competency in depth in Chapter 8. If the course you teach leads to certification, then there is most likely an exam associated with the material. You should remind the students how this particular course fits into the certification sequence, and if an exam is part of the course, then assure them that the skills you are covering will prepare them for the test.

The course introduction sets the stage for the rest of the course and determines the initial tone and expectations for the students. The introduction also assists you with determining any modifications that you will have to make to your teaching strategies, based on your audience. This initial presentation needs to be well planned to make sure that you start the course on a positive note. Use the introductions suggested previously for icebreakers or come up with your own, but the key is to do something that will assist you with analyzing the students' needs and expectations. At the same time, you want to put the students into a positive and attentive state of mind.

Adapting Your Style to the Students

After the initial presentation, you might discover that you have to adapt your delivery style to accommodate the audience. Chapter 1 discussed various types of students with varying backgrounds, job experiences, skill levels, and reasons for attending the class. Although it might be too late to completely restructure your course, if you are properly prepared, you can make changes that will accommodate your students better.

You might find that the students are more advanced than expected. If this is the case, you can increase the pace of the lecture or add optional information that will supplement their skills. You could also reduce the number of practice exercises if they grasp the material more quickly or use more complicated exercises that will challenge them more. You have to be careful, however, that your decision to modify a course does not adversely affect any of the students. For some students, the accelerated pace might be too fast. You should not modify the course just to accommodate students who have enrolled inappropriately in a course that is too basic for them. Most likely, you will find that your class consists of students of different skill levels and backgrounds. Teach to the median level of the class as long as this approach is congruent with the course objectives. This technique will address the needs of most of the students, and then you can address the rest individually.

Your ability to adapt to a variety of students' needs starts with planning. If you have taken the time to analyze the course materials and have prepared a variety of exercises and activities, you will be able to adapt to any surprises that the students might present. If you have researched the types of students who are expected to enroll in the course, you will be able to tailor your examples to situations to which they can relate. If you are teaching a course on creating spreadsheets and you discover that your students are teachers, using a grade book as an example will hold their interest longer then an expense report. To reiterate, your ability to adapt your delivery to learner characteristics is directly related to the planning and preparation that you have put into the course.

Managing Time

The students should have received a copy of the course schedule during the introduction. One of the trainer's many jobs is to stick to the schedule. If this course is a component of a certification series or receives approval from one of the certification groups, it is expected that all of the necessary material will be covered. If you do not effectively manage the time, you might not be able to cover everything. Three areas that can challenge the schedule are pace, questions, and breaks.

Pace

To manage time effectively, you need to be prepared if a lesson takes significantly more or less time than you planned because the students are having a difficult time with a particular concept (or if they grasp the concept more quickly than you planned). To accommodate this possibility, be prepared with practice activities of different lengths. Dictating the length of a lesson is fairly easy when the lesson consists of only lectures, but lectures alone cannot teach students to become proficient in most skills. In fact, there are often better ways to introduce a lesson than through lectures. Chapter 10, "Using Instructional Methods Appropriately," will discuss a variety of instructional methods in depth, many of which involve group activities. Group interaction is a great way to learn a subject, but it opens the door to many time-management issues that we will discuss shortly. You will have to determine which activities are appropriate based on how much time is available. You should also determine ahead of time whether optional material exists and whether you can omit that information if time limits require. Always be conscious of your schedule and whether or not you are on track.

Student Questions

Students ask questions when they are involved in the learning process. In this situation, you have done a good job of creating a positive, interactive learning environment. Student questions, however, can take a significant amount of time. Although you should encourage students to ask questions, you need to stay on the topic with your answers. If you feel that a question is off topic, you might have to ask the person to hold the question and discuss the topic during the next break. You must handle this situation with tact so that you do not discourage the student from asking other questions.

You need to determine what level of understanding on a particular topic is necessary for the course. The students should understand the theory behind their actions, but the explanation of the theory might be beyond the scope of the particular course, and you might lose many of the other students. One example would be a lesson on the creation of Web pages. A short course might teach only the use of a *Hypertext Markup Language* (HTML) editor, which hides the code from the user, whereas an in-depth course could address the fundamentals of creating a Web page by writing HTML codes. The first course requires only a familiarity with a graphical word processor, whereas the second requires an understanding of a markup language and proper syntax. If someone asks a question in the first course regarding the syntax of the HTML codes for creating a table, the explanation, although relevant for a true understanding of Web-page creation, is not necessary for the student's success in this particular course. The explanation might confuse some of the students and discourage them from attempting to create a Web page. You have to know when a question is related and necessary to the topic.

Students will sometimes ask questions about topics that you will cover later in the course. You should create a question box on the board, pictured in Figure 4-2, where you write down questions that you will address later. This procedure will enable you to move on with the lesson but will remind you to address the question at the appropriate time. This technique also enables the students to know that their questions are important and that you will answer them later.

Breaks

As mentioned previously, you need to adhere to and enforce the start and end times of the sessions and breaks. Losing half an hour each day just getting the students back to their seats after breaks is easy. Remind the students how long the break is, and start promptly. Often, you will have students that have outside commitments that they feel they need to check on during each break. These check-ins with the office often delay their return. If this situation happens regularly, you should address the issue with

Figure 4-2
Question box

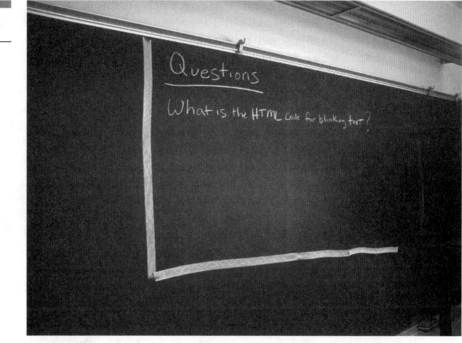

them privately. Let them know that you will have to start on time to cover all of the material, and if they miss something, you will not be able to delay the rest of the class while you re-explain the item. Be understanding and polite with problem students, but do not let them impact the rest of the class.

Learning to monitor and control the pace of the course, student questions, and breaks will augment your time-management skills. Two other areas that can significantly affect your schedule are group interactions and dealing with conflicts. We discuss these two topics in depth in the next chapter. When you learn to manage and control these situations effectively, you will be better equipped to manage the timing of the entire lesson.

Group Interaction

When designing the training session, you should strive to create an active learning environment where students interact with the instructor, other students, and the technology. In other words, you need to involve the learners in the lesson. In Chapter 10, we will discuss in depth a variety of instructional methods that will enable you to teach a topic in multiple ways, depending on the students' needs. At this point, realize that several modes of delivery exist and they require you to develop competency in understanding and managing individual and group dynamics. Regardless of which delivery mode you use, you will have to respond to the reactions and behavior of the students. As the instructor, your responsibility is to create a positive and supportive environment that encourages students to ask questions and experiment but that discourages any inappropriate behavior. Interactions occur between you and the students and among the students. The following section discusses types of interactions and some suggested reactions.

NOTE: *To create a positive and supportive environment, you must remember to treat all of the students fairly and give equal attention to each of them.*

Interactions: You and the Students

Naturally, you will have more in common with certain students and will thus feel more comfortable with them. Make sure that you do not subconsciously give them special attention or treatment. Make sure that you learn the names of all of the students. Do not call just some of them by name, or you will alienate the others. If you have difficulty remembering the students' names, use nametags. Chapter 5, "Demonstrating Effective Communication Skills," discusses communication skills in depth. At this point, you should realize that unfortunately, even if you do everything right, you will still have negative situations with students. This section addresses some of the types of students that you might encounter and provides suggestions for dealing with them.

In general, if you think you have a problem student, follow these steps:

Steps for Dealing with Problem Students

1. The first step is to evaluate the situation and determine whether the situation is having a negative effect on the class. Sometimes you might

decide that the best course of action is to do nothing and see how the rest of the class responds, because their reactions might be enough to discourage further problems.

2. If you feel that you must take action, try the specific steps discussed in the following descriptions of the various behaviors. Always remember that you should strive to maintain the dignity of the student. Many times, the students are unaware of the behavior in question or how their actions are affecting the rest of the class.

3. If you cannot resolve the problem through indirect measures, you will have to speak to the student about the situation. Make sure that you speak in private so that you do not embarrass the student, the rest of the class, or yourself. Be tactful but direct, and explain how the situation is adversely affecting the class and what possible solutions are available.

4. If the problem continues after you have discussed the problem with the student and you determine that the success of the class is at stake, your last resort is to remove the student from the class. This might be the hardest task that you will face as a trainer, but every student in the class expects and deserves a positive learning environment—and your job is to create and maintain this environment. If you have to remove the student, make sure that you document the situation and follow up after the class with the appropriate people. You do not want this type of situation to blemish the reputation of you, the course, the sponsor, or anyone else involved.

The following descriptions are examples of the types of students that you might have to deal with in your class. You will find that some of the behaviors and solutions are related and will overlap. After each description are some suggested steps for remedying the problem.

The Know-it-All Sometimes, you will have a student in the class who feels that he or she knows the answer to every question that you ask (and many that you do not ask). He or she will work ahead, thinking that he or she already knows what you are demonstrating. This situation often leads to the student making mistakes, which you will then have to help them fix by repeating something that you just said. The student might also try to assist other students and end up showing them the wrong way to do something. This situation can cause several problems for you and for the rest of the class. First, this person can dominate the class discussion and discourage others from asking and answering questions. Second, the person might be wrong and can lead other students astray. The know-it-all will hinder the learning process for other students and will dominate and sidetrack group discussion.

The know-it-all might not realize the effects of his or her actions on the rest of the group. This person might just be trying to get the most out of the training session and think that by sharing his or her knowledge, he or she is helping everybody else. You have to be careful that you do not stifle this student's enthusiasm and interest in the topic when you deal with the situation.

Solution(s) Several possible solutions exist for this type of behavior, depending on its severity. When you ask the class questions, call on other students. When waiting for an answer, avoid eye contact with the know-it-all. Look for other students who might want to respond. If the student has already answered a question, try saying, "Thank you [student's name], does anybody else have thoughts on this?" or "Thank you [student's name], let's hear from somebody else on this next one." The goal is to encourage other students to respond, which will minimize the problem student's responses.

If the student continues to dominate the class, talk to that person during a break. The know-it-all is often looking for recognition of his or her knowledge. Tell that person that you really appreciate the input, but you need to encourage other students to participate so that you can evaluate their level of understanding.

The Challenger The challenger is a person who questions your skills and competence. This person might have years of experience and might be an expert in the field. The person might be taking the training because it is required or to learn a new version of the software. The student might disagree with the way you teach a task and try to find your weakness by asking many obscure questions. The first thing to remember is to not turn this situation into a competition between you and the student. This attitude is unprofessional and will end with one or both of you looking bad. You must address this problem, however, because this type of person can be the most detrimental to a class by generating a stressful and adversarial environment that will frustrate many of the other students.

Solution(s) If the student is asking a legitimate question about the course material, then you must know the answer. Being well prepared and establishing your credibility (discussed in Chapter 3) will prevent this type of problem.

NOTE: *If you do not know the answer, do not try to make one up. Acknowledge that you cannot answer the question immediately but that you will follow up later.*

Write down the question and remember to answer it later. If the student asks questions that are outside the realm of the course, you should defer the questions until a break and then either answer the questions or refer the student to courses or resources that will.

Try to determine the cause of the student's behavior. Is the student bored because he or she already knows the material? If you determine that the student will benefit more from another course, during a break, discuss with the student the option of switching classes. If this course is required, acknowledge the student's skill level and ask him or her to make the best of it. Remind the student that this material is new to most of the other students and that you have designed the course to address their needs. Although the student might disagree with the way you teach the topics, your experience has taught you what works best with most new users. You can also suggest for the student to move through the material at his or her own pace and try to provide some additional materials to keep that person occupied. You should also remind the student that he or she might learn a new and more efficient method of doing something if he or she pays attention.

Is the student insecure about learning the material, challenging the instructor as a way of coping with this problem? If this is the case, you need to reinforce the assumption that making mistakes in class is acceptable and that you do not expect the students to grasp everything immediately. Have this discussion with the entire class so that it does not draw attention to the insecure student. If you feel that it is appropriate, discuss the problem with the student during a break and try to determine the root of the insecurities. The student might not have the prerequisite knowledge for the course and might need to review the material outside of class.

Is the person angry about everything? In this situation, there are probably other issues in this person's life that are causing the negative behavior. You need to talk to the person privately. Try starting the conversation with a statement similar to the following: "I have noticed that you appear to be unhappy about something. I may be misreading you, and if I am, I'm sorry. I don't mean to pry, but I just wanted to make sure that the course is meeting your expectations. I would like to remedy any problems that I can so they do not negatively affect you or the rest of the class." This non-aggressive opener will give the student a chance to vent or discuss any difficulties. If the student does not want to talk, at least he or she will understand that the behavior is affecting the rest of the class. If you discover that the student is dealing with outside issues and cannot concentrate on the course, suggest for the student to reschedule and take the class at a later date when everything is under control.

Does the student appear to have a problem with you personally? As a trainer, you need to develop strong interpersonal skills that should prevent this situation from arising. If you determine that a personality conflict exists and you are not able to reach an understanding with the person, your best option is to suggest a course with another trainer. You cannot let a problem with one student impact the rest of the class.

The Overwhelmed Student   The amount of information that you cover might overwhelm some students. You have to determine whether the person really does not have the required background for the course or just lacks confidence in his or her skills. Many people underestimate their own technical abilities and just need reassurance that it is normal to not understand the new concept immediately. Remind them that you are there to assist them.

Solution(s)   If you determine that the student does not have the prerequisite knowledge required for the course, you will have to discuss the option of transferring to a course that is better suited to his or her needs or suggest review material to get up to speed.

You can also partner students together to work on the projects. One of the best ways of learning a task is to teach it to another person; therefore, the group work will benefit both the students who need extra help and students who are beginning to master the material. This technique will also help students gain confidence in their own abilities. One caution when partnering students is to make sure that the more knowledgeable students do not become frustrated with the overwhelmed students.

The Class Clown   The class clown is the person who makes a joke out of everything and always strives to be the center of attention. Humor is not bad in a class and can be helpful in reducing the tension that sometimes accompanies learning new things. The problem occurs when the humor breaks the concentration of the students and interferes with the learning process. The trainer must constantly evaluate the learning environment and determine when the humor starts to become a problem.

Solution(s) One of the first methods to try when dealing with a class clown is not acknowledging the jokes. Combining this technique with the other students' groans or comments might discourage the class clown. This action could, however, have the opposite effect and cause the class clown to try even harder to get a reaction. If this situation happens, address the situation with the individual privately. Explain that although you appreciate his or her participation, the jokes are a distraction to other students.

The Introvert Some students will sit through an entire course without talking to anyone. This person might go unnoticed because he or she does not ask questions or make any comments. The introvert will generally not cause problems in the class, but you do need to monitor that person's progress to make sure that he or she is learning the material.

Solution(s) In Chapter 7, we discuss effective questioning skills that you can use to determine the students' levels of understanding. You should try to involve the introverted student in the class discussions while not making that person uncomfortable.

Student versus Student Another responsibility of the instructor is to monitor student interactions to make sure that the students are productive. If you notice one student criticizing another, you need to intervene immediately.

Solution(s) When addressing problems between students, you should follow the same strategies that we discussed previously. The following suggestions will assist you with overcoming negative student interactions.

If a student disparages another student's question, remind the class that there is no such thing a stupid question. Others in the class might have the same question but be hesitant to ask it. Remind students that not asking a question is stupid. You should always encourage questions, but you might have to postpone the answer until a later section or a break. Effective questioning and feedback skills are an essential component of competencies 7 and 8, and we will discuss these in depth in those chapters.

Remind students that they have different backgrounds, and something that might be easy for one of them might not be as easy for others. Even students who already know how to do something might learn another, more efficient method.

If you have the students working in groups, rearrange them if there are problems. You can also expand the number of students in the group, which might minimize the impact of the negative student. The most important rule for dealing with students is to strive to maintain everyone's dignity and privacy. When you have to deal with a situation, do so privately if possible. If the situation becomes heated, suggest a break or review period so that everyone can calm down. The group and coaching strategies that we discuss in the next section also can assist you with handling student interactions.

Group Strategies

Breaking the students into groups to discuss scenarios or to work on projects can greatly benefit the learning environment, but it can also be a significant waste of time if not managed properly. The following list offers suggestions for successful group work:

Steps for Successful Group Activities

1. Define the size of the groups, and be sure that everyone is included.
2. Define the objective of the task or project clearly. If the students do not know what you expect of them, they can waste time doing the wrong task or just socializing. If the groups need to report back to the larger group, define the scope and extent of the report.
3. Set ground rules regarding group interaction. For example, reinforce the idea that everyone should have a chance to participate in the groups and that members should be able to finish their thoughts without interruptions.
4. Set a short time limit to focus the students and to keep the conversations on track. Conversely, do not make the time limit so short that the groups cannot accomplish the task.
5. Make sure that the room layout is conducive to group discussion. If the room is not, you should plan ahead of time how to rearrange the room or reserve another room.

6. Check in with each group to make sure that the members are on track. If they are practicing a skill, let them make mistakes—but be sure to show them the correct procedures. If they do not make mistakes, they will not know how to correct them later (when you are not there to help). Have each group report any problems that they encounter to the class so that everyone can learn from the mistakes.

7. Do not perform the group's work by providing the right answers. If you do not give the students a chance to think about the questions and come up with their own answers, right or wrong, they will not learn the information as well.

Coaching Strategies

As the instructor, you also fill the role of coach to the students. You are there to provide support, encouragement, and advice. You establish this role at the beginning of the class during the introductions. You need to gain the students' confidence and trust so that they are comfortable asking questions and revealing their weaknesses to you. The following list of coaching strategies will assist you with filling this role. We have mentioned some of these points previously as steps toward conflict resolution. By successfully creating a positive environment, you will eliminate many of the problem behaviors that could arise.

1. Interact with each student. To develop a positive rapport, you should greet students as they arrive and talk to them. Use small talk to build their comfort level. During breaks and lunch, socialize with all of the students. They should see you as a colleague who is there to help them, not as an aloof expert who is gracing them with your presence.

2. Making mistakes is acceptable and is a necessary part of the learning process. They are certainly not the first to make a particular mistake and will not be the last.

3. Mistakes create learning opportunities. Turn mistakes into learning experiences by discussing how to overcome the mistake and exploring various situations where the problem might arise.

4. Congratulate students on their successes. Make sure that you point out the things that they do correctly, as well as their mistakes.

5. Be accessible. Remind students that if they need to talk to you individually, you are available during breaks and lunch.

6. Be enthusiastic about the material. The students will share in your excitement.

7. Do not personalize disagreements. If you disagree with something a student says, discuss the topic or idea but do not personalize it. You do not want the student to feel attacked. If the student is wrong, let the student save face in front of the class.

8. Relate the information to the students. Help the students relate to the information so that they see how learning the material can benefit them directly.

9. Be supportive. Create an environment that encourages learning.

Feedback

To manage the learning environment effectively and to meet the needs of each student, you must be attune to both verbal and nonverbal feedback. By constantly observing the students, you will note their reactions to the material and will be able to adapt the lessons accordingly. Throughout the session, you should monitor their responses. You should ask the students how they feel about the material and see whether there are any problems or concerns. Performing this task frequently will prevent any surprises at the end and will encourage a sharing environment. Some instructors have found it useful to establish a signal in order to determine the students' comfort level. One example is using the thumbs up sign for understanding, thumbs down for confusion, and thumbs horizontal if they are not sure. After you introduce each new topic, you can give a quick thumb check to determine the group's level of understanding. Chapters 7 and 12 discuss a number of questioning and evaluation techniques that you can employ to determine a student's level of understanding.

The Instructor: Keeping Your Sanity

Some of your students will possess a variety of these characteristics, and they will challenge you and turn your hair gray. The first trait that you need to develop as a trainer is a thick skin. Do not take any negative situation personally. Do your best to remedy the problems and strive to prevent them in the future, but do not blame yourself for every situation that occurs. Despite your best planning efforts, students sometimes bring baggage that is difficult to handle. The best you can strive for is to offer the students a supportive and organized learning environment that gives the students the opportunity to grow.

SUMMARY

By this point, you should realize that there are a number of factors that help determine the success of training session. The first two chapters dealt with the planning and organization of the course materials and learning environment, as well as analyzing any information that you have about the students. The next chapter provided an in-depth discussion of professional, interpersonal, and social behaviors to help you establish and maintain your credibility. In this section, we dealt with the most important section of the class with regard to establishing a positive learning environment: the initial presentation. Prepare and practice this presentation so that you can set the stage properly and place the students in the right frame of mind for the rest of the course. This preparation will minimize the number of problems that could occur. Remember that all of the competencies interrelate. In Chapter 6, we discuss in depth the specific skills that are necessary to be an effective presenter.

Throughout the course, you should continue to monitor the learning environment to make sure that you are on track and that the students are involved. The communications, presentation, and questioning skills discussed later in this book will enhance your evaluation skills and provide additional tools for responding to students' needs. When a problem with a student does arise, remember to address it swiftly and tactfully, because it is your responsibility to maintain a positive learning environment for the class as a whole.

The following list summarizes the key items to be aware of throughout the course:

- The course introduction
- Adapting your delivery to the match the students' needs
- Managing time
- Managing group interactions
- Involving the learner
- Ongoing evaluation of the effectiveness of the instruction

The instructor *must* keep these issues in mind throughout the preparation and delivery of the course in order to ensure that the students have the best possible learning environment.

QUESTIONS

There might be multiple correct answers for some questions. The answers are located at the end of the chapter.

1. What is the purpose of the initial presentation in a training session?

   a. To familiarize students with the course objectives
   b. To get to know everybody
   c. To tell everyone when lunch is served
   d. To share the instructor's expectations of the students
   e. All of the above

2. What is the best way to address a behavioral problem with a student?

   a. Ignore it; the class is only one day long, and everyone can put up with it.
   b. Meet privately with the student as soon as possible.
   c. Immediately halt class and discuss the concern with the student on the spot.
   d. Tell the student to stop whatever he or she is doing wrong and then continue with class.
   e. Embarrass the student so that he or she does not repeat the behavior.

3. What types of questions are appropriate to ask students at the beginning of class?

   a. Any question is appropriate.
   b. What are their expectations for this course?
   c. How old are they?
   d. What is their favorite music group?
   e. What is their background with regard to the course topic?

4. What is the most appropriate dress code for a training class?

   a. Suit and tie
   b. Jeans and T-shirts
   c. Anything in which the students are comfortable
   d. Leisure suits
   e. Leave it up to the students, as long as the dress does not offend anyone

5. What actions might be successful for handling a student who is a know-it-all?

   a. Tell the student to "be quiet and let someone else answer a question."

   b. Say, "Thank you [student's name], does someone else have an answer for this one now?"

   c. Keep calling on the student, and he or she will eventually tire of answering questions.

   d. Avoid eye contact with the student when asking a question.

   e. None of the above

6. What information should you look for during student introductions that might affect your course delivery?

   a. The students' current duties

   b. Favorite colors

   c. Prior experiences with the topic

   d. Course expectations

   e. All of the above

7. What should you do if you realize that some of the students already know the material that you are teaching?

   a. Keep the current pace to accommodate the rest of the students.

   b. Increase the pace of the course.

   c. Tell the students who understand the material to leave early.

   d. Provide these students with additional material to keep them busy (if they desire).

   e. Team them up with the other students during labs.

8. What do you do if a student does not return from breaks on time?

   a. Start without that student.

   b. Wait until everyone is there so that you do not have to repeat any material.

   c. Chastise the student when he or she returns.

   d. Make negative comments about the student so that the other students will say something to him or her.

   e. Talk to the student privately about the problem if it persists.

9. What methods can you use to encourage a comfortable learning environment?

   a. Greet the students when they arrive and make small talk.

   b. Leave them alone during the breaks and lunch so that they can form group unity.

   c. Ask them to call you by your proper title (Dr., Mr./Mrs./Ms., and so on).

   d. Participate in the introductions.

   e. Tell lewd or risqué jokes.

10. What is the best policy for addressing students in class?

    a. Use their proper titles.

    b. Memorize their names and call them by names.

    c. Make up nicknames for each of them.

    d. Do not use names; just point.

11. What is the first step that you should take if you think that you have a problem student?

    a. Observe and evaluate the situation to determine how the problem impacts the class.

    b. Confront the student immediately.

    c. Talk to the student in private.

    d. Kick the student out of class to show everyone else that you mean business.

12. What reason(s) might cause a student to challenge you in class?

    a. Boredom

    b. Insecurity about the material

    c. They feel that you do not know the material.

    d. They just do not like you.

    e. All of the above

13. To effectively manage the learning environment, the instructor should do the following:

    a. Include time for introductions.

    b. Start the lesson immediately.

    c. Tell students not to ask questions.

    d. Plan the lesson ahead of time.

    e. All of the above

14. What actions might be successful for handling a student who is an introvert?

    a. Ignore the student.

    b. Involve the student in the lesson as much as possible.

    c. Call on the student frequently.

    d. Force the student to answer questions.

    e. None of the above

15. What step should you take to prepare for a group activity?

    a. Define the size of the group.

    b. Set a time limit for the activity.

    c. Check in with each group.

    d. All of the above

    e. None of the above

16. Which of the following are philosophies of an effective coach?

    a. No pain, no gain

    b. Making mistakes is acceptable.

    c. Never make mistakes.

    d. Ridicule the students when they make mistakes.

    e. Provide constant encouragement.

17. What actions might be successful for handling a student who is the class clown?

    a. Ignore the jokes and antics of the class clown.

    b. Laugh at every joke that the class clown tells.

    c. Make fun of the class clown.

    d. Talk to the class clown privately.

    e. Discuss the rude behavior with the entire class.

18. When should a trainer solicit feedback?

    a. At the beginning of the session

    b. Throughout the session

    c. At the end of the session

    d. All of the above

    e. None of the above

19. What strategy can you use to keep the course on time?

    a. If the class is running late, skip the hands-on practice.

    b. If the class is going too fast, give the students a long break.

    c. If the class is running late, skip a topic.

    d. Prepare a variety of exercises that vary in length in order to accommodate the pace of each class.

    e. None of the above

20. What actions might be successful for handling a student who is overwhelmed with the material?

    a. Repeat the lectures several times to the entire class.

    b. Ask the student to team up with another student.

    c. Ask the student to drop the class.

    d. Explain to the student that he or she must work harder, because he or she is holding back the rest of the class.

    e. Assist the student outside of class.

21. Which of the following methods are useful for soliciting general feedback from the students?

    a. One-on-one evaluations

    b. Multiple-choice tests

    c. Thumbs up, thumbs down

    d. Observing students throughout exercises

    e. All of the above

22. What strategies might be successful if you discover that a student does not have the prerequisite knowledge for the course?

    a. Start with the basics for each topic.

    b. Ignore the student.

    c. You should ask the student to drop the course and start with a more basic class if he or she becomes overwhelmed.

    d. If the course lasts more then one day, suggest supplemental material for the student to review outside of class.

    e. All of the above

23. What actions might be successful for handling a student-versus-student conflict?

    a. Treat the student as an adult, and let him or her work it out.

    b. Intervene immediately if one student disparages another student.

    c. Talk to the students privately, determine the problem, then address the problem.

    d. Admonish the students publicly.

    e. None of the above

24. What should you do if a student disagrees with you during class?
    a. Explain to them that you are the expert and are always right.
    b. Ignore the student.
    c. Discuss the topic and determine the validity of the student's argument.
    d. Tell the student that he or she is wrong and that he or she should listen to what you say.
    e. Do not personalize the issue.

25. Which of the following items are important aspects of managing the learning environment?
    a. The course introduction
    b. Adapting your delivery to the match the students' needs
    c. Managing time and group interactions
    d. Ongoing evaluation of the effectiveness of the instruction
    e. All of the above

ANSWERS

1. e
2. b
3. b, and e
4. e
5. b and d
6. a, c, and d
7. a, d, and e
8. a and e
9. a and d
10. b
11. a
12. e
13. a and d
14. b
15. d
16. b and e
17. a and d

18. d
19. d
20. b and e
21. c and d
22. c and d
23. b and c
24. c and e
25. e

Demonstrating Effective Communication Skills

Introduction

By the end of this chapter, you will be able to perform the following tasks:

- Use verbal communication appropriately:
  - Identify components of a message
  - Understand tone, volume, and pace
  - Recognize fillers
  - Realize the importance of proper grammar

- Using nonverbal communication appropriately:
  - Appearance
  - Movements
  - Gestures
  - Body language

- Monitor and evaluate student communications
  - Listening skills
  - Frames of reference

Competency 5 of the ibstpi Standards deals with the trainer's ability to communicate effectively. All of the skills that we discuss in this chapter are necessary in order to master the next competency, which addresses effective presentation skills. The ability to communicate effectively is an essential skill for trainers, and without this skill, they will not be able to succeed. Communication skills consist of more than just being able to form proper sentences in a particular language. Such skills include the awareness of the messages being sent to the students through both verbal and nonverbal signals and the messages that the students send to the instructor. The ability to control these signals and use them to enhance discussions is crucial. When you perceive that the students do not understand the message, you need to be able to adjust your style to better suit their needs. One component of such an adjustment involves understanding the students' frames of reference and being able to use this understanding to relate to them.

To master all of these skills, you must first understand the various components involved in a message. One model that describes this concept, pictured in Figure 5-1, breaks communication into three components: the sender, the message, and the receiver.

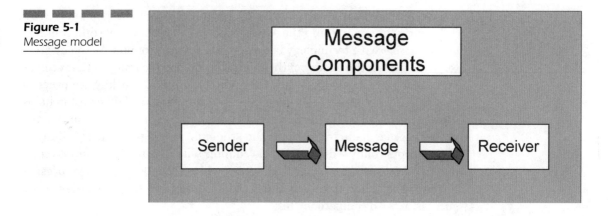

Figure 5-1
Message model

The sender refers to the person who is talking. You are the sender when you are giving a lecture, and the student is the sender when he or she asks a question. The message refers to the concept or idea being conveyed. The receiver refers to the person for whom the message is intended. This model seems to be an obvious and simplistic view of communications, but it conveys an important point. The sender and the receiver each have their own frame of reference, derived from past experiences, that will be a factor in how they interpret the message. If they are not on the same wavelength, the message might be misinterpreted. This is the reason misunderstandings often occur.

NOTE: *Throughout this section, keep the message model in mind when you think about the various communication strategies that we discuss.*

If you are the sender, understanding the receiver's frame of reference is a significant factor in determining how successful you are in delivering the message. A common example is the difficulty that people of different generations sometimes have in communicating. Children growing up today have never experienced a time when computers were not commonplace. Many children can sit down at a computer and intuitively figure out everything, but many older people who grew up before the advent of computers have VCRs that still blink "12:00" because they cannot figure out how to set the clock. This situation is mostly related to comfort level, rather than to ability. You would approach teaching a technical topic to the younger group differently than you would the older group, because they have different levels of comfort with technology because of their backgrounds. As the instructor, who is often the sender of the message, you need to analyze the receiver and tailor your message so that they will understand. Luckily, we practice this activity subconsciously in our daily interactions. This chapter helps illustrate the verbal and nonverbal cues that you can use to convey the proper message and to interpret the students' messages properly. Many of the concepts that we discuss in this chapter will also directly relate to competency 6 (covered in the next chapter), which focuses on effective presentation skills. Therefore, you must master competency 5 in order to be successful with competency 6.

Verbal Communication

Verbal communication refers to the messages that you send when you speak to others. The message consists of more than just the words that you speak; the message also derives from how you say the words. By being conscious of the message that your voice is sending and learning to control it, you will convey the appropriate message to your students. The following list includes the components of verbal communication that we discuss in this chapter.

Components of Verbal Communication

- Tone, volume, and pace
- Fillers
- Proper grammar
- Emotions

Tone, Volume, and Pace   Think back to when you were in school. Each of us had classes that seemed to drag on forever and ones that flew by. Teachers who spoke with a monotone voice that seemed to drone on and on could easily put students to sleep, whereas teachers who varied their tone and spoke with enthusiasm could make any topic exciting. To be an effective instructor, especially if you are teaching technical information, you need to become a dynamic speaker who can excite the students about the material. To become dynamic, you have to vary the tone of your voice appropriately. Tone refers to the pitch of a sound or word, and by varying the tone you can impart different meanings or emotions. If you speak in a monotone voice, your words have little variation, and they all seem to blend together. Following thoughts becomes difficult, and you impart little excitement to the listener. In normal conversation, most people vary the tone of their voice depending on what they are saying. When asking a question, people often raise the pitch of their voice at the end of the last word. When finishing a statement or being sarcastic, the pitch of the voice often lowers at the end of the last word. These actions come naturally to most people, but if you find that you do have a monotone voice, you should work on varying the tone of your speech.

The volume of your voice also conveys a message to the listener. If you speak softly, the listener might have to strain to hear your words, which is frustrating and often leads to misunderstanding. Speaking too softly can also leave the impression that you lack confidence in yourself regarding the topic of discussion. Conversely, speaking too loudly can intimidate and scare people.

The third component of speech is the pace, or the speed at which you speak. The pace at which you naturally speak is related to the environment in which you grew up. When people move to a different part of the country, they often notice that they speak faster or slower than those around them. You probably have noticed that when people get excited about something, the pitch of their voice will often rise, they will speak more loudly, and they will speak faster. The problem occurs when someone who naturally speaks quickly gets excited and speaks so fast that people cannot understand them. This situation is especially true when teaching technical subjects, because people often need to think about each word in order to follow the details involved in a particular task.

The tone, volume, and pace at which you speak are difficult to change, because these are habits that you have formed throughout your lifetime. One of the best methods for identifying any speech patterns that might be detrimental to your instruction is to tape yourself while speaking. Most people find that the sound of their voice seems different when listening to it on a tape. We are used to hearing our voice as it reverberates through our skulls, but not from across the room as other people hear it. Tape yourself when you give a speech, talk on the phone, and carry on normal conversations. Put yourself in your students' place, and ask yourself if you would enjoy listening to your voice for an entire training session. If not, you need to identify and rectify any weaknesses.

Fillers   When you tape yourself, you should also listen for any filler words that you use, such as "umm," "er," "alright," "OK," and so on. People use these words subconsciously in order to fill the silences in their thoughts. When someone asks you a question, you often use one of these words while thinking of an answer. People also use filler words when they are nervous or unsure of themselves. The other reason for using filler words is that many people are uncomfortable with silence, so they use these words to bridge other words. As a trainer, you should become comfortable with silence, because it is a tool that you can use to your advantage. If you do not provide an end to the silence, others will feel compelled to speak—whether answering a question that you asked or asking one of their own. Remember this point when reading Chapter 7. Wait time is an important questioning technique.

Once you start consciously thinking about these fillers, you will notice that almost everyone uses one or more of them regularly. One down side of this awareness is that you might find it difficult to sit through presentations from people who repeat a filler word frequently, because you will start counting the number of times that they say the word. You might become so caught up with this word that you will not be able to pay attention to anything else (I speak from my own experience). Tape your presentations, identify any fillers that you use, and work to eliminate them. Ask a fellow trainer to attend some of your sessions, and have that person alert you whenever you slip. This process will take work, but you can eliminate these words from your speech.

Proper Grammar   Learning to vary your voice patterns and eliminate the fillers will improve your communication skills, but if you do not know how to use proper grammar, you will lose credibility in the eyes of the students. Although your language skills and knowledge of the technical subject matter are unrelated, using poor grammar could cause some to question your education and knowledge. Examples include using the word "ain't" or using double negatives, such as "can't do nothing." Some improper words are harder to identify. One example that comes to mind is the plural for the word *software*. Many people say softwares, which is not a word. Some people will judge you based on your ability to speak properly, and if these skills are weak, you could find that you are unable to relate to the audience.

You also need to be sure that you speak to the level of your students. Do not speak over their heads by using every technical term that you can think of (unless they are engineers, who will probably expect this situation and will understand what you are saying). In technical training, you will need to use technical terminology. The point is to make sure that your audience understands what you are saying.

Emotions When you speak, use words that grab people's attention. Which of the following sentences would you rather hear at the beginning of a training session?

"Class, next we will be discussing spreadsheet formulas."

or

Next we are going to be learning about the most powerful aspect of spreadsheets! We are going to learn how to create formulas that will do all of our calculations for us!"

Which one of the lessons would you rather attend?

Remember from Chapter 4 that one of your roles is to be a coach. You need to convey your excitement about the topic to the students. The students will feed off of your emotions, share your enthusiasm, and become interested in the topic. You convey emotions with the sound of your voice and the words that you choose, so think not only about what you want to say but also how you want to say it.

Putting It All Together

Remember that the best way to improve your verbal communication skills is to tape yourself while speaking, then analyze your speech patterns. Use the following checklist for assistance:

Verbal Communication Checklist

■ *Tone, Volume, and Pace*
  ▪ Do you vary your speech to highlight points, convey emotion, and sustain the students' attention?
  ▪ Are you speaking too quickly or too slowly?
  ▪ Are you speaking too loudly or too softly?
■ *Fillers*
  ▪ Do you use any fillers ("umm," "ah," "er," "like," "OK," "you know," and so on) when speaking?
■ *Silence*

- Do you feel comfortable with silence?
- Do you take advantage of silence and use it to encourage participation?
- *Grammar*
  - Do you use proper grammar?
  - Do you use any slang terms?
  - Do you speak in terms that your students understand?
- *Emotions*
  - Do you use words that will excite the students?
  - Are you interested in the topic?
  - Would you fall asleep taking a class from yourself?

Nonverbal Communication

Although the way in which you communicate verbally is important, this communication is only half of the message. The nonverbal signals that you send are just as important in conveying your attitude and mood. Look at the images in Figures 5-2 and 5-3 and ask yourself what message the instructor is sending to the students.

In the following list, we include some of the items that contribute to nonverbal communication:

Nonverbal Factors

- General appearance
- Eyes
- Hands
- Movement and distance
- Body language

General Appearance   Chapter 3 briefly discussed the issue of proper attire for different situations. The way in which you dress communicates a message to your students. The important thing to remember regarding clothing is to dress appropriately based on the clientele. If you are teaching a group of presidents, you should wear a suit—because that is what these people are used to wearing. If you are teaching a group of technicians,

Figure 5-2
Nonverbal signals

Figure 5-3
Nonverbal signals

you should dress more casually—because a suit might cause them to associate you with management, which is not always conducive to a relaxed learning environment. Regardless of what you wear, you want to dress neatly. The disheveled, absent-minded professor look might work in college, but it would signal to your students that you might not care about or remember the small details. Your goal is to put the students at ease. One method that instructors often use (when appropriate) to indicate that it is time to get started and dive in to the topic is for the trainer to remove his or her jacket and roll up the sleeves. This action removes some of the formality that a suit imparts and makes the statement that the trainer is getting ready to work with the students to assist them with mastering the skills. Your general appearance makes a strong statement to the students, so think about the message that you want to send.

Eyes What should you look at when you are standing in front of the class and are speaking to the students? Remember, if you can draw the students in, involve them, and make them comfortable, you will increase their chances of learning the information. Your eyes are a powerful tool. If you look at a person, he or she feels as if you are paying attention to them. If you look away, they might feel neglected. Someone shared an incident with me that illustrates the subconscious power of looking at someone. A high school history class decided to test this theory on their teacher. (I am not endorsing this prank, but this story illustrates the point well.) The class started the semester by looking at the teacher when she was standing on the left half of the room and ignoring her when she was on the right half. After a while, they found that she spent most of her time on the left half. They continued to narrow the area in which they would pay attention. By the time the end of the semester arrived, the teacher remained in one spot during the entire class, because it was the only place in which she received any attention. Being a teacher, I think that this action was an awful thing to do, but it does prove the power of eye contact.

Make eye contact with each student throughout the day. Include a smile, and they will feel even better. Work around the room with your eyes, stopping for a moment on each student. Make your actions look natural; do not move up one row and down the next. We also do not mean that you should stare each student down until they look away, because doing so will either intimidate or anger them. The purpose of eye contact is to make the students feel as if you are talking *with* them, not *to* them or *above* them. Become a member of the learning environment, not the "sage on the stage."

Hands Use your hands to enhance, rather than distract from the message. Some people cannot talk without moving their hands to emphasize what they are saying. Motion is one way to draw the students' attention back to you when their minds might be wandering. Too much motion, however, can make people dizzy. As with the other factors in verbal and nonverbal communication, you must strive to achieve a happy medium.

Your hands can also reveal your feelings to the audience. If you are nervous, your hands might shake. If this situation occurs, hide your hands from view or rest them on the desk until you relax. If your hands are shaking, try not to hold them over the overhead projector, because doing so will augment the problem. Another common nervous behavior is to jingle the change or keys in your pocket. You should empty your pockets before you start a class, so that even if you do put your hands in your pockets, you will not make noise.

Instructors often use their hands to point to items. Try not to call on students by pointing at them with your index finger. Subconsciously, this action can be threatening to some people, because your hand takes on the appearance of a gun. Another motion that you can use instead is to point toward the person with your hand open and palm facing up. This action is seen as a welcoming and inviting gesture, rather then an accusatory one. Figures 5-4 and 5-5 illustrate the difference.

When you first meet the students, you should greet them with a handshake. Your handshake should impart a feeling of confidence and friendliness, which means that you should not have a weak handshake, which people often refer to as a "dead fish." This type of handshake could leave an

Figure 5-4
Pointing incorrectly

Figure 5-5
Pointing correctly

impression of weakness and a lack of sincerity. You do not want to squeeze so hard, however, that you hurt the other person's hand. Like every other nonverbal signal, you need to find a happy medium.

Movement and Distance   You can use movement in a variety of ways throughout a lesson. Chapter 8 will mention movement as a method for responding to students' needs. This chapter will focus on movement as a communication tool. Moving around the room while you are teaching is similar to hand movements in that there is a happy medium for which you should strive. I have been to presentations in which the speaker stood behind the podium and did not move for the entire talk, and in other lectures, the presenters made a point of walking around the stage and down into the audience. The presentations were on similar topics, but the presentation in which the instructor moved and joined the audience was much more interesting because I felt involved in the conversation. Similar to hand motions, the movement drew my attention and helped keep me focused. In contrast, a trainer once shared a course evaluation with me. The trainer was upset because of a student's comment that the class "learned nothing because the trainer was too busy dancing around and entertaining himself . . . I couldn't concentrate at all!" When teaching a topic, especially a technical topic, instructors need to give students a chance to absorb the material. Do not distract them with unnecessary pacing.

Movement affects another nonverbal issue of which the instructor needs to be aware: personal space. Each person has an area that he or she considers personal space, and people can become uncomfortable if another person invades that space. The perimeter of this personal space varies in size from person to person and in different cultures. If you approach a person who backs or leans away from you, then you are inside his or her personal space. If this situation happens, nonchalantly back up a little.

Because your goal when you are teaching is to engage the students, you do not want to turn your back to them. If you need to point at something on the board or screen, point to it while facing the students, as opposed to turning away from them. Figures 5-6 and 5-7 illustrate this point.

Body Language: The Messages You Send   Body language is the combination of all of the elements of nonverbal communication discussed previously. How you sit or stand sends a positive or negative message to your students. The following list illustrates some of the more common situations

Figure 5-6
Facing the screen

Figure 5-7
Facing the students

and the message that they send to the students (even if you do not feel the way you are indicating):

Common Body Language Messages

- *Folded arms*   You are blocking the student's access to you.
- *Open arms*   You are welcoming the students and inviting them to join you.
- *Leaning forward*   You are interested in the students and want to hear what they are saying.
- *Leaning back*   You want to distance yourself from the students. You do not want to associate with them. They are invading your space.
- *Feet on the desk*   You are completely relaxed and in your own world. You are out to lunch.
- *Tapping your foot*   You are impatient. The students are taking too long.
- *Sweat rings*   You are nervous. Never let them see you sweat.
- *Scratching your head*   You are confused.
- *Slouching in the chair*   You are tired or exhausted.

- *Swallowing frequently*   Your mouth is dry, and you are nervous. (Note: This sound might normally go unnoticed, but a microphone greatly accentuates it.)

- *Clenching objects*   You are nervous. Do not hold on to things if you notice this habit.

- *Smiling*   You are enthusiastic and enjoy what you are doing.

We can add many other actions to this list of messages that we experience (and respond to) every day.

Checking Your Nonverbal Communications

You should evaluate the nonverbal messages that you are sending to your students in the same way that you check the verbal ones: tape your training sessions and ask colleagues to evaluate your presentation. You should also consciously look for the signals that people send you. This technique will increase your awareness of what you could be teaching them.

Use the following checklist to assist with analyzing your nonverbal communications:

Nonverbal Communication Checklist

- *General appearance*
  - Are you dressed appropriately for the intended audience?
  - Is your outfit distracting?
- *Eyes*
  - Are you making eye contact with each student?
  - Are you staring at the students and intimidating them?
- *Hands*
  - Do you greet the students with a firm handshake?
  - What are you doing with your hands?
  - Are your hands distracting?
  - Are you fidgeting or playing with anything in your pockets?
  - Are you clenching objects?
  - Are you pointing at the students?

- *Movement and distance*
  - Are you moving about the room and involving the class?
  - Are you invading anyone's personal space?
  - Do you turn your back to them?
- *Body language*
  - Are you sending your students positive or negative messages?

Once you have identified your strengths and weaknesses, you need to strive to eliminate your weaknesses. You can accomplish this task practice and continuous self-evaluation.

Listening

The communications model at the beginning of this chapter contained three parts: the sender, the message, and the receiver. The items that we have discussed so far concern the sender and the message. Probably the most important skill in communications that many people seem to forget is listening. The receiver cannot hear the message without listening for it. As an instructor, you must develop your listening skills so that you understand the questions the students are asking and can respond appropriately. Listening is easy, if only people would concentrate on just listening. The problem is that the human mind can process information at a much faster rate than people can speak, which is the reason why some people say that they can watch television and carry on a conversation at the same time. Therefore, we have to concentrate if we want to give someone our undivided attention. If you are unsure of what a student has said, it is better to ask the student to restate the question than to answer the one that you think you heard. If you answer the wrong question, the receiver will know that you were not really listening.

Another problem that instructors often have is the overwhelming desire to help a student work through a problem. When the student is trying to formulate an answer, instructors will constantly chime in and help. The problem is that the instructor is not giving the student a chance to think through the problem, analyze various options, and figure out why something is right or wrong. Without the chance to think about the answer, students do not learn the why; instead, they only have a chance to memorize the answer that the instructor helps them figure out. Remember the discussion about silence? You must learn to not interrupt the students when they are asking questions or trying to work through the answers. Try to encourage the same behavior from your students.

Another facet of listening is the ability to clarify the question before you answer it. A good habit to develop is to restate the question to the student in order to verify the question. This action confirms that you are listening and that you understand the question. This technique also gives you an opportunity to see whether other students can answer the question. Listening is a crucial skill for the instructor and students to develop. We will cover more of this topic in Chapter 7, which discusses effective questioning skills.

Student Communications

All of the verbal and nonverbal items discussed in terms of the instructor also apply to the student. In other words, by learning to recognize and control these items yourself, you are also learning how to read your students and understand their point of view. This knowledge will enable you to anticipate and respond to their needs based on their verbal cues. One caution to keep in mind when trying to read the students is to not try to overinterpret every signal that they give you. After studying your tapes, you will find it easy to determine what your actions signify, because you know what you were thinking at the time. When observing the students, in many cases, you will never have met them before the class. Therefore, the constant fidgeting that you interpret as boredom might be a result of the wet pants that they are wearing because of the coffee that they spilled during the drive to class. You do not want to overreact to your interpretations. Having made this statement, we encourage you to continue observing the students to detect any signals that they are sending you.

There are a couple of nonverbal signals to add to the list that specifically relate to the students. Where they choose to sit in the classroom (if they have a choice when they arrive) might indicate their comfort with the material or excitement about being in class. Students who sit in the back (especially the corners) could be planning an escape route and be potential problem students. If the class is in a computer lab and a student turns the monitor away from you and the other students, it might be a sign that the student is doing something other than participating in the class (such as playing games, browsing the Internet, or checking e-mail). If the student paid for the training and does not want to benefit from it, that is his or her choice; but if the student's performance on the material will affect your evaluation (and your company's reputation), you need to address the issue.

With regard to verbal communication, you should listen to the tone of the students as they speak so that you can try to identify when they are excited, frustrated, or bored. This technique will assist you with managing the learning environment by adjusting the pace and instructional methods that you employ based on the students' reactions. Remember, however, the same caution applies to verbal skills regarding overinterpreting. A student who is constantly yawning through class might not be bored; instead, he or she might just be tired from a late night at the office.

Frames of Reference

A frame of reference refers to how people look at life based on their background, experiences, job duties, and so on. You need to tailor your lessons so that they fit the students' frames of reference. The example mentioned previously referred to teaching a class of college professors how to use a spreadsheet. To relate to their frame of reference, the worksheet they made in class was a grade book. The frame of reference refers to more than just work. If you were teaching a course in Europe and were discussing a device that dealt with temperature, using numbers based on the Fahrenheit temperature scale would not be as familiar to the students. If you were teaching a computer class to students who have used only a Macintosh computer, referencing the *Disk Operating System* (DOS) throughout the discussion would be useless and probably confusing. The following example illustrates how one instructor properly used frames of reference to help students relate to the topic. The course was on creating a Web page by using *Hypertext Markup Language* (HTML). The instructor asked the students how many of them were familiar with the word-processing program WordPerfect®. When he discovered that most of them were, he discussed the similarities between the codes viewed in the word processor when selecting Reveal Codes from the menu and the structure of HTML. This correlation assisted the students with relating to the new topic by creating an association with something with which they were already familiar. If you are not familiar with either WordPerfect® or HTML, the comparison I just made is an example of not adjusting to your frame of reference. One of the primary purposes of the course introduction is to learn about each of the students and determine their frames of reference so that you can adapt the learning environment and choose examples to which they can relate.

Checking Learner Understanding

Throughout this chapter, we have discussed the verbal and nonverbal signals that you and the students send. An important component of this competency is that you must be aware of each learner's level of understanding. Your skills at interpreting the signals that each student is sending you will be crucial to your success in this task. Chapter 7 will discuss questioning skills that will assist you with determining the students' current level of understanding, and Chapter 12, "Evaluating Learner Performance," will cover methods of evaluating each student's progress. Your job as the instructor is to learn to interpret the students' verbal and nonverbal signals and react to them appropriately.

SUMMARY ▬ ▬ ▬ ▬ ▬ ▬ ▬ ▬

The keys to effective evaluation of your communications skills are constant observation of the students and the awareness that your body language and how you are speaking is as important as the words that you are saying. Remember that these skills take practice, and the best method for self-evaluation is to tape your training sessions. Critique these sessions by using the checklist provided previously in the chapter. Finding colleagues to assist you will make the job much easier.

Once a training session is complete, the evaluation form that you distribute should have a section regarding your communication skills. This feedback will also assist you with spotting any weak areas, which you can then work on to improve for future sessions.

This chapter discussed essential verbal and nonverbal communications skills that you must master to be an effective trainer. You must learn to constantly monitor the messages that you are sending to your students and adapt them to their needs. Remember to use frames of reference to which they can relate and constantly observe the students to be certain that they understand the topic. The next chapter will build upon these skills and discuss effective presentation skills to improve your delivery even more.

QUESTIONS ▬ ▬ ▬ ▬ ▬ ▬ ▬ ▬

There might be multiple correct answers for some questions. The answers are located at the end of the chapter.

1. What is the message model discussed in this chapter?

   a. Message, emotion, results
   b. Sender, message, receiver
   c. Sender, receiver
   d. Sender, emotion, results
   e. None of the above

2. Which of the following are components of verbal communication?

   a. Emotions
   b. Body language
   c. Fillers
   d. Eye contact
   e. All of the above

3. Which of the following are components of nonverbal communication?

   a. Fillers
   b. Distance
   c. Hands
   d. Proper grammar
   e. All of the above

4. What should you do if you ask a question and there is silence?

   a. Answer the question immediately so that no one feels stupid.
   b. Change the subject.
   c. Use small talk or jokes to ease the discomfort.
   d. Wait; do not say anything.
   e. None of the above

5. What are examples of verbal communications that might be detrimental to the lesson?

   a. Using proper grammar
   b. Speaking in a monotone voice
   c. Speaking quickly
   d. Using technical terms when needed
   e. All of the above

6. Which is more important, verbal or nonverbal communication?

   a. Verbal communication
   b. Nonverbal communication
   c. Both are equally important.
   d. Neither are important.

7. What should you be looking at when you are teaching a lesson?

    a. Your notes
    b. Pick out the students who are paying attention and focus on them.
    c. Look at each student, one at a time and row by row.
    d. Look at each student, moving randomly from one to another.
    e. None of the above

8. Which is the best way to call on students?

    a. Point at them with an open, upturned hand.
    b. Shout their name.
    c. Point at them with your index finger.
    d. Say, "Hey you!"
    e. Draw names from a hat and randomly call on students by name.

9. What message are you sending when you face the board with your back to the students?

    a. You trust them.
    b. You are confused and are trying to focus on the problem on the board.
    c. You are ignoring them.
    d. It is time for them to do their own work.
    e. None of the above

10. What might students who choose to sit in the back of the room indicate to you?

    a. They do not like you.
    b. They have to leave early.
    c. They are upset at having to be in the class.
    d. They are unsure of the material.
    e. All of the above

11. What should you do if students appear bored?

    a. Observe and evaluate the situation to determine whether they are paying attention.
    b. Confront the student immediately.
    c. Talk to the student in private.
    d. Kick the student out of class to show everyone else that you mean business.

12. Why should you vary the tone of your voice?

    a. To keep the students' attention
    b. To keep your voice from fading
    c. To keep yourself awake
    d. To emphasize points and convey emotions
    e. All of the above

13. What do we mean by personal space?

    a. The classroom

    b. The desk

    c. The home

    d. The zone around a person that another person should not enter

    e. The distance that one should stand from a person in order for that person to hear you easily when you are talking in a normal voice

14. What actions might indicate to students that you are interested in their opinion?

    a. You stare at them throughout the class.

    b. You listen to them when they speak without interrupting them.

    c. You talk to them during breaks and lunch.

    d. You call them by name.

    e. You give them their space and talk to them only when they show interest.

15. What subconscious message can pointing at students send?

    a. You are encouraging them to take a risk and answer a question.

    b. You are pointing a gun at them.

    c. You are interested in their opinion.

    d. You are accusing them of something.

    e. None of the above

16. How often should you move around the room?

    a. Always

    b. Never

    c. When it is necessary to make a point

    d. If you need to get the class's attention

    e. Only when the students are doing exercises and might need your help

17. Which of the following are examples of positive body language?

    a. Crossing your arms

    b. Leaning toward the audience

    c. Leaning away from the audience

    d. Smiling

    e. Jiggling the change in your pocket

18. Which of the following are examples of negative body language?

    a. Turning your back on the audience

    b. Shaking their hands firmly

    c. Moving around the room

    d. Crossing your arms

    e. All of the above

19. What signal could indicate that you have entered a person's personal space?

   a. A smile
   b. A step toward you
   c. A step back away from you
   d. Nervousness
   e. Asking questions

20. What is the best way to assist students when they are having difficulty answering a question?

   a. As soon as you realize the problem, explain the answer to them.
   b. Tell them to ask another student for the answer.
   c. Tell them they have to work harder.
   d. Let them work through the problem, giving them hints if necessary.
   e. None of the above

21. What method(s) can you use to evaluate your verbal and nonverbal skills?

   a. Tape yourself while teaching a lesson.
   b. Ask a colleague to evaluate your presentation.
   c. Place questions on the student-evaluation forms regarding your communication skills.
   d. Observe others to practice identifying communication skills.
   e. All of the above

22. What do we mean by the term *frame of reference*?

   a. A student's willingness to learn new things
   b. A student's plans for the future
   c. A student's past experiences and how those experiences relate to the topic
   d. A student's attitude
   e. All of the above

23. In terms of verbal communication, what does the term *filler* refer to?

   a. The optional information that you discuss in class
   b. Using words such as "umm" or "like" to fill the silence between words
   c. The course manual
   d. The required information that you discuss in class
   e. All of the above

24. What is the recommended way to shake a student's hand?
    a. Squeeze as hard as you can to convey your confidence and power.
    b. Let the student do the squeezing so that you do not hurt him or her.
    c. Do not shake hands with the students.
    d. Shake hands firmly, based on the amount of pressure that the student applies.
    e. Any of the above

25. What information is useful for determining a student's frame of reference?
    a. Job duties
    b. Past experiences
    c. Favorite hobby
    d. Educational background
    e. All of the above

ANSWERS

1. b
2. a and c
3. b and c
4. d
5. b and c
6. c
7. d
8. a
9. c
10. e
11. a
12. a and d
13. d
14. b, c, and d
15. b and d
16. c and d
17. b and d

18. a and d
19. c and d
20. d
21. e
22. c
23. b
24. d
25. e

Demonstrating Effective Presentation Skills

■ ■ ■ Introduction

By the end of this chapter, you will be able to perform the following tasks:

- Plan effective presentations
  - Utilize Outlining
  - Organize content effectively
  - Utilize anecdotes, stories, analogies, and humor appropriately
  - Visual aids
  - Handouts
- Deliver effective presentations
  - Coping with stress
  - Presentation styles
  - Verbal and nonverbal signals

Competency 6 of the ibstpi Standards deals with the trainer's ability to effectively present each topic. To teach a lesson effectively, you need to use a number of instructional methods—one of which is a lecture or presentation. Even if the course focuses primarily on lab work, where the students work on projects most of the time, there will come a time when you need to present a topic to the students. Teaching a topic to a group of people involves more than just standing in front of the group and reading from your notes. You have probably attended presentations or lectures where this situation occurred, and like most people, you probably found this style to be extremely boring and had trouble concentrating on the subject. You might have attended other sessions in which the presenter was so exciting and personable that you could listen for hours without losing interest. You must strive to be a dynamic speaker who creates and sustains excitement and enthusiasm for the audience. Chapter 5 discussed verbal and nonverbal communications and the need to be aware of the signals that you are conveying to the audience. This chapter expands on these topics by discussing the details of preparing and giving a presentation. Throughout the chapter, always keep in mind the messages associated with your words, body language, and visual aids.

■ ■ ■ Presentation Basics

The first step toward being an effective presenter is preparation. Anytime you stand in front of the class and speak about a topic, you are giving a presentation or lecture. The presentation can be a five-minute overview of a topic or a two-hour, in-depth discussion. Either way, the lecture will contain the same elements—and you should prepare for it. Previous chapters discussed preparing the learning environment and planning the lesson. You still need to think about how you will convey the message to the students—not just what you want to say, but how you want to say it. To determine your approach, you should work through a number of steps each time you plan a presentation. We describe the essential preparation steps in Figure 6-1.

Determining the Objective

The first step in preparing a presentation is determining your objectives for the particular lesson. Decide what you want the students to learn from the lecture, and focus on that topic. Do not introduce too many concepts in the same lecture, or you could overwhelm the students. By continually refocusing on the objective while you prepare the lesson, you will eliminate any extraneous material. If you have ever sat through a lecture and afterwards were unable to determine the point of the discussion, you quickly realized the necessity of concentrating on the objective.

Evaluating the Audience

In previous chapters, while we discussed the preparation and management of the learning environment, we also discussed audience evaluations. While

Figure 6-1
Preparing
presentations

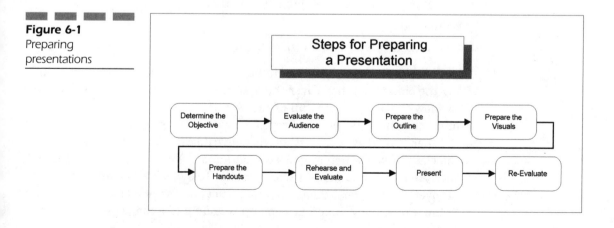

audience evaluation is not specifically part of this competency, it is a necessary step in order to become an effective presenter. You *must* recognize the fact that people will react to a presentation differently based on their backgrounds (occupation, technical ability, and so on). A fellow trainer told me about a class on computer viruses that she recently taught. Before the course, she called the clients and discovered that the class consisted primarily of network managers who were concerned about the safety of their networks. This knowledge radically altered her presentation, which she originally intended for home users, because she had to discuss network anti-virus software options instead of the more common standalone versions. Do your homework, and learn as much as you can about the students before the session begins. This preparation will assist you considerably when you prepare your presentation.

Preparing the Outline

The presentation outline is the most important component of the planning process. Outlining enables you to organize the content effectively. Unless you are an exceptional speaker who knows your material inside and out and never becomes flustered or sidetracked, you should develop an outline based on the course objective. The purpose of the outline is to keep you on track and to ensure that you cover all of the necessary information. This component is a crucial part of the distinguishing characteristics of the competency, specifically the reference to structuring the content. The outline should contain the key ideas that you wish to discuss. The outline also needs to follow a logical order. Many speech courses teach that you should use the following formula for organizing a presentation:

1. Tell them what you are going to tell them.
2. Tell them.
3. Tell them what you told them.

This simple formula states that every presentation should start by listing the objectives, then cover the material, and then review the objectives to show that you covered all of the objectives. If you keep this concept in mind, the students should always be aware of the point of the lecture.

When you create your outline, do not write complete sentences to read to the class. If you watch any news program on television, you can often tell that the reporter is using a teleprompter. Television reporters often stumble over words, repeat themselves, or do not add the proper voice inflections to the words. They sometimes end up sounding like robots reciting lines.

Once, I observed a student teacher who had this problem. He was not comfortable speaking in front of the students, would quickly become nervous, and would lose his place. He was always fumbling through his notes and often lost complete control of the class. I realized that each day he had written out his entire lecture and was trying to read through it. The class lasted one-and-a-half hours. He had a script of at least 15 pages that he worked from each day. There were several problems with this method. First, he was exhausted because it took him hours each night to write the script. Second, whenever he lost his place, he became flustered—which the students sensed and capitalized on (this class was a summer-school course and consisted of seventh and eighth graders).

The point is that you need to be comfortable enough with your material and presentation that you feel confident without a script. In fact, it is much easier not using a script; you will not mess up your lines because there are not any. Your course outline is simply a road map for you to follow that includes key words or notes that will help you remember to cover all of the necessary information.

You can develop your outline in many forms. You should choose the one that works best for you, whether it is a note card, bullets on a sheet of paper, or yellow Post-It® notes. Some people use props or visual maps instead. When teaching about the basic components of a computer, I sometimes bring in a computer, which I use as my outline. I simply pull out each component and talk about it. If I think that I have forgotten something, I just look inside the computer to see what is left. A visual map, depicted in Figure 6-2, is like a flow chart. You could draw pictures representing the key

Figure 6-2
Visual map

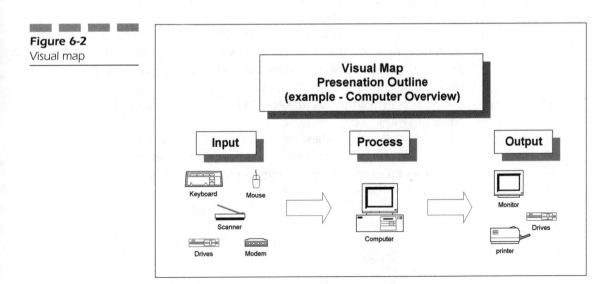

components in the presentation, using arrows to show the flow of the presentation. A well-organized outline will lead to a well-structured class that covers all of the necessary information. You will find that after you have presented the same material several times, you might never even look at your notes—but you will still be confident that they are there to assist you if necessary.

Preparing Visuals

Once you have developed your outline and know exactly what you plan to talk about, you should develop visual aids to complement the lecture. Numerous studies prove that preferred learning styles vary greatly among people. The mind can also absorb information much faster than people can speak. Therefore, the instructor needs to acknowledge and accommodate multiple learning styles. Imagine sitting in a lecture hall listening to a presentation with all of the lights off. Would you be able to concentrate on the discussion? Now, imagine sitting in a classroom with windows and a computer sitting in front of you with a screen saver sending fish across the screen. All of these visual distractions could significantly diminish the amount of material that you will retain. We discussed how to eliminate these distractions, or at least minimize them, in Chapter 2; however, your eyes will always find something to watch. Thus, it is in the best interest of the instructor to provide something for the students to watch. Whenever possible, you should always include visuals with your presentation.

Luckily, a variety of software programs are available that enable you to create presentation slides quickly and easily, such as Microsoft® PowerPoint or Lotus® Freelance. With most of these programs, you can begin with an outline that you then transform into a colorful presentation. While you are creating your outline, you are also creating your visuals. If you do not have an LCD projector available for your presentation, you can print the slides on overhead transparencies (which you should do for backup purposes anyway).

Figures 6-3 and 6-4 show two examples of visuals.

Which one is better, and why? Whenever you create slides that you will project on an overhead or LCD projector, you need to consider the following items:

- Font size
- Font type
- Amount of text

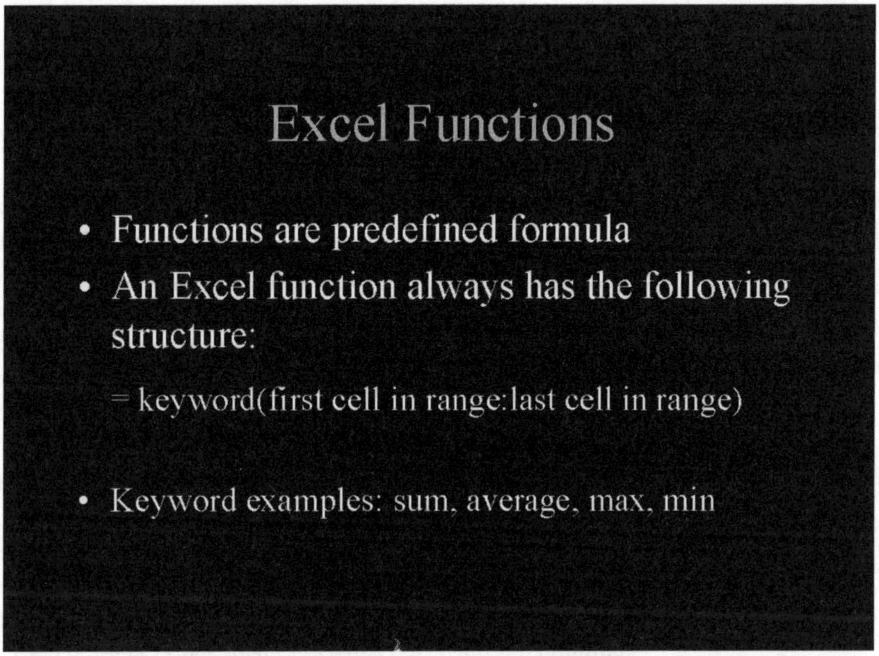

Figure 6-3
A good slide

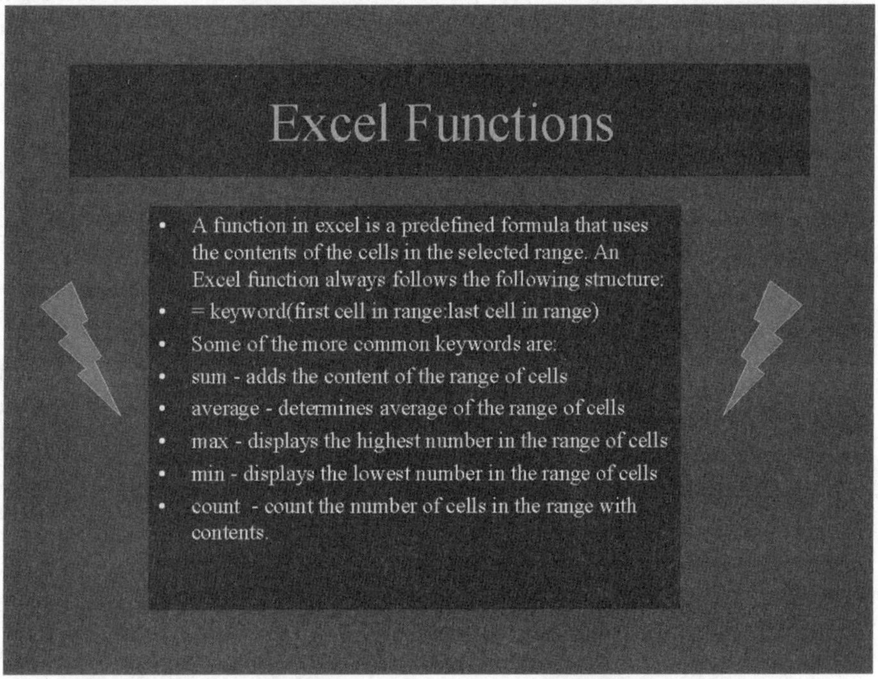

Excel Functions

- Functions are predefined formula
- An Excel function always has the following structure:

  = keyword(first cell in range:last cell in range)

- Keyword examples: sum, average, max, min

Figure 6-4
A bad slide

Excel Functions

- A function in excel is a predefined formula that uses the contents of the cells in the selected range. An Excel function always follows the following structure:
- = keyword(first cell in range:last cell in range)
- Some of the more common keywords are:
- sum - adds the content of the range of cells
- average - determines average of the range of cells
- max - displays the highest number in the range of cells
- min - displays the lowest number in the range of cells
- count - count the number of cells in the range with contents.

- Graphics
- Color
- Templates

The font size must be large enough to be read from any distance. I have attended many presentations in which the instructor made overhead transparencies of pages taken from a book. The text was impossible to read unless you were sitting in the front row. Depending on whom you talk to, the minimum font size should range from 18 points to 30 points (72 points equal one inch). One way to test the readability of your handouts is to stand and place the visual on the floor at your feet. If you can easily read the text, then the type size is large enough—assuming, of course, that you have normal vision.

There are literally thousands of fonts (or letter styles) available on computers. You can divide all of these fonts into two categories: serif fonts and sans-serif fonts. A serif refers to the slight enlargement or curl that appears at the endpoints of the lines in font styles. Fonts that have these feet are serif fonts; those that do not have the feet are sans-serif fonts. Studies have shown that serif fonts are easier to read because your eyes follow the curves that flow from letter to letter. You will find that the majority of the text in books and magazines uses serif fonts. Sans-serif fonts stand out and draw your attention more, so people use this type of font more often in titles. Keep this point in mind when creating your visual aids, and choose the appropriate size and type of font.

Even if you adhere to the suggested minimum font size, you can still get into trouble by placing too much text on a slide. Another general rule is that there should not be more than six to eight lines of text on a given slide. In other words, you cannot present long paragraphs of text on a slide. Luckily, this limitation fits perfectly with the standards that you should follow for your outlines. Use short, bulleted lists of information to remind you (and the students) of the necessary information.

One danger with using presentation software is that inserting extraneous information on a slide is too easy. One example is the use of graphics. Because adding graphics is so easy, many people add any graphic that they can find to spice up the presentation. Nothing on the slide should be gratuitous. Everything you place on a slide should enhance the message that you are delivering. If a graphic is not needed, then do not add it. The graphic will just be a distraction. The same can be said for transition effects between slides. Transitions enable a seamless move from one slide to the next and can help build continuity. Do not use every transition that the program offers, however, just because you can. This action might cause the students to spend more time guessing what the next transition will be, rather than paying attention to the subject. The same rules apply for sound effects and animations. A well-placed transition can focus attention on an item, but use this feature intelligently.

Think carefully about the use of color, because color can have a subtle but powerful effect on the students. Consider the following example. A fellow trainer was hired to teach a technical course for a local company. Throughout the day, he noticed that whenever he presented material to the class, the students appeared to be tense and distant. He had a difficult time encouraging participation, and at the end of the day, he felt that few of the students grasped much of the required material. After the course, he pondered the situation but could not think of anything that he had done to offend the students. He had taught the course many times before and was always successful and well received. That evening, while watching the news, the reason for the problem became quite clear. He was watching a segment announcing that the company might possibly be taken over by its largest competitor, and the report mentioned that some employees might lose their jobs. The other company's corporate colors were green and white. In fact, they were the exact shade of green and white that he used in his presentation. With each presentation, the colors reminded the employees of the possibility of layoffs. Rarely will your colors have such a drastic effect, but each color is associated with a particular emotion. Figure 6-5 shows this relationship for several of the more common colors. Be aware of the impact of your choice of colors.

If you are using presentation software to create your visual aids, another issue is the use of templates. Templates provide you with a predefined design incorporating graphic elements, color, and font type. All of the design work is already done for you. The only problem is that there are a limited number of formats and a large number of people using them. Commonly at a large conference, you will see many presenters who have the same design. To set yourself apart, make minor changes to the design so that it is different from everyone else's.

Once you have completed your handouts, ask yourself the questions in the following checklist to eliminate any problems.

NOTE: *This checklist is also useful when addressing competency 11, "Using Media Effectively."*

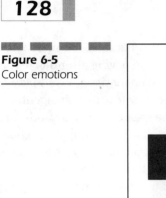

Figure 6-5
Color emotions

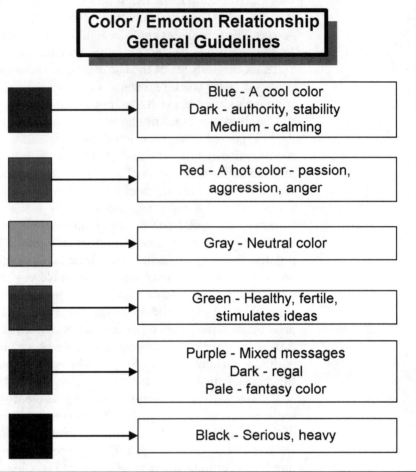

Presentation Visuals Checklist

- Is all of the necessary information covered?
- Can the text be read easily from a distance?
- Is there too much text on the slide?
- Does each of the graphics have a purpose?
- Are the colors appropriate from the students' viewpoint?
- What emotions do the colors convey?
- Do you have a backup of the visual aids in case the computer or projector fails?

Preparing Handouts

Unless the students have course manuals that cover all of the material you are lecturing on, you should provide them with handouts of the presentation so that they will always have a resource to refer to. If you have used presentation software to develop visual aids, printing the handouts is simple. Most programs offer options of printing one, two, four, or six slides per page and will add lines for note taking.

Deciding when to pass out the handouts is debatable. One side of the argument states that if you hand them out before the lecture, the students will read ahead and not pay attention to what you are saying. The other argument states that the students can use the handouts as a reference, and rather than frantically taking notes on everything you say, they can take notes on their reactions to the presentation. I believe that handing them out before the class is the better choice. Those students who do not want to pay attention will find something else to distract them (if it's not the handouts).

Remember the Verbal and Nonverbal Signals

Chapter 5 discussed the numerous issues regarding your verbal and non-verbal signals. Once you have prepared your outline, notes, visual aids and handouts, ask yourself what signals you are sending to the students. Remember the emotions that certain colors can convey. If you are teaching a course on graphic design and all of your handouts are plain black-and-white overhead slides, what message are you conveying regarding your abilities? Possibly, you are communicating that you are not too knowledgeable about the newest technologies. If you have attended a conference with a technology theme lately, you will be hard pressed to find a presentation that does not use some form of presentation technology. Those who do not use this technology are "behind the times," and they lose credibility. Each of your actions sends a signal to the students, so do your best to make your message positive.

Rehearse and Evaluate the Presentation

Once you have finished creating the presentation, you need to practice it. The first time that you think through the actual words that you will use to discuss your notes should not be when you are standing in front of the class. Being an expert on the subject matter does not automatically mean that you know how to teach the topic. This problem exists in many technical fields. Someone tells the expert to teach everyone else in the department how to do something. As this book demonstrates, there is a lot more to being a good presenter than just knowing the subject matter. Test your presentation on a colleague, and get that person's reactions.

When you rehearse the presentation, remember to keep track of time. You want to make sure that you can cover all of the material in the time allotted. If you discover that you cannot get through everything, you need to either eliminate some of the material or increase the length of time. If you rush through the presentation, the students will feel rushed and will never get a chance to ask questions. Evaluate the length of the presentation and make sure that the pace is appropriate.

Use the following checklist to determine whether anything is missing from your presentation:

Presentation Rehearsal Checklist

- Was the objective communicated clearly?
- Was the information appropriate for the level of students?
- Did the visual aids support the presentation, or were they distracting?
- Was the presentation the proper length?
- Did you summarize the material at the end?
- Did you monitor all of your verbal and nonverbal signals (refer to Chapter 5)?

Presenting the Topic

Now that you have worked through the steps for preparing the presentation, the time has come to present your information. At this point, most people look forward to and fear standing up in front of the group and teaching the material. Public speaking is one of the activities that many people fear. Even if you are a seasoned presenter, it is still normal to be a little nervous before the presentation (or course) begins. A colleague of mine once said that if you are not a little nervous, you either do not care about the topic or you are comatose. The nervous energy that you experience before a stressful event is a natural human reaction. This nervousness is the body's way of preparing for a potentially dangerous situation. Many of the world's best actors, athletes, politicians, and teachers experience extreme cases of nervousness before the big event. If you do experience this nervousness, it will eventually decrease as you become more comfortable presenting the topic and teaching in general. I speak from experience in this matter.

Dealing with Stress

You can take steps to reduce stress-induced problems. The first step, which we mention repeatedly throughout this book, is to be well prepared. If you are confident in your knowledge of the subject matter and have followed all of the steps for preparing the learning environment and the lesson, then you will have reduced the most significant cause of stress.

The second step is expecting the unexpected. This statement sounds impossible, but it reverts back to preparation. Expecting the unexpected means imagining what could go wrong and trying to have contingency plans in place. After you present a topic several times, you will know what questions to expect and where the students will have the most difficulty. Each time you teach a topic, your experience will become easier.

If you find that you still have problems with stress, you should try to develop a routine that you stick to before each class. This routine will help relieve your stress, because it adds structure to the preparation process. A former colleague of mine who traveled around the country offering three-day training sessions on a proprietary software program consistently followed the routine described next in order to put her in the proper frame of mind (and to relieve her nerves) for each training session:

1. The first thing that she did was plan her travel so that she arrived at the location on the afternoon before the day of the session and checked into her hotel room.

2. Next, she checked out the training facility to identify any potential environmental problems that might arise.

3. Next, she made sure that all of her handouts and notes were in order.

4. She returned to her hotel and had a relaxing dinner (room service) and watched a movie to relax and not think about the course.

5. She then reviewed her notes one last time and went to bed at a reasonable hour (after making sure that she had set her alarm).

6. She awoke several hours before the session, had a relaxed breakfast, then arrived at the training facility about 45 minutes before the session.

7. She checked on any final details and reviewed the material until about 15 minutes before the course.

8. She then took a five-minute walk to calm her nerves, checked herself in the mirror, and returned to the room prepared to greet the students as they arrived.

9. She made a point of talking to each student in order to learn their names and to set them at ease.

10. When the starting time arrived, she was ready.

This schedule might seem extreme, but this routine enabled her to be organized and ready for any session. The most important point is that when the students arrived, she was not worrying about anything but greeting them; all of her other preparations were complete. An important step in her routine that all trainers should do is greet the students as they arrive and talk to them. This socializing not only sets the students at ease, but it also helps the trainer relax and get into "presentation mode." If you have problems with stress, find a routine that works for you and stick with it.

Presentation Style

The style of the instructor when presenting the material has a significant impact on the success of the lesson. Recall the verbal and nonverbal signals discussed in Chapter 5. If you stand at the podium and clutch it while you read your lecture in a monotone voice to the students, they will not only sense your insecurities but also will most likely fall asleep. To be an effective teacher, you need to be a dynamic speaker—one who can capture the students' attention and maintain their excitement regarding the material. The most important thing that you should strive to do is to act naturally. You want the students to know that you are genuinely interested in being there and teaching them the material. Share your excitement with them. Everyone is different, and you will develop your own style of teaching. No one style is the best. Describing the styles that you should strive *not* to adopt is easier (such as the ones described in the following sections).

Haughty and Condescending   No one wants to be treated condescendingly. Chapter 3 discussed establishing your credibility, but we do not mean that you should try to intimidate the students with all of your degrees, certifications, and experience. They must perceive you as knowledgeable, but also approachable. If a student challenges your presentation, do not become defensive and "put him in his place;" instead, use this opportunity to discuss the topic in more detail.

The Best Buddy   The opposite of being haughty and arrogant is to be overly friendly. The students are attending the session to learn a new skill, not to find a new best friend. (If they are, they are in the wrong place.) Although you want to set them at ease during the presentation, you do not want to be overly chummy with the students. Do not make up nicknames for them or joke with them in any way that they might feel is offensive or suggestive.

The Joker   You can use jokes to lighten the atmosphere and relax people, but jokes can also backfire. Similar to the best-buddy example, the students are not attending the session to see a comedian. Use humor only when it relates to the topic, and stay away from any humor that might be offensive to anyone. For example, I work in western New York, and people constantly make references about the winters. Personally, I like snow, and I chose to live here. If I attend a session where the presenter starts by complaining about the awful, snowy winter and how he or she would hate to live here, these comments automatically offend me. Use humor only when it is appropriate and nonoffensive.

The Sarcastic Presenter   The use of sarcasm follows the same reasoning as that for jokes. Some people are used to sarcasm; others are not. Some will misunderstand what you are trying to say. Sarcasm has no place in your presentation.

Bored   The emotional state of the participants often mirrors that of the presenter. If you act bored with the topic, the students will definitely sense this attitude and become bored or discouraged as well. You must make them believe that there is nowhere else that you would rather be than in the room with them, presenting your topic. They will share in your excitement. If you find yourself becoming bored with the topic, either stop teaching it or find a new way to approach the material.

Bundle of Nerves   We have discussed nervousness several times in this book already. If you are nervous, the students will sense it—and the nervousness will erode your credibility.

The Reader   *Do not constantly read from your notes.* Remember the student teacher described previously in this chapter. The notes are there to remind you to cover certain topics. You cannot be a dynamic presenter who speaks with emotion if you are reading a script. If you know your material (and if you do not, then you should not be teaching it) and have practiced the presentation, the words will come naturally—especially after you have presented the information several times.

The Angry Presenter Everybody has a bad day, but as the presenter, you must hide any negative emotions from the students. If a student tries to argue with you, do not become angry. Expect to be occasionally challenged on the topic of the presentation, so be prepared to answer the questions that might arise. If you are attacked personally, *do not* respond with anger. You are expected to act professionally, regardless of the students' behavior. Once the students detect that you are angry with them or do not like them, re-establishing a positive learning environment will be difficult.

The Liar This point should be obvious, but never ever make up an answer that you know is incorrect. Not only will the students sometimes sense that you are not being truthful, but this approach will destroy your credibility when they discover the truth.

The Right Style If you can eliminate all of the behaviors mentioned here, you will be on your way to becoming an effective presenter. Listed are a number of positive traits that you should strive to include in your style:

- Be natural.
- Be sincere.
- Be dynamic (voice, motion, enthusiasm, and so on).
- Be relaxed.
- Interact with the individuals (remember the discussion regarding eye contact).

If you can incorporate these characteristics into your style, you will be effective. Remember that there is no one right way to do things. You have to find out what works for you, always keeping in mind the verbal and non-verbal messages that your style sends to the audience.

Varying the Presentation

If you present the same topic repeatedly, you might find yourself going into auto-pilot mode occasionally. You will find yourself so comfortable with the presentation that you will say the same words and use the same examples over and over again. This repetitiveness can cause the material to become boring for both you and the audience. To prevent this boredom, remember to vary the content of your presentation regularly and use different examples, new stories, and any other modifications that make sense.

Using Stories, Anecdotes, and Analogies

When you are presenting a topic, you want the audience to be able to relate to the subject and internalize the information. One of the best tools available to you is telling stories or describing scenarios. You probably still remember some of the stories, anecdotes, or analogies that you heard when you were a child. One of the purposes of these stories is to teach children something. We all have heard the phrase, "The moral of the story is . . . " Stories such as these help audience members remember concepts that they would otherwise forget. If you choose your stories wisely so that they match the audience's frames of reference, you will be even more successful.

The Opening

Now that we have discussed the various components of a presentation and what to avoid, we will discuss the most important part of the presentation: the opening. The words you say in the first couple of minutes will set the tone for the entire session and will determine the receptiveness of the audience. You need to capture the audience's interest and get them excited about the topic with your words and your actions.

Remember the verbal and nonverbal signals that we discussed in Chapter 5, and implement them. The following list suggests several strategies that you can implement singly or together to start the presentation:

- Start by opening up to the audience with your hands and posture.
- Step toward them to show that you are interested in being there with them; some presenters will walk down the rows in the audience to get close to them.
- Move around the stage.
- Use your voice to draw them into the topic; speak with conviction and excitement.
- Start by telling a story to which they can relate (remember to be careful about humor).
- Start with an exciting multimedia presentation or video (related to the topic) to grab their attention.

■ Tell them why they need to be at this presentation and what knowing the material will do for them. Get them to buy into your presentation. (Chapter 9, "Providing Positive Reinforcement and Motivational Incentives," addresses this topic in depth.)

Your knowledge of the audience and your style will help determine the appropriate opening. The key is to capture the audience's attention and build students' excitement about the session.

SUMMARY

This chapter discussed the mechanics of creating, practicing, and giving a presentation. Remember that you must address many of the topics discussed in previous chapters, including communications skills and preparation, before you can master this competency. The underlying theme throughout this process is being aware of the verbal and nonverbal messages that you are sending to the audience while you present. Through preparation and practice, you can eliminate the negative messages and emphasize the positive ones. The result will be that you become a dynamic and exciting presenter who can excite the audience and encourage them to learn. The primary role of a trainer is to build a positive, interactive learning environment, and effective presentation skills are necessary for succeeding at this endeavor.

QUESTIONS

There might be multiple correct answers for some questions. The answers are located at the end of the chapter.

1. What is the first step in becoming an effective presenter?
   a. Writing a word-for-word script
   b. Preparation
   c. Being able to "wing it"
   d. All of the above

2. What is the purpose of a presentation?

   a. To show the students how smart you are
   b. To teach the students everything about a particular topic
   c. To teach the objective of the lesson
   d. None of the above

3. Why is it useful to know the students' backgrounds before the presentation?

   a. You can use examples that are relevant to their jobs.
   b. You will know their names.
   c. You will understand their frame of reference.
   d. All of the above
   e. None of the above

4. Which of the following is an example of a good course outline?

   a. A page listing the key topics to cover
   b. A word-for-word narration of everything you want to say
   c. A page with pictures representing each topic of the presentation
   d. The training manual serving as the outline
   e. Memorizing everything so that you do not need an outline

5. Why should you use visual aids for a presentation?

   a. To keep the audience's attention
   b. To explain complex topics
   c. To give the students something to follow as you talk
   d. None of the above
   e. All of the above

6. Which of the following items could affect the quality of the visual aids?

   a. Font size
   b. Font type
   c. Amount of text
   d. Color
   e. All of the above

7. Which of the following colors can represent anger?

   a. Blue
   b. Red
   c. Green
   d. Yellow
   e. Orange

8. Which of the following colors can be soothing?

   a. Blue
   b. Red
   c. Green
   d. Yellow
   e. Orange

9. What is the purpose of adding a graphic to a visual aid?

   a. To add some pizzazz to the slide
   b. To take up space
   c. To illustrate a point of the discussion
   d. To show an example

10. What are the traits of a good presenter?

    a. Confidence
    b. Knowledge of the material
    c. Well prepared
    d. Exciting
    e. All of the above

11. What should you do if you are always nervous before presentations?

    a. Find a new line of work.
    b. Develop a routine to follow before every presentation.
    c. Do not look at the audience, and your listeners will not know that you are nervous.
    d. Keep you hands in your pockets so that the audience does not see them shake.
    e. Make sure that you are well prepared.

12. What is the best presentation style for which you should strive?

    a. Peppy and exciting
    b. Funny
    c. Serious
    d. Being yourself

13. What strategy can you use to help a student remember a concept?

    a. Tell stories relating to the concept.
    b. Tell the students that it is important for them to memorize the information.
    c. Explain the concept slowly so that they will understand the information.
    d. Relate the skill to their job.
    e. None of the above

14. Why is the opening of the presentation important?

    a. The opening sets the tone for the entire presentation.

    b. The opening tells the students what they will be learning.

    c. The opening builds excitement.

    d. The opening helps you establish a rapport with the students.

    e. All of the above

15. Which are more important: verbal or nonverbal skills?

    a. Verbal skills

    b. Nonverbal skills

    c. Both are equally important.

    d. Neither is important.

16. What is a good method for improving yourself as a presenter?

    a. Practice

    b. Observing other presenters

    c. Getting plenty of rest before each presentation

    d. Having others observe and evaluate your presentation

    e. All of the above

17. What is the final step of the presentation preparation process?

    a. Sleeping

    b. Presenting the topic

    c. Evaluating the audience

    d. Preparing the handouts

    e. Re-evaluating the presentation

18. How much information should you include in a single presentation?

    a. Cover all of the objectives of the course.

    b. Cover the objectives of the current lesson only.

    c. Cover as much as time allows.

    d. None of the above

19. When should you give the students their handouts?

    a. Before class

    b. In the middle of the lecture

    c. After the lecture

    d. Never

    e. It depends on the purpose of the handouts.

20. What types of jokes are acceptable for a presentation?

    a. Jokes that relate to the topic and that are not offensive

    b. All jokes are acceptable.

    c. Jokes are not acceptable.

    d. Jokes that are not directed at the audience

    e. Jokes about yourself

21. When is sarcasm acceptable in a presentation?

    a. When you need to put students in their place

    b. Never

    c. When you want to put the students at ease

    d. As an icebreaker

    e. When you know a member of the audience and know that person will not be offended

22. What can you do to keep a presentation exciting for you to present?

    a. Change the stories that you use.

    b. Modify the structure of the presentation.

    c. Accept that the topic can be boring.

    d. Take a break from teaching the topic.

    e. None of the above

23. What traits could indicate that you are nervous?

    a. Reading your notes word for word

    b. Smiling at the audience

    c. Playing with the change in your pocket

    d. Speaking loudly

    e. Shuffling your papers constantly

24. What are some of the signs of a poor visual aid?

    a. Too much text on the page

    b. Using fonts that are larger than 30 points

    c. Improper use of color

    d. No graphics

    e. All of the above

25. What is the proper length for a presentation?

    a. No more than 20 minutes

    b. Long enough to cover the objective of the lesson

    c. No more than 45 minutes

    d. No more than an hour

    e. The presentation length does not matter.

ANSWERS

1. b

2. c

3. d

4. a and c

5. e

6. e

7. b

8. a

9. c and d

10. e

11. b and e

12. d

13. a and d

14. e

15. c

16. e

17. e

18. b

19. e

20. a

21. b

22. a, b, and d

23. a, c, and e

24. a and c

25. b

Demonstrating Effective Questioning Skills and Techniques

Introduction

By the end of this chapter, you will be able to perform the following tasks:

- Use questioning skills effectively
  - Select appropriate types of questions
  - Encourage learner participation
  - Appropriately respond to student questions
  - Evaluate student progress

Competency 7 of the ibstpi Standards deals with the trainer's ability to use questions effectively. The ability to effectively ask and answer questions is an essential skill for trainers without which it would be impossible to evaluate the students' level of understanding. This chapter discusses the various factors that determine the success of a question. Questioning strategies are discussed that will enable you to evaluate student skills, stimulate and direct discussions, and encourage a positive, interactive learning environment.

Strategies for answering students' questions also are discussed. It is important to know when and how to answer students' questions so the students learn the necessary material. Questioning skills are the foundation for generating positive classroom interactions.

Why Ask Questions?

Why do you ask students questions? When should you ask questions? How do you ask the questions? Questions can be used for a number of reasons during a class. Asking and answering questions are the instructor's best tool for determining the progress of the students and the success of the lesson. However, questions are more than just an assessment tool. The following list summarizes some of the most important reasons.

- Questions allow the instructor to check the understanding of the students on a particular topic
- Questions are a method to encourage student participation in the lesson
- Questions can be used to shape a discussion by leading the students toward the desired solution and keeping the lesson on track; questions also put the students in the proper "thinking" mode

■ Questions are necessary to build the interaction that creates a positive and participatory environment

A question is the instructor's best resource for creating and maintaining an active learning environment. Active learning means that the participants are involved in the process rather than just listening to a lecture. Think back to classes that you attended as a student. I would bet that you had classes where you knew the instructor would randomly call on people. This encouraged you to listen during class and be prepared in case he or she called on you. In classes where the instructor never asked questions, it was easier to let your mind wander because you knew there would be no immediate consequences. The questions encouraged you to follow the discussion and to be prepared to participate. If you, as the instructor, notice a student starting to "drift off," you should ask an easy question to draw that student back into the session without embarrassment.

Questions are an important tool that can assist you in creating a supportive environment where students are comfortable answering and asking questions, which is one of the distinguishing characteristics of this competency. When the students see that you respond positively to their questions and answers, their fear of participating will quickly diminish.

If you discover that the discussion is moving away from the topic, you can use questions to redirect the students and lead them in the right direction. This is a good way to keep them on track without giving them all of the answers. If you have a student who is monopolizing the discussion, questions directed at other students can shift the focus away from the overbearing student. Once you have mastered the art of asking questions, you will have a powerful tool in your teaching arsenal.

Levels of Learning

It is easy to ask the wrong types of questions and draw the wrong conclusions regarding a student's level of understanding. When asking a question, you must realize that there are two parts to every question: the question and the response. As illustrated in Figure 7-1, this is a two-way relationship.

You need to first think about the type of response that you are looking for to determine the type of question you should ask. To do this properly, you need to determine the level of understanding that you are expecting the students to achieve.

Figure 7-1
Question/Answer

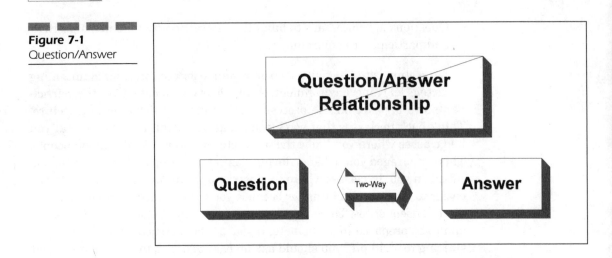

Benjamin Bloom organized the various levels of thinking complexity into six levels. These can be used to determine a person's depth of understanding on a particular topic. Figure 7-2 depicts the progression through the six levels of learning.

The six levels of learning are defined as follows:

1. *Knowledge* The first level of learning is defined as a basic memorization of facts. For example, memorizing that the acronym RAM stands for random access memory would indicate that students have reached this level, but they would not necessarily know what random access memory is.

2. *Comprehension* The second level of learning is defined as an understanding of what the memorized facts mean. An example of this level is knowing that RAM is the temporary memory, or "workspace," on a computer and is used to hold all of the information you are currently working with and that it is erased when the computer is turned off.

3. *Application* The third level of learning is defined as the ability to apply the knowledge to a specific task. For example, you know that data is stored temporarily in RAM, so you remember to save your work to the hard drive before you turn off the computer.

4. *Analysis* The fourth level of learning is defined as the ability to break a concept into components, recognizing the relationship between the components and understanding how to use the components to explain the concept clearly. For example, you might find that your computer is slowing down or unable to open a program and determine that, as RAM is the "workspace," there is not enough RAM in the computer to run the program.

Figure 7-2
Levels of learning

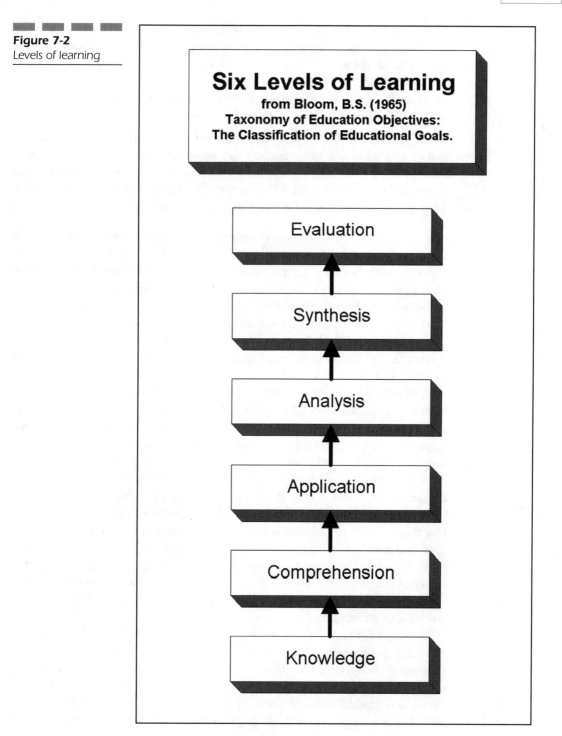

5. *Synthesis*   The fifth level of learning is defined as the ability to develop a new concept by applying previous knowledge. For example, you know that RAM is the "workspace" into which programs are loaded and the speed that the data can be transported in the RAM determines the speed of the computer. You study the existing types of RAM and discover a new design that will speed up the data transfer.

6. *Evaluation*   The sixth and final level of learning is defined as the ability to evaluate a new concept and access its viability and usefulness based on existing knowledge and past experiences. For example, you compare the new design with the design of existing products and determine whether it will work properly and more efficiently.

Notice that each level is a progression from the previous one. Realize that you do not need to progress to the sixth level to be proficient at a task. Think about when you learned math. In grade school you memorized the multiplication table. Later you learned how to determine the area of a circle by using a special number called π. You memorized that π was approximately 3.14. Most people do not know (nor care) about the origins of π or how to calculate it. In fact, you do not need this information to use it in equations. You only need to progress to the application level to be able to use the concept of π.

As the instructor, you need to determine what the necessary level of learning is for the topic you are teaching in a given class. This will determine how extensively you must cover a topic, how much time will be spent in practice and review, and the types of questions that you will be asking the students. In a perfect world, you would want and expect everyone in the class to rise to the level of evaluation regarding the topic of the course, but obtaining this level of understanding will require a significant amount of time. Therefore, you need to refer to the objectives of the course. If an objective is to be able to perform a task, such as inserting a graphic on a page, then you need to bring the students to the application level. They do not need to understand how to create or modify the graphics. This additional information might be useful, but it should not be the focus of your questions. Your questions should determine whether they have memorized the steps for inserting graphics.

Identifying the required level of knowledge will also assist in distinguishing the questions that should be answered immediately from those that should be reserved for after class. Suppose your course objective is that the students will be able to create a new calendar in Microsoft® Outlook. Suppose a student asked the following question: "What are the advantages and disadvantages of setting permissions from 'owner' to 'reviewer'?" Although this is an important question, it is beyond the course objectives and you might defer the question until a break. Keeping the desired level of understanding in mind will greatly assist you in determining the type of questions you should (and shouldn't) ask and answer.

The Basics

Questions are only useful if you establish the proper conditions for a correct response. Before we discuss the specifics of when and how to ask questions, we need to discuss the environment necessary for questions to be successful. The following conditions must be present for questioning to be successful:

- A positive learning environment
- Adequate time
- No interruptions

In Chapter 4, one if the key points was the development of a positive learning environment. When students answer questions, they place themselves in a position of risk, because if they answer incorrectly they may look bad in front of the other students. If you have not developed a positive environment, no one will feel comfortable taking these risks. You must continually remind students that they are expected to make mistakes and that this is the place to do it, so they can learn from them. You must also enforce the rule that negative behavior from other students (ridicule, impatience, etc.) is not acceptable.

Once a concept is taught, the students must have adequate time to practice so they can absorb it before they are questioned on the material. It is easy as a trainer to forget how difficult it was to learn a concept initially and assume that the students will master it quickly. If you fail to give them adequate time, they will feel rushed and quickly become discouraged. When you plan your lesson, make sure you provide adequate time for practice.

When students begin to answer a question, give them a chance to work through the answer. Do not interrupt them; save your comments until they have finished answering it. Imagine the following scenario.

Scenario

You have asked a student to explain how to format a floppy disk in Windows 95.

Student: Well, I think one way to do it is . . . , um, you double click on the icon on the desktop, the umm . . . .

Instructor:	The My Computer icon?
Student:	Yes, that's the one. . . . Then you click on the 3½" floppy icon and . . .
Instructor:	Right click, right?
Student:	Yes, that's what I meant. Then you click on, umm . . .
Instructor:	Format on the menu, right?
Student:	Yes, and then click on Start.
Instructor:	Once you make sure you have the right options selected.

Was the instructor being helpful in this situation? It is human nature to try to help people, so it is natural to assist them if they hesitate while answering. The problem is that by "helping" them with the answer, you are preventing them from working through the problem themselves. They must be given the chance to figure out the problem to truly understand the topic. They may memorize the answer you give them, but they will not be able to apply it when the situation changes slightly and you are not there to help them. This does not mean that if they are truly lost you wait forever, but make sure you give them a chance.

The second problem with the scenario is that you lose the opportunity to involve the rest of the class in the question. Once you let the student finish answering the questions, you have a perfect opportunity to ask the follow-up question, "What does everybody else think about this solution?" Let the students work through the answer (and do the work for you!). Only intervene if you determine that the students will not reach the proper conclusion. Letting the student and the class work through the problem might take longer, but it will allow them to internalize the solution and better understand it.

Types of Questions

There are several types of questions that can be asked, depending on the type of information you are trying to ascertain. Once you understand the types of questions, you will then have to determine the most appropriate one for each situation. All questions can be divided into two categories: closed questions and open-ended questions. A closed question is one that asks about a fact.

The following questions are examples of closed questions:

- Does everyone understand the topic?
- Did you like the training session?

- What does "CD-ROM" stand for?
- Are you hungry?

When you ask a closed question, there is a specific answer, which does not lead to discussion or debate. It can be answered with a "yes," "no," or a short response. This type of question is most useful for determining whether students have memorized required material. Think back to when you learned the multiplication tables. There was only one possible answer for each problem, e.g., two times four always equals eight. In technical training, closed questions are useful for assessing the students' knowledge regarding facts or procedures.

An open-ended question is one that cannot be answered with a simple "yes" or "no" or with a fact.

The following questions are examples of open-ended questions:

- What are the key points of this lecture?
- What did you like or dislike about the training session and why?
- What are the advantages and disadvantages of a CD-ROM compared with a floppy disk?
- What is the healthiest food choice for lunch and why?

Notice that each of these questions requires the student to think about the topic because there are often multiple answers that could be correct. Open-ended questions can often generate a discussion, whereas closed questions do not. If you want to discuss the strengths and weaknesses of various disk drive back-up strategies, open-ended questions would be used to stimulate the discussion. Both types of questions have their place, and it is your job as the instructor to determine this. Figure 7-3 illustrates the differences between the two types of questions and the responses they solicit.

When to Ask Questions

When should you ask questions? If you remember that one of the primary purposes of a question is to assess the students' level of understanding, then you should be able to determine when to ask the questions. Note that this skill is an important component of student evaluation, which will also be addressed in Chapter 12. Also recall that questions are one of your best tools for engaging students in the topic and creating an active learning

Figure 7-3
Question types

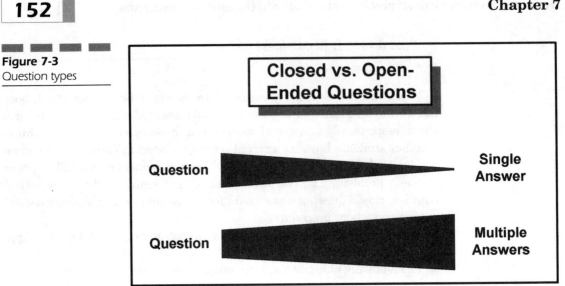

environment. You can ask questions at anytime to involve the students, but you should always assess their understanding at the following times:

- At the beginning of each class
- After a break or meal
- At the end of an exercise or unit
- At the end of the course

In Chapter 4, which covered managing the learning environment, we discussed using questions as icebreakers to encourage participation and raise the comfort level of the class. You should also include a number of questions that will assess each student's current knowledge level on the topic of the lecture. This will impact the pace of the lecture, the number of exercises, and the amount of review that may be necessary. Some of this initial evaluation may not be necessary if there are prerequisites for the course, but you should still determine their level of understanding. If the course is more then one day, each day should start off with several review questions to reinforce what was taught previously to check whether the students are ready to continue to the next topic. The review should also occur after breaks and lunch. You always need to make sure the students are where you think they should be before moving on to the next topic. Questions should be asked at the end of each exercise or unit to check whether the objectives of the lesson have been attained. At the end of the course, you also need to evaluate the success of the session.

Asking questions at each of these points throughout a class may seem redundant or time consuming, but this is your best tool for engaging each student in the activities and evaluating progress. Also, the questions are not just for your benefit; they challenge the students and assist them in learning about the topic. Make sure you provide sufficient time in the course for questions. Conversely, you do not want to spend all of your time questioning; therefore, you should determine the appropriate questions to ask ahead of time. You can use closed questions to quickly check if students have memorized facts or procedures.

How to Ask Questions Effectively

Remember the two parts to every question: the question and the response. Now that you have determined the level of understanding that is required and when to ask the question, you need to decide how to ask the question and how to respond to the answer. Ask yourself the following questions:

- What is the purpose of the question?
- Who should answer the question?

The answers to these questions will determine the best way to ask the question effectively.

What Is the Purpose of the Question? Everything you do as the instructor must have a purpose. Before you ask the questions, determine the result you are looking for. In the following scenario, the class has just returned from lunch and the instructor asks several questions. As you read it, think about each question and ask yourself if it had a purpose.

Scenario

Instructor: Welcome back everyone! How was the food at lunch?

Students answer . . .

Instructor: Does anyone have any questions about the topic we covered
right before lunch?
Students answer . . .

Instructor: Susie, can you explain the steps for creating an account in
Windows NT?

Susie answers . . .

Instructor: Next we are going to learn about account management. Can anyone see any issues that we need to be concerned about based on the privileges we chose for the account we created?

Students answer . . .

Each question in this scenario had a purpose and was planned before the session began. The first question about lunch was not just small talk. The instructor was interacting with the students and drawing them back into the learning environment. The second question gave everyone a chance to ask any final questions regarding the previous topic. The third question elicited the details of the previous topic. The last question connected the new topic with the previous one. Another important point to notice is that each question clearly focused on one point, which makes it easier for the students to focus on the topic. Always think about the purpose of each question you ask. This may seem like a daunting task, but as you gain experience teaching a course, the "right" questions to ask will become automatic.

Who Should Answer the Question?   There are three possible answers, which depend on the purpose of the question. Each possibility is listed.

1. You can ask a question to an individual
2. You can ask the group a question
3. You can ask a rhetorical question to which you do not expect an answer

Asking an individual a question is useful for involving a student in the discussion and assessing the level of understanding. Be aware that this also puts the student in the spotlight, which could be an uncomfortable situation, especially if the student does not know the answer. If you have developed a positive learning environment, then this will not be a problem because the students will not be afraid to take risks. When you ask individuals questions, you need to constantly remind them that there is nothing wrong with making mistakes. Directing questions to an individual is the best way to challenge them because they are forced to think about the problem and attempt to determine a solution.

An alternate method that is non-threatening is to ask the group a question. It offers everyone a chance to participate and does not place anyone "on the spot." This type of question is often referred to as a general question, does not focus on an individual. It is good for a quick assessment of the class. An example of this type of questions is "Does anyone have any questions about this topic?" The downside is that you may not get a true indication of each student's level of understanding. Also be careful that you do not exclusively ask general questions because it is often difficult to accurately assess student performance with them. General questions can sometimes become "trivial" if they are the only type that is asked. Students will realize that they will never be directly questioned and may not concentrate as much on the material.

NOTE: *If you are preparing for the CTT certification video, do not use general questioning techniques exclusively.*

Asking a rhetorical question is useful for stimulating thinking. One method for ending a training class is to ask several open-ended questions and then send the students on their way. This will leave them with questions to think about and work through, which will increase their comprehension of the material.

Putting It All Together: Asking Questions

We have discussed the elements of a question: why, what, when, and how to ask questions. When you put all of these elements together, you end up with a well-thought-out question that is directed at a group or person for a purpose. Questions become your best tool for challenging the students to master the material.

Despite all of your planning, you may have students who just are not comfortable answering questions in class. They may be self-conscious, lack confidence in themselves, or just not like talking to people. You can employ the strategies described next to access their skill level without creating an awkward situation.

One method for quickly assessing the comfort level of the students on a particular topic, which was mentioned in Chapter 4, is the "thumbs up" or "thumbs down" question. I have seen some instructors hand out color-coded cards that can be held up upon request. Each color indicates a different level of comfort. Another strategy is to create a comment/question board where students can leave notes anytime during the class or breaks. The instructor then addresses each note later in class. You will have to determine whether these methods are appropriate based on the type of students you have in each class.

A more direct method for assessing students' understanding of a topic is to ask them to restate the concept in their own words or to summarize the information. You could have them assemble into groups to perform this task. You can have them work on a group response or have them summarize it for each other. Having the students work in small groups, questioning and teaching each other, is a great method for involving all of the students and helping them identify weaknesses and master the information. It can also be less threatening for some students because they are not being questioned in front of the entire class or revealing their weaknesses to the teacher.

Another type of question that deserves some thought is the follow-up question. If the response to your initial question is not complete, you should use other questions to lead the students through the thought process for determining the correct answer.

The best way to become skilled at asking questions is through practice. You will know instantly when a question doesn't work the way you intended it to. Just like the students, you will make mistakes and learn from them. You should also observe other trainers whenever possible to learn their tricks and strategies. Use the following checklist to assist you in preparing good questions.

Question Checklist

■ What is the purpose of the question? (knowledge check, stimulate discussion, focus discussion, etc.)

■ Who is expected to respond? (a specific individual, anyone in the group, no one)

■ What is the appropriate response? (is there more than one response)

■ What follow-up questions are appropriate?

■ When should the question be asked?

■ How should the question be asked? (open-ended, closed, written format, etc.)

■ Have the students been given sufficient instruction and time to be able to answer the question?

Figure 7-4 illustrates the thought process you should work through when you are planning questions.

Figure 7-4
Question flow chart

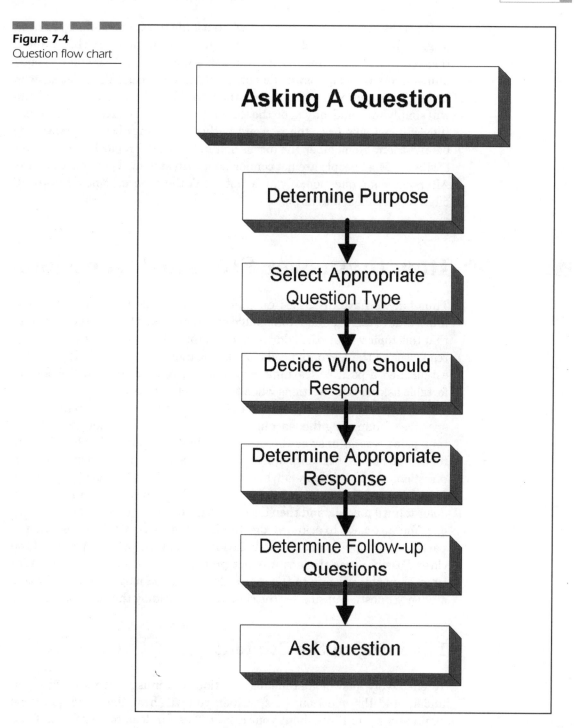

One other item to keep in mind when asking questions is that you need to give the students a chance to come up with an answer. This is often referred to as "wait time." When you ask a question and no one responds immediately with an answer, do not simply give the class the right answer. If they learn that you will not force them to think about it, many students will simply wait and let you do the thinking for them. The result will be that they will just memorize the answers, without thinking about the reasoning behind them. Remember the discussion in Chapter 5 regarding the power of silence. Most people are not comfortable with extended periods of silence. After you ask a question, if you do not break the silence, someone else will often feel compelled to do so.

How to Answer Students' Questions

Thus far, we have discussed questions asked by the instructor. It is also important to consider how you handle questions asked by the students. Note that this topic will also be addressed in Chapter 8, which covers appropriate responses to the learners needs for clarification and feedback. If you have established a positive learning environment, your students will feel comfortable asking you questions when they do not understand a topic. Chapter 4 discussed several strategies for handling students' questions from the perspective of managing the learning environment. To review, the most important point was to answer the questions that were directly related to the topic, but not let students' questions sidetrack the discussion or lead in directions that were more advanced than the intended focus of the course. If you determine that a question is outside the scope of the course, always defer it until a break and then decide if it is appropriate to answer it one on one. You also have to acknowledge the fact that there will be times when a particular student cannot master the material at the pace of the rest of the class. Possibly that student was not prepared at the start or needs extra time. Your obligation is to the entire class, and you may have to defer this student's question until after the class to avoid holding the entire class back.

Listening to the Student

To effectively answer a student's question, you must first make sure you understand the question. As a trainer, you will hear the same questions again and again throughout your career. This can lead to a problem if you are not paying close attention to the student asking the question. I have observed trainers who start to answer the question before the student finishes asking it. This caused a number of problems. First of all, no one likes to be interrupted. Second, the question that the trainer answers may not be the question the student is asking. Third, this will quickly deteriorate the learning environment.

The most important step in answering a student's question is to listen to the entire question before answering it. The next thing the instructor should do is to restate the question to the student. This will guarantee that the instructor and all of the other students heard and understood the question. Once you are sure that you are both on the same wavelength, you need to determine the appropriate response.

Responding to the Question

When a student asks you a question, the following options are available to you:

- Answer the question immediately
- Defer the question until later
- Redirect the question
- Do not answer the question at all

Each strategy can be appropriate depending on the situation. If the question is directly related to the current topic, it is reasonable to answer the question immediately. If one person has a question, it is likely that another has the same question and this will clear up any problems before you move on.

Another option is to redirect the question to other students. This is an excellent way to generate a discussion and involve other students. It is especially useful if you have students in class with experience in the subject. In many technical courses, you will have students who have a significant amount of hands-on experience, and this is a good way to involve those students in the discussion. Redirecting the question is also a good strategy if you are unsure of the answer. If you are teaching a course in PhotoShop, you should be an expert in the program, but you may not have graphic designer skills. Your students might and could readily answer design questions.

If the question is not directly related to the current topic it is appropriate to defer it until later. Recall the "question box" mentioned in Chapter 4, where an area of the board is used to write student questions so they can be asked at a later time. It is also acceptable to defer a question to which you do not know the answer. Remember, never try to "fake" an answer. If you don't know the correct answer, acknowledge this to the students and get back to them with the answer.

There are times when you will choose not to answer a question, which could occur if you know that the question is not within the scope of the course and is too involved for a quick answer. You should, if possible, refer the student to another course or resource to find the answer. If an inappropriate question is asked, you may chose to ignore it. If it is an isolated event, this is sometimes a good strategy. However, if inappropriate behavior persists, you must address it.

Putting It All Together: Answering Questions

To summarize the process of answering questions, whenever you are asked a question, you should follow these steps:

1. Listen to the entire question
2. Restate the question to the student to verify that you are answering the proper question
3. Determine who, if anyone, should respond to the question
4. Determine the appropriate response

The flow chart in Figure 7-5 illustrates this thought process.

Each time a student asks a question, you have an opportunity to evaluate the student's knowledge level and involve the class in the learning

Figure 7-5
Answer flow chart

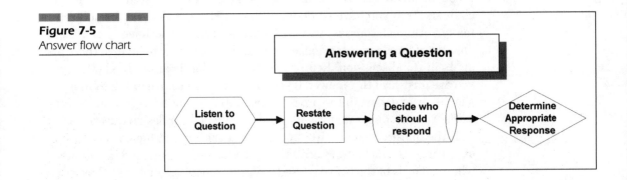

process. Remember that when one student asks a question, other students will most likely have the same question. This gives you an opportunity to reinforce the concept for the entire class. If the same question is asked each time you teach the course, it may also indicate a weakness in your lesson. At the end of each class, think about the questions that students asked and determine if you can improve the lesson so it covers the questioned material better. Trainers should always be monitoring, modifying, and enhancing their courses, and questions are a useful tool in this process.

Evaluating the Questions

Throughout each course, you need to ask yourself how successful your questioning strategies are. Are the students responding appropriately to your questions? If your questions indicate that the students understand the material, do their performances during the exercises also indicate this? If the answer is no, then you need to evaluate and modify the questions you are asking.

You also need to evaluate the questions the students are asking. If you find that students are not asking any questions, you need to ask questions to determine their level of understanding. If they all understand the material, then you know the class is a complete success. However, if you discover that students are having problems, you need to address two issues: their weaknesses and the learning environment. Remember that a positive learning environment is the most important factor in student success.

SUMMARY

This chapter discussed the questioning skills that enable the instructor to be aware of each student's progress throughout the course. The questions are designed to determine whether the students have reached the necessary level of learning, which is determined by the course objectives. The concepts of why, how, when, and to whom to ask the questions were discussed. Questions are also used to encourage and focus discussions and promote an active learning environment. Responding to student questions appropriately is also an important factor in creating a positive learning environment. Remember that questioning skills are acquired through experience.

At the end of each session, evaluate your performance and try to identify weak points for improvement.

QUESTIONS

There may be multiple correct answer for some questions. The answers are located at the end of the chapter.

1. Why should you ask students questions?

    a. To check the students' understanding of the material
    b. To embarrass the students
    c. To encourage student participation
    d. All of the above

2. If you notice a student is not paying attention, what should you do?

    a. Ask a difficult question
    b. Speak loudly to startle the student
    c. Ask an easy question
    d. Ignore the student

3. What two parts of a question should you always consider?

    a. Original questions and follow-up questions
    b. Question and response
    c. The right answer and the wrong answer
    d. None of the above

4. Which is the proper order of Benjamin Bloom's six levels of learning?

    a. Application, knowledge, comprehension, analysis, evaluation, synthesis
    b. Knowledge, comprehension, analysis, application, evaluation, synthesis
    c. Knowledge, comprehension, application, analysis, synthesis, evaluation
    d. Comprehension, knowledge, application, synthesis, analysis, evaluation
    e. Knowledge, synthesis, comprehension, analysis, application, evaluation

5. What is an example of reaching the knowledge level of learning?

   a. Memorizing that RAM stands for random access memory

   b. Knowing that RAM is the temporary storage space on a computer

   c. Knowing that you must save your work because anything in RAM is lost when the computer is turned off

   d. None of the above

   e. All of the above

6. What is an example of reaching the application level of learning?

   a. Knowing that RAM stands for Random Access Memory

   b. Knowing that RAM is the temporary storage space on a computer

   c. Knowing that you must save your work because anything in RAM is lost when the computer is turned off

   d. None of the above

   e. All of the above

7. What level of learning should you always expect the students to reach?

   a. Knowledge

   b. Comprehension

   c. Application

   d. Evaluation

   e. It depends in the objectives of the course

8. What conditions must be present for questions to be successful?

   a. A positive learning environment

   b. The students must be smart

   c. Adequate time for answers

   d. No interruptions

   e. None of the above

9. What should you do when students hesitate when answering a question?

   a. Immediately assist them so they are not embarrassed

   b. Give them time to figure out the answer

   c. Ask another student the question

   d. Tell the student to hurry up

10. Which if the following questions are open-ended?

    a. What does "CPU" stand for?
    b. Who is currently having problems with the course and why?
    c. Do you understand the course material?
    d. What is the meaning of life?
    e. Do you like this course?

11. Which of the following questions are closed-ended?

    a. What does "CPU" stand for?
    b. Who is currently having problems with in the course and why?
    c. Do you understand the course material?
    d. What is the meaning of life?
    e. Do you like this course?

12. Why are the advantages of open-ended questions?

    a. The are a quick method for determining student understanding
    b. The student has a chance to explain the answer
    c. They can require a deeper understanding of the material
    d. They can be used to generate a discussion
    e. They only have one correct answer

13. What are the advantages of a closed-ended question?

    a. The are a quick method for determining the classes understanding of the topic
    b. They are easier to correct
    c. They may have multiple answers
    d. They can be used to generate a discussion
    e. None of the above

14. When should questions be asked?

    a. During a break
    b. At the beginning of a class
    c. At the end of class
    d. During the training session
    e. All of the above

15. What effect do you have on students comprehension when you help them answer a question?

    a. You build their confidence
    b. You help them learn the material more quickly
    c. You prevent them from working through and internalizing the solution
    d. None of the above
    e. All of the above

16. What is the purpose of asking questions at the beginning of the class?

    a. To get the students involved immediately
    b. To show them how difficult the material will be
    c. To maintain control of the course
    d. To determine their initial skill level
    e. All of the above

17. What should you determine before you ask a question?

    a. The purpose of the question
    b. How to word the question so it is difficult
    c. Who the question is directed at
    d. None of the above

18. What is an advantage of directing a question at an individual student?

    a. It will challenge the student
    b. The student may be unprepared to answer the question and be embarrassed
    c. It will assess a particular student's skills
    d. It can involve students in the discussion
    e. None of the above

19. What is an advantage of asking a question to the entire class?

    a. It does not put anyone on the spot
    b. It will assess an individual's skills
    c. It will determine the class' general feelings regarding the topic
    d. All the students have a chance to participate
    e. None of the above

20. What is the first step to answering a student's question?

    a. Answer the question immediately

    b. Listen to the student as she asks the question

    c. If the student hesitates while asking a question, finish the question for them and then answer it

    d. Restate the question

21. What acceptable options do you have when answering a student's question?

    a. Answer the question immediately

    b. Defer the question until later

    c. Redirect the question

    d. Do not answer the question at all

    e. All of the above

22. Why would you redirect a question to other students?

    a. You should never redirect a question because the students will lose confidence in your abilities

    b. To get other students to contribute their experiences

    c. To see if anyone else knows the answer when you are unsure of it

    d. To generate a discussion on the topic

    e. None of the above

23. When is it appropriate to not answer a question?

    a. Never, you should always answer students' questions

    b. When you do not know the answer

    c. When the question is unrelated to the topic

    d. None of the above.

24. How can you improve your questioning skills?

    a. Practice and experience

    b. Planning

    c. Listen to the questions that others ask

    d. All of the above

ANSWERS

1. a and c
2. c
3. b
4. c
5. a
6. c
7. e
8. a and c
9. b
10. b and d
11. a, c and e
12. b, c and d
13. a and b
14. e
15. c
16. a and d
17. a and c
18. a, c and d
19. a, c and d
20. b
21. e
22. b, c and d
23. b and c
24. d

Responding Appropriately to Learners' Needs for Clarification or Feedback

Introduction

By the end of this chapter, you should understand the following concepts:

- Feedback
  - ibstpi-defined
- Types of Feedback
  - Verbal
  - Nonverbal
- Communication
  - From instructor
  - From students
  - Two-way street
- Focusing on the issue, not the person
  - Pointing out strengths
  - Pointing out weaknesses
- Follow through
  - Initiating some discussion
  - Generating scenarios
  - Testing for understanding
  - Having students do it

Competency 8 of the ibstpi Standards is interrelated with the skills outlined in several of the other competencies. For example, competency 9, which deals with motivational incentives, plays a major role in responding to student needs during a class. Competency 7, which involves questioning skills, also plays an integral part in ascertaining and addressing students' needs for clarification. competency 8 involves finding out how the class is going for the students, concept by concept. We will address the optimum relationship between the trainer and his or her students, but first, we will learn ibstpi's definition of competency 8. Next, we will focus on the types of feedback that the instructor can expect—verbal and nonverbal. In the remainder of the chapter, we will discuss a model for managing feedback between the instructor and the students.

ibstpi Definition

In its simplest form, Competency 8 involves the ability of an instructor to "respond appropriately to learners' needs for clarification or feedback."[1]

This competency is about discovering what your students are thinking. You first need to be able to get a heartbeat or pulse—a reflection of how the class is going. After making your assessment, you need to choose a positive approach to facilitate learning. While you are teaching a complex topic, you must pay attention to whether students are actually understanding and grasping the principles.

ibstpi defines positive feedback as follows:

> Learners learn in different ways and at different rates. Additionally, learners' needs for clarification and feedback vary with the learner, the content, and the instructor, the conditions and the environment. An instructor must be aware of and seek out cues that learners need additional clarification or feedback and respond appropriately. An instructor must verify interpretations of these cues to be sure the response is adequate and appropriate for the situation.[2]

An instructor's job is to find out whether a student understands the principles that he or she is teaching. Instructors must gather and ascertain whether or not a student requires additional information. The trainer must meet the learner's needs for clarification or positive feedback.

Whenever you introduce a new concept or when you outline a new rule or principle for the first time to a group of students, you must stop and ascertain what the students learned. Students will not always provide the instructor with requests for clarification. When students do request additional information, they usually ask for help in a variety of ways.

No matter how students ask for help when they do not understand a concept, the instructor must meet the student's needs for additional understanding of the topic at hand. Instructors must follow three basic rules.

---

[1]Original source: *Instructor Competencies: The Standards*, Volume 1, International Board of Standards for Training, Performance and Instruction, ISBN: 881326–03–9, 1993.

[2]Original source: *Instructor Competencies: The Standards*, Volume 1, International Board of Standards for Training, Performance and Instruction, ISBN: 881326–03–9, 1993.

1. They must focus on the issue, not the student.

2. They must keep the interaction as positive as possible. Instructors should point out the strengths and weaknesses of the learner's current understanding of a principal topic.

3. The instructor should follow through and verify that the student actually learned from the additional teaching.

These are the basic principles of responding to students' needs for clarification and feedback. The purpose of this chapter is to explore these principles.

Types of Feedback

The feedback that students provide to their trainer will be either one or both of the following:

- Verbal
- Nonverbal

Verbal

Verbal feedback from students comes in many ways at various times throughout the learning process. Student mutterings, jokes, questions, and answers are all great starting points when you consider feedback. During the course of explaining a concept, you should give all student verbalizations attention. This competency is based on two-way communication (refer to Figure 8-1).

A telephone conversation is a good illustration of the appropriate communication needed in the classroom setting. Students and their instructor should be able to interact. We try to stay away from the "I lecture, you listen" type of communication (in other words, one-way communication). We could compare this style of teaching to using a microphone or bullhorn (refer to Figure 8-2).

The problem with the "I lecture, you listen" approach to teaching is that only the instructor is speaking. This situation is sometimes called "instructor speaks, students listen" or a lecture approach to teaching. No interaction exists in this model. The exact opposite is true with the telephone model, which enables a two-way conversation.

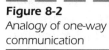

Figure 8-1
Analogy of two-way communication

Figure 8-2
Analogy of one-way communication

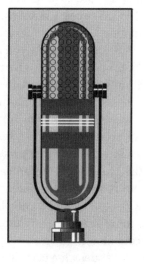

Instructors must enable students to ask questions. Students must also have an environment that lends itself to the exchange of ideas, even if these ideas are counter to the concepts that the instructor is teaching.

Pauses by instructors, sometimes referred to as wait time, are a required part of instruction. After each major introduction to a new concept, we must stop for a moment to enable the concept to sink in for the students. All we need is a moment of time. This time is necessary to enable the learners to consider the new information. We must be open for related questions, as well. If learners are confused or just misunderstood the information, then they might need a few seconds to verbalize a question. Often, instructors will state a new point and then move on without any interaction with the students. The knowledge being transferred can be rushed or pushed at the students. Sometimes, the student feels that he or she was not a part of the process. If there is confusion on the student's part, then learning will become more difficult—especially if the new information is required for learning more complex ideas that follow the original concept. Asking the learners if the pace is too fast or too slow might be an option here for the trainer.

Ultimately, trainers must follow a two-minute rule. We must solicit interaction every couple of minutes in order to keep the class moving ahead. How do we maintain such a rule? Trainers must plan and be prepared ahead of time for this type of interaction to occur. We must preconceive scenarios, real-world examples, and basic questioning skills that we can apply during class time. Every couple of minutes, we must prod people to participate. People want to be included in the process. A bystander will not cognate and think about the concept at hand nearly as much as a participating player. If you are participating in a tennis match, you must identify where the ball is going and how to react properly to the ball's trajectory and speed. If you are an observer, you will only have to react to the player's actions. This scenario describes active thinking versus passive thinking. Active thinking and cognition is far more exciting and meaningful to the participant than passively observing an event. In part, for this reason, kinesthetic (or hands-on) learning is required in the learning process.

For this reason, we prefer the two-way communication model, because people are more likely to receive requests for feedback. The desired communication model is much like the analogy of a telephone conversation. A telephone enables both parties to interact. We advance ideas and allow for the students to interactively consider them and respond with either an agreement of understanding or a request for clarification. When we build such a model in the learning environment, there is a better chance that people will actually learn during their time in a classroom. In the end, the desired result is having students who are able to understand the concepts that you are presenting.

Student questions are the most direct examples of their need for clarification. If a student does not understand a concept, he or she should feel free to ask a question. The responsibility of the instructor is to respond in kind, positive ways to the student's question. Previous competencies outlined how the instructor should praise the student for asking a good question (" . . . that is a great question, Johnny . . . ").

We praise students for asking good questions in order to encourage more questions from all of the students. An instructor giving a contradictory response would aggravate the student and the rest of the class, instead of keeping the environment positive.

After a student asks a question, the instructor should repeat it to make sure that everyone has heard the question. Then, the trainer should respond with a clear, brief answer. The reason for brief answers is twofold. First, students quickly accept or reject brief and concise answers. The other reason for brief answers is to ensure that the class as a whole does not perceive its time as wasted. Try to remember that students consider class time valuable as long as the instructor is credible, the subject matter is pertinent, and the time is properly applied to the subject at hand. When an instructor responds for 15 or 20 minutes to a single question that other students do not perceive as on subject, then they will feel that their time is being wasted. If a student asks a question that the instructor will cover in the class, the instructor can cover the topic immediately or defer it until later:

> "That is an excellent question, and folks, we were going to cover this point in a moment or two, so let us go ahead and discuss this issue now!"

or,

> "That is an excellent question that we will be covering during the next section."

These quotes are a great way to keep everyone on track and involved.

Other student verbalization could include disapproval of, or disagreements with, the instructor about the material. Instructors must be cautious about how they react to such verbalizations. The first step is to listen to the students. Do not be too quick to react to a student's disagreement with the material. Listen, and then confirm what the disagreement is about in the context of the subject matter. Consider the point that if a person is disagreeing with the material, then at the least, the person is thinking about the subject.

Trainers must not react with a defensive posture. Try to perceive the statement with which the student disagrees. If the student is actually correct in his or her understanding of the concept, then the instructor must acknowledge this reality. The worst thing that a trainer can do is be incorrect and defend the incorrect statement as though it were true in order to save face. We must leave our egos at the door when we enter the classroom. Defending and arguing a point with a student in the classroom would be unprofessional. Sometimes there might be a minor misunderstanding on the student's part. Often, the only step that the instructor must make is to clarify a finer point that he or she already declared. Above all else, the last thing that an instructor wants is to have a confrontation in the classroom. Confrontations in the classroom will only result in the loss of credibility with the entire class.

Other students will observe how an instructor responds to a student. If an instructor shouts down a student or simply tells him or her to shut up, then other students will recognize that the instructor will not accept their comments in a positive way. The learners will then be less likely to interact within the classroom. Such events are disastrous to the learning environment and will interfere with future students' needs for clarification throughout the learning process.

We highly recommend the instructor to attempt to understand the students' motives. Some of the students' issues might well be valid.

If possible, you should discuss derogatory student issues outside the classroom. At all times, the best course of action is to pay attention to student needs before the issues boil over into the classroom.

By the end of each main concept, trainers must follow Competency 12 and evaluate learner performance. This process is sometimes the only way in which the instructor will know for sure that the students actually understand. A common type of student is one that nods his or her head as if he or she grasps a concept. Sometimes when I ask the student a question about something he or she seemingly understands, he or she responds with either the wrong answer or no answer at all. I then discover that this student actually does not understand the concept at hand, and we can now move forward and figure out what points need clarification. A student's body language is not always a good barometer for assessing his or her level of understanding.

Nonverbal Feedback

Students do not always respond verbally when they either do not understand or do not care for the subject matter. Try to think of all of the ways in which a person can express that he or she is happy about what he or she is learning. The list could be quite extensive—everything from looking directly at the instructor to head nods and smiling. Now, try to imagine the things that someone might do if he or she is uncomfortable or is having difficulty

Figure 8-3
Example of a bored person

understanding an idea. Nonverbal or body language could also suggest that the person is bored, tired, or worried (refer to Figures 8-3 and 8-4).

Of course, many of these issues can have sources that come from outside the classroom. Instructors often have to respond to these varying nonverbal forms of communication in order to understand how the students are grasping the concepts.

If many of the students are fidgeting, sometimes a simple question, "Does anyone need a break?" will result in a quick answer by everyone getting up and running to the restrooms and to the coffee room. There was a class in which the instructor had just finished explaining what should have been exciting news, and the group appeared to be extremely unexcited. The instructor promptly asked if there was a reason for this mood. The students all replied that they were actually happy with the news, but they were just so tired from the long day.

If nothing else, a question will help the trainer relax a little bit and feel more comfortable knowing that the students are understanding the concepts being explained.

Focus on the Issue, not the Person

The first step to proficiency in teaching is determining whether or not your students are actually learning. The next step is to help the student gain a better understanding of the ideas being explained. This process is usually

Figure 8-4
Example of an
excited person

procedural. One could call this process "student troubleshooting 101." We try to figure out exactly what the student did understand, and we can accomplish this goal by diligently asking questions or by having the student give an illustration of the idea being presented. Once we have a better understanding of what the individual is learning, we can begin to resolve any misunderstandings.

During this troubleshooting process, the instructor must not emotionally bruise the student. Trainers must treat all students in a professional manner. At times, you might have to remind yourself (and possibly even the student) that you are there to help them in the learning process. Keep in mind that the instructor must keep the entire experience positive. Try to remember that the learning experience can seem painful. When a person does not understand an idea, trainers should try to be compassionate. You should focus on the issue and never decide that the person is to blame for not learning quickly. Everyone learns differently. Some people learn better from listening to lectures, while others respond better to watching demonstrations or reviewing diagrams drawn on the board. No matter what method facilitates learning, actually applying the knowledge gained will help students enhance their understanding of the material.

Pointing Out Strengths

Trainers must work diligently to keep the learning environment a positive experience. When someone is having difficulty either applying an idea or performing a lab, the instructor needs to determine what the student has actually learned. Then, the trainer can say something like, "Well, Tim, you have the first two steps down, now let's take a look at the third."

Giving the student positive reinforcement is essential before moving on to those areas that need additional work. This technique makes the entire experience more satisfying for the student. What is interesting is that other students will respond positively to the praise that an instructor gives to the original student. The others then become more likely to ask questions and point out their own lack of understanding so that they can receive assistance, as well.

Acknowledging what the student correctly understands about the subject prior to correcting the student is important. A large part of pointing out student strengths is actually a part of the instructor's gathering of information about the student's understanding. Before you can begin the learning process again or restart the learning process, instructors must discover where to begin with the learners. By pointing out what a learner has correctly surmised from the learning experience, instructors assist the learner with moving forward. Learners need clarification and structure from the trainer, and they will gain added understanding by reviewing the subject with the trainer. Resynchronization of the material is a positive way of refreshing and restructuring the information. This step aids in the learning process when the instructor adds new and correct information to what the student already knows, generating a single picture of the concept.

Pointing Out Weaknesses

People need to know what they are doing well and what they have yet to learn. We must be forthcoming and focused on the subject matter. Properly articulating what students do not yet understand can be extremely difficult for instructors. Students want and need to know what they are not correctly learning. At the same time, students do not enjoy failing to learn. Try to remember that learning can be difficult, and learning is not always fun. The students appreciate instructors that remember how hard it can be to work through the learning process. On the other hand, students need to know when their answers are correct and incorrect. When you, the trainer, think that the students are getting the information, then the next step should take place: testing for understanding or following through.

Following Through

Following through is the most satisfying aspect of feedback. By this point in the interactive exchange between the instructor and the student, we have identified that the student has failed to learn certain sections of the material. We have discovered what the student has properly learned, and we have ascertained where the learner requires further assistance in the learning process. We then aid the learner in correcting the issue or misunderstanding. The goal is to verify for the instructor and the student that the student actually understands the reinforced learning. The student finally got it. The student's job here is to prove that he or she really understands.

In the lab environments where the students are performing the hands-on learning phase, following through consists of the student performing the required steps correctly. If the instructor realizes that students do not understand a step or are misunderstanding a concept during the initial presentation of the topic, then the instructor must create a scenario to verify student learning. In this setting, we could use a live version of the software and get the students to guide the instructor through what should be the proper steps for a specific procedure. This part is the best part of instruction. We can see students applying the material that they have learned. As a class or as an individual, students generally enjoy applying knowledge. This process is much akin to shouting out the answer when you know it. As instructors, we often think of this part of the learning process as the most rewarding and positive aspect of training.

Initiating Some Discussion

Utilize your questioning skills. Suggestions for this technique begin in the preparation and planning stages for the trainer. Try to plot out in the planning stages ideas of how you will get the students to interact. Plan exercises or quick samples of the project where students can apply the knowledge that they just learned interactively with the students. Get the students to interact early in the day so that their self-esteem increases. Increased self-esteem will aid in getting the student to verbally announce that he or she does not understand a concept later in the learning environment. If you were to wait until the afternoon to get people to interact, then they are actually less likely to become involved in the discussion. Start with simple questions at the beginning. Later, develop more complicated questions that encourage the students to stay involved in the process. Interactively review the previous day's learning with the students. Above all, keep the learning environment positive. Even if student responses are not correct, praise them for their interaction. Say things like, "That was a good try." You should consider and acknowledge partially correct answers. "Part A of Tom's answer was correct; someone else help us get the full answer" is a statement that helps generate a positive learning environment that assists in getting the students to verbally declare that they need more information about a subject.

Generating Scenarios

In the planning stages, instructors should plan scenarios that are pertinent to the subject and to the students. Create examples that will help clarify the subject without requiring the students to announce their lack of understanding. Once in the classroom, we can map out a scenario to apply what we have just taught the students. Interactively with the students, we build an example of applying abstract information to a concrete example of what the students should learn.

SUMMARY

In this chapter, we discussed the importance of having a good relationship between the instructor and the students in regards to learner clarification and feedback. In order for the learning environment to be effective, people need a positive atmosphere. Instructors can provide this atmosphere in a number of ways. Answering and asking questions in such a way that creates a warm group dynamic is one way of promoting learning. We point out what students verbalize. We ask questions that require verbal answers from the students. We call the students by name. Even when students ask inappropriate questions, the instructor still regards the students with respect. Instructors should focus on the issue and not the student's lack of understanding. Remember that learning is a two-way street. The student creates feedback verbally and nonverbally. The trainer's job is to respond appropriately and in a positive fashion to the student's feedback. Trainers should point out what students are doing or saying correctly. Finally, instructors should follow through and verify that the students are actually learning the material. When the students show that they are getting the information correct, this situation is the most satisfying moment for everyone involved. Rewarding students with praise is an essential part of the learning process.

At a training session, the goal for both the student and the instructor is for learning to take place. Maintaining a positive learning environment so that students can actually learn is a complex job. People who take on the job of training other adults need to follow the rules of credibility, structure, motivation, effective questioning skills, and positive reinforcement within the learning process.

QUESTIONS

There might be multiple correct answers for some questions. The answers are located at the end of the chapter.

1. (True/False) All learners actually learn at the same rate and in the same ways.

2. Student feedback can come in two ways: _____ and _____.

3. You can usually see _____ feedback on the students' faces or through their body movements.

4. Praise (IS/IS NOT) involved when an instructor responds to a student's question.

5. Having the students involved in the process could require:
   a. Two-way communication
   b. Asking students questions
   c. Getting annoyed when students ask questions
   d. Getting irritable when students ask silly questions
   e. a and b
   f. c and d

6. Among the rules outlined for responding to students are:
   a. Pointing out student strengths
   b. Pointing out student weaknesses
   c. Asking questions that test understanding
   d. Following through (having them do it)
   e. All of the above

7. When measuring student competence in a subject, instructors can:

    a. Go home wondering whether people are learning.

    b. Interactively build a scenario with the students' input.

    c. Ask open-ended questions.

    d. Pass out exams at the end of each day's lecture.

ANSWERS

1. False

2. Verbal, nonverbal

3. Nonverbal

4. IS

5. e

6. b, c, and d

7. e

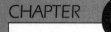

Providing Positive Reinforcement and Motivational Incentives

Introduction

By the end of this chapter, you should understand the following concepts:

- Motivation
  - Defined by ibstpi
  - Dictionary definition
  - Real-world definition
- Differing levels of motivation
  - At the class introduction
  - When introducing new topics
  - Maintaining a motivated, enthusiastic class
  - Meeting learner expectations
  - Positive reinforcement

Competency 9 of the ibstpi Standards deals with positive reinforcement and motivation. Motivation is an important requirement for student success and should be of primary consideration for all instructors. Motivation is one of the most powerful tools that an instructor uses when teaching his or her students. Positive reinforcement is one of the tools that an instructor can use to motivate his or her students.

One might assume that because students are sitting in a classroom, they are primed to learn the information presented. This situation is not always the case, however. Instructors must create motivational incentives for students to want to learn and must continually motivate them as the class progresses.

There are many ways to motivate people who want to learn information. Some forms of motivation are explicit and easy to observe in a teaching session. Other forms of motivation are more complex, intertwined with other competencies that we already discussed in this book. To fully explain motivation, we will first define motivation as a standard. Then, we will address types of motivational incentives and discuss explicit methods of motivating people in the learning environment.

One of the fundamental rules of motivating students is to explain how students will benefit from learning the information presented, especially when instructors introduce a new topic or concept. Our examples will include motivations that instructors use at the start of a class and motivations that instructors use at the beginning of a class period. Next, we will discuss motivating students on a topic-by-topic basis and using interactive methods to motivate students to buy into a concept presented in class.

Defining Motivation

- Common dictionary definition
- ibstpi definition

Motivational speakers tend to follow the definition of motivation presented in the modern dictionary. According to Webster's dictionary, to motivate is "to move to action, or that which causes a person to act."[1]

Motivational speakers often prompt people to act or to take action in a positive way. For most speakers, though, the interaction and motivation ends at the conclusion of the speech or seminar. Classroom instructors also want students to take action by learning, but instructors also must work hard to provide incentives for continued learning throughout the course, no matter what the length.

Consider how different ibstpi's definition of motivation and motivational incentives are compared to Webster's definition. The ibstpi definition of motivation includes the following:

> "Helping learners want to learn is one of the critical responsibilities of an instructor. Learners must identify appropriate reasons for expending time and energy in learning. They must want to translate new skills and knowledge into meaningful payoffs for their work and personal lives before they are willing to attend to instruction. Rewards, encouragement, feedback and support are essential to keep learners focused and energized toward learning goals. This is even true for well-motivated learners . . . Since every learner comes to training with a unique set of needs, interests, motives and concerns, positive reinforcement and incentives help learners translate their personal objectives into a willingness to learn and to apply new skills and knowledge."

According to ibstpi, instructors must apply five basic criteria in order to provide reinforcement and motivational incentives:

---

[1]Original source: *The Merriam Webster Dictionary*, Merriam-Webster, Inc. ISBN: 0–87779–606–8, 1995.

- Match learner and organizational goals with a realistic objective.
- Utilize introductions in a manner that stimulates learner enthusiasm.
- Structure and successfully implement interactivity that aids in promoting positive reinforcement.
- Evaluate the effectiveness of suggested incentives provided to the learners.
- Adjust learning methodologies to meet different needs of the learner, organization, or company.

In the classroom, each student will decide what is motivational to him or her and will decide if and when to participate and learn. Often, however, students do not have the resources to determine the benefits of learning the material. For this reason, instructors must try to give students effective reasons for learning. Instructors must work to convince each student that the concept at hand is worth learning and give them reasons for continued participation in the classroom learning process.

In its rawest form, motivational incentives are used to hook the students into considering that the information is valuable and that they will use the information in some fashion. In essence, we are trying to help students make a positive value judgment so that they will want to learn and keep learning. We want to create an environment in which the audience will be receptive to the discussions, both at the start of the learning process and during the ongoing presentation of the material.

Of major importance is the need to establish for students the reasons why they need this instruction and how they will benefit from it. This effort is determined and purposeful on the part of the instructor and begins the motivational process in the classroom.

Instructors must know who their students are and why they are attending the class. This knowledge enables them to create positive motivations for the different learners in their classroom. What makes something worthwhile to one person does not always make the subject interesting to someone else. What makes you, the instructor, interested in something will not always be an effective motivator for your students initially. Therefore, as the instructor, you will have to change your motivational incentives to meet those of your students. This technique is important, and you should keep it at the forefront of your mind throughout your teaching.

Many simple, yet effective sentences exist that instructors can use to motivate students to participate in the learning process. You can use some of the sentences when you begin each new topic; others you can use to foster continued interest. Here are some examples of effective motivational sentences:

When introducing a new topic:

"You will benefit from learning this, because . . ."

"On my last project, we really needed to know this information because . . ."

"If anyone has ever wanted to know how to do this, here it is."

"When I was learning this, I needed to understand this next point in order to understand the next major topic."

For promoting continued interest:

"You will really want to pay special attention to this next topic, because . . ."

"John, you asked about this next subject earlier in the week."

"Remember the old problem that caused hours of difficulty? Well this next step cures that."

"This next section is one of the most important of the week."

Phrases such as these often get the students' attention. From this point on, the instructor will then continue to provide additional motivations to keep learner interest high.

Instructors must have a sense of excitement about the course content and its usefulness so that they can pass this excitement along to their students. If the instructor is excited and positive about the material being presented, he or she will in turn convey this enthusiasm to the students—and the students will be more motivated to learn. An instructor's own experiences and background also add motivation to the classroom. The instructor should offer his or her own unique perspectives on the subject and provide positive feedback and reinforcement throughout the learning process. When students leave your class, they should go back to work with new skills and the confidence to use those skills. If so, you have done your job well.

Selling the Class

- Learner information
- Student introductions
  - Learner/student expectations
- Explaining the format of the class

- Meeting student expectations
- A realistic approach to meeting student expectations

Chapter 1, "Analyzing Course Materials and Learner Information," included information about knowing as much as possible about your students before the actual class. The better informed you are about the backgrounds and expectations of your students, the better prepared you can be in terms of motivating your students during the class.

For example, you are about to teach a class that has been using Corel WordPerfect at work, and they are all being switched to Microsoft Word after completing this class. Because you know this information about your students, you will be better prepared to handle the situation and provide positive motivation. In this example, you might anticipate that some students are unhappy about having to use a new program at work and might be resistant to learning. You will then be able to consider methods of motivation ahead of time and develop ways to foster a positive learning experience. Your enthusiasm for the material and ability to convey its benefits might just be the ticket that you need to turn around the class. The key point is that knowing your students ahead of time would, at the very least, give you some time to prepare methods of motivation that are appropriate for the class. Review Chapter 1 for strategies concerning gathering student information.

Next, you will need to learn something about the students when the class begins. This approach can include asking for information about each student's immediate background or asking what their employer will expect of them when they return to work after the class is over. You can gather this information during student introductions, which are another way to determine how best to motivate each student.

In this section, we will address the following ibstpi approaches to positive reinforcement and motivational incentives:

- Utilizing introductions in a manner that stimulates learner enthusiasm
- Matching learner and organizational goals with a realistic objective
- Structuring and successfully implementing interactivity that aids in promoting positive reinforcement

Utilizing Introductions in a Manner that Stimulates Learner Enthusiasm

At the start of a class, the instructor and the students must introduce themselves. Instructors should not wait until later in the teaching process to provide background information about themselves or to find out background information about the students. The introduction is also the time to introduce the topic or course that you will teach. At this moment, you can begin positive motivations and promote learner enthusiasm. Class introductions should be the first step of every class, and we discussed this topic in Chapters 3 and 4.

You should use a structured approach for introducing and beginning the course. First, the instructor announces the pattern of events that will occur in the beginning of the class:

> "Welcome. We are about to begin the class. First, I will introduce myself and tell you something about my background (as it relates to the course about to be taught). I will then ask you to introduce yourselves, tell me what your background is, possibly where you are working, and something about what you are currently doing. I will then go over each of the chapters that will be covered in this class. After that, I'll explain some housekeeping—where the parking spots are, where the coffee and phones are located, where the restrooms are. And then we will take a quick five-minute break before getting started with Chapter 1."[2]

We give instructions about housekeeping (for example, proper parking, Internet access for e-mail, and when lunch is scheduled), to help the students feel comfortable and more knowledgeable about their surroundings.

Establishing Credibility

The instructor establishes credibility by confidently explaining his or her background (specifically pertaining to the subject matter). Training instructors must show exuberance and confidence from the start. We want to instill confidence in the students that a) we will not waste their time, that b) we will properly answer their questions during subject-matter discussions, and that c) their learning experience will be valuable.

The instructor introduction always happens at the beginning of the class or presentation. We have to make people aware of who we are and answer unspoken questions about our capabilities as soon as possible.

An analogy for explaining the effectiveness of establishing credibility at the beginning of the course is comparable to a person walking onto a stage and explaining a complex thought about human genetics. With no introduction of any kind from the speaker, some of the audience would listen to

---

[2]Original source: Andrew Zeff, ZTAC Inc. Copyright 2000.

what the person had to say, and others would listen lightly. Still other members of the audience would not listen at all. In this example, audience members discover later that the speaker was a Nobel Prize winner in the field of human genetics. If the speaker had given an introduction and stated his credentials at the start of the program, the audience would have been more inclined to participate in the event. Some of the audience members would have been more enthusiastic about the opportunity to participate in such a discussion, and their level of motivation would have been much greater. Some might have even wanted to ask questions of the speaker.

The bottom line is that establishing one's credibility effectively at the start makes for increased cooperation, participation, and motivation from the learners. An instructor must establish credibility early and maintain it throughout the learning process.

Student Introductions

During student introductions, the instructor should ask for the following information from the students: 1) experience with the product to be covered in class, 2) current job responsibilities, 3) expectations from the class, and 4) nonverbal clues about the person's original attitude towards the class. These items can explain some of the incentives that this student will have during the class.

The student introductions always occur right after the instructor's introduction. For the purposes of motivational incentives and promoting a positive learning environment, student introductions are significant.

Student introductions can take on a variety of approaches, including having students learn about and introduce each other, creating a game out of the introductions, or simply having each student tell about himself or herself. The instructor should let the students know how he or she will handle the introductions. We list a few types of introductions in this section.

Students can introduce each other. The instructor can give them five minutes to ask questions about each other's backgrounds, then introduce each other to the class. This technique is great for getting students to talk with their neighbors and is one form of breaking the ice in the classroom. Often, this type of introduction will enable camaraderie to begin early in the training session and is quite beneficial.

One method is to have the students perform a game of sorts and have them explain their answers to the class as part of their introductions. An example could include making as many words from the class title as possible while waiting for other students to arrive. This game is another type of icebreaker.

The instructor could meet with the students as they arrive and interactively discuss the class with each student. This technique might be beneficial for large groups of people or when the instructor prefers the one-on-one approach. This approach is excellent for the instructor/student relationship but does require early participation that many students might not be ready for yet.

The most common approach to student introductions is to have the student talk about himself or herself. As mentioned previously, the trainer must announce the specific information that he or she needs to know about each of the students. Then, the instructor walks to each of the students and has the student present to the class the requested information.

This information is invaluable to the instructor. While the students give their introductions, the trainer monitors each student's response. Sometimes the trainer will interact with the student to obtain more specific information if necessary. The goal is to try to understand the student's possible motivations for being in the class, what his or her aptitudes might be, and what benefits the student thinks that he or she might derive from the lessons. The trainer must also determine whether the students' perceptions of the class are realistic. The trainer must have an idea of the pulse of the class as soon as possible—determining whether the students have met prerequisites, if they seem eager to learn, whether possible problem students exist, and so on. The trainer must keep in mind what is going on at this point in the learning environment.

This interaction between the instructor and the students also helps provide valuable information to the students themselves. As students participate in the introduction process, they might learn that others are at the same or similar skill level. This knowledge often helps them relax and feel more confident about participating and interacting throughout the class and might increase motivation dramatically.

Experience with the Product

Students who come to a class with previous knowledge of the product are usually great students. They have already made mistakes in the real world when using the product, and they want to correct those mistakes. These students are often ready to learn and will have many good questions for the instructor.

Sometimes these students can also be confrontational, however ("I want my answer now!" "This just doesn't work in my environment, and it never will!"), but they do not have to be a menace to the class. If the instructor can show the student positives about the subject matter and answer questions effectively, most of these students will be satisfied and happy.

On the other hand, if a student has no previous experience with the product or subject matter or has not been working with it very long, the instructor will know that these students might need more help in order to understand the material. Determining this situation early in the introductions will help the instructor know which students will need more assistance during lab exercises or who might need further explanations and demonstrations throughout the course.

Determining which type of student will require more support and positive reinforcement is difficult. Most often, having a mixture of both types of students in the class helps interaction throughout the course. Interaction, in turn, helps the students become more self-motivating. They will enjoy the learning process more. At the least, having students explain their level of expertise in the subject will enable the trainer to begin evaluating the motivation that students will need in the class.

The following are two typical scenarios that an instructor might expect to see in the classroom relating to motivation:

Scenario 1:

Student: "I have never worked with Microsoft Systems Management Server, and I don't ever want to."

Turn a negative into a positive. You might only have to show this person the benefits of the new product in order for them to develop motivation in the classroom. Hearing this type of comment might lead the instructor to ask whether the student has a preferred software that he or she likes to work with currently. Then, briefly highlighting what users can do with the new software versus the one that the student is currently using might just be the ticket to creating a positive learning experience for the student. Perhaps by the end of the course, the student will be able to enjoy what he or she can do with this new product instead of (or in addition to) the one that he or she uses on the job. The student might have deeper issues causing a negative reaction, however. You might need more information to better evaluate the situation. The instructor should dig deeper to understand the student's perspective and offer additional motivational incentives.

Scenario 2:

Student: "I have been working with *Structured Query Language* (SQL) 6.5 for three years and am looking forward to seeing the changes made with SQL 7.0."

What a great perspective—positive motivation right from the start. This individual only needs positive reinforcement to know that he or she will get what he or she wants from the class. The instructor needs to show the student that he or she is excited along with them and glad that the student has decided to attend the class. Also, try to find out specifics on the subject that would interest the student—and remember the specifics when you cover the outline of the course.

Prerequisites

People who do not meet the prerequisites for a class can be a motivation challenge. These individuals can be the most intimidated, fearful, and possibly least-cooperative people in the class. On the other hand, if the instructor assists the student with finding benefits from the class while still pointing out the necessity of the prerequisites, the student tends to enjoy the class to a larger degree. Because prerequisites are usually required for a person to understand that material, and because the courseware writers use the prerequisites as a starting point for the topical discussion, instructors announce the prerequisites at the start of the course. Refer to Figure 9-1 for an example of prerequisites for a particular course.

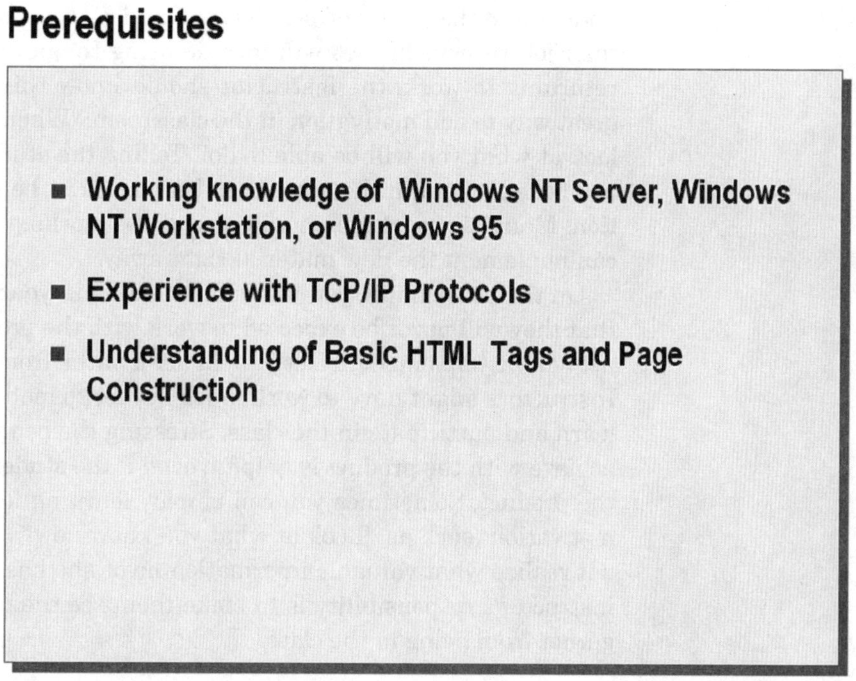

Figure 9-1
Example of
prerequisites

Prerequisites

- **Working knowledge of Windows NT Server, Windows NT Workstation, or Windows 95**

- **Experience with TCP/IP Protocols**

- **Understanding of Basic HTML Tags and Page Construction**

When interviewing the students, during their introductions, make attempts to find out whether the person meets the prerequisites. If students fall short in some areas, instructors should be understanding and reassuring. Remind the students that you will be with them to assist with any difficulties during the labs or hands-on exercises. This statement provides positive motivation to encourage students to participate, despite their lack of knowledge.

You should work hard to remember the students who did not meet the prerequisites. Motivationally, you need to closely monitor these individuals during the hands-on exercises. You need to handle their questions in a more positive light. Let these students know that they can ask all of the questions they want and that you will do your best to answer them. Also let them know, however, that there might not be sufficient time to cover all of the questions during class, so ask them to write down their questions. Tell them that you will be happy to discuss these questions during a break. These students are then reassured and receive positive reinforcement.

Current Job Responsibilities

Knowing what the students do in their current jobs can help the instructor understand the students' perspectives and reasons for being in the class. If their job responsibilities will include using the new product quickly after returning to work, the instructor should know this information. What a great way to add motivation in the classroom: "When you get back to work, look at what you will be able to do!" Telling the students how the product can benefit them in their work environment can be a really great motivation. Many times, students will already be working with the product and can implement the new material right away.

On the other hand, you will find students in your classroom who know that they will never be expected to work with the product or that the product will be implemented in the next six months from the time of the class. Instructors might have to work much harder to motivate these students to learn and participate in the class. Stressing the benefits that students can achieve with the product is helpful, even if the student has no plans to use the product. Sometimes you can employ learning for learning's sake as a motivation (such as, "Look at what you know now!"). Often, a student does not realize what valuable information he or she has readily available. The instructor's responsibility is to make them see the positives that they can gather from being in the class.

Students who come to the class because they are currently working with the product initially might be more enthusiastic about participating in the class. Trainers must work closely with such individuals to ensure that they answer those students' questions when applicable.

Students who do not perceive the current subject matter as useful to their jobs might become lazy during the learning process. Sometimes you might encounter a student who chooses not to participate:

> "I won't be doing this part of the course back at my job, so I am just going to skip this part of the lab."

This statement should elicit a red flag to the instructor. If you handled class introductions well, you might know that this administrator is working with the product currently, although he or she might not see the need for learning all of the concepts. A positive response would be to further motivate the student as follows:

> "You should know how to do this task, even if you aren't currently working with this aspect of the product, because on your next job, or next assignment, you might just need to know this."

Instructors need to try to remember as much as possible about the students' introductions in case this kind of situation occurs.

Certifications

Not all students attend class because they will be using the product on the job. Certification is a common reason why students take instructor-led classes. Many times, students enroll in classes to prepare for exams and become certified in various products. This certification might mean a salary increase or promotion for these students, and this fact in itself is a great motivator for learning. During introductions, the instructor should look for these types of students so that he or she can stress important aspects of the course for them.

On the other hand, sometimes these certification-bound students just want to know how to pass the exam. They might create problems for the instructor because they want fast answers with little detail or follow-through. The instructor must find ways to show these students that learning how the product works can be of great use even after the exam, in the real world. Sometimes short-term satisfaction is necessary for these students to be motivated and happy, however. Make sure to get them the information that they need and answer all appropriate questions. Point out to students both the benefits of certifying to prove their capabilities and the benefits of learning to gain hands-on expertise. Together, these are important motivators to prepare them for the future.

Expectations from This Class

During introductions, students will not always directly state what they want or expect to gain from the class. For the instructor, however, obtaining this information at the start is imperative. If we can find out why people are actually taking the class, we can find out how potentially dedicated they are to the learning process. We can better perceive the questions that students ask. We can also tailor the class to better meet the needs of the class as a group, to motivate them, and to meet their expectations.

With this information in hand, we can make the class as a whole more interesting, satisfying, and motivating. For instance, one of the first things that generally occur after the instructor/student introductions is an explanation of the class format (for example, what the instructor will cover in the course). Here is your opportunity to use student information and expectations to your advantage.

If the course materials are divided into chapters, introduce each chapter, pointing out highlights of each. When you come to a section in which a student has shown interest, stop and touch on that point. Stress that this concept or section will meet the student's expectation, which he or she mentioned during the introductions. Make a big deal out of it, adding your own excitement and enthusiasm. For example, you might say, "John, you said you wanted to learn how to set up Remote Access service. Well, in Chapter 14, we are going to cover that subject!" By interacting in such a way, the students begin to make positive value judgments of how this class will meet their needs. This approach is like yelling, "Don't touch that dial . . . stay tuned for more good things to come." This way, students will know that they will get what they came for and will recognize the benefits they can achieve.

Keeping Expectations Realistic

Meeting students' expectations while keeping these expectations realistic can be a challenge for the instructor. This challenge is another reason why instructors must be aware of the students' expectations at the start of class. If a student arrives with an expectation that you will not meet in this class, a potential problem exists. Either the student did not receive proper information about the subject matter to be covered in the course, or he or she needs the instructor's and administrative staff's guidance.

An example could be a student who wants to learn advanced SQL when the class covers SQL administration. The information that the student .seeks is not part of the class curriculum. In this particular case, we can sometimes help the student become more realistic in finding satisfaction with the present class. The instructor could inform the student that he or she will need to attend this class and master these skills before moving toward the next class that would train him or her on SQL. This help might satisfy the student. The instructor might also be able to find additional reading materials for this student in order to help him become more motivated. The instructor should honestly inform the student, though, that you might not meet his or her initial expectations—although he or she will definitely benefit from the course material.

One further tip for assuring students that the class will be a success and that you will meet their expectations is to say something as follows:

> "This is an excellent mix of people. We have a wide variety of experiences and backgrounds, and I can't wait to hear from each of you during the length of this course. We will be covering information that will be useful to all of you."

The best thing that can happen is that the students' self-esteem will rise, that they will begin to ask questions as the class goes on, and that they will get what they came for from the class.

Format of the Session Discussions with the Class

- Review of each chapter described
- Reference to students' explicit motivations cited
- Request acceptance from the class as a whole
- All changes announced and rationalized
- Make motivational throughout

The last phase of the class introductions that we will discuss here is the announcement of the format of the course. Announcing the course format has two purposes: developing structure and building and reinforcing the students' own incentives.

All learning environments require structure, as we discussed in Chapter 4. We point out the structure that the course will follow from the first day to the last day. We announce the chapters that we will cover and the main points of each chapter. Because this phase is the last phase of the introduction process, we already know why each student is attending the course. If we discuss the materials to be covered, there should be no surprises in the classroom for the students. This knowledge makes them feel secure.

You should explain the format of a class anytime you expect something different or unusual from the student. For example, if the students are going to perform some role in class, give a speech, or present a demonstration, you should give them as much advance notice as possible. This time helps them prepare for what is to come and keeps the learning process positive.

A great example is the participation of students in the formal introductions at the start of class. If we are to expect students to interactively introduce themselves, then the instructor should provide the format for the students:

> "OK class, I am going to go around and have each of you introduce yourselves. It is good to start with your name and where you are presently working. I would like to know if you are currently working on SMS 2.0, or if you have any plans to roll out this product. Also, I need to know what you would like to get out of this course, and if there is anything in particular that you need to take away with you by the end of this course."[3]

In some courses, students might need to do preparatory work prior to attending the class and require clarification of the course format ahead of time. In ZTAC's Train-the-Trainer Instructional Techniques Workshop, attendees receive student packets as soon as they register for the class. According to Eve Lempert, ZTAC's operations manager,

> "We send out our workshop packets to the students to make sure they know ahead of time what is expected of them in the class. Because each student is going to perform several practice teaching exercises in front of the class, we want them to know this in advance and be prepared."[4]

---

[3]Original source: Andrew Zeff, ZTAC Inc. Copyright 2000.

[4]Original source: Eve Lempert, ZTAC Inc. Copyright 2000.

As the course introduction proceeds, we introduce each chapter and explain the highlights and benefits of each. We are selling the class first thing Monday morning. We mention and reinforce the students' own incentives whenever possible:

"And David, you wanted to learn how to set up Remote Access Services. Well, on Wednesday we will be covering just that topic in Chapter 15!"[5]

This phase of the introductions reinforces the expectations of the students as a group. During the introduction of the class format, the students and instructor might determine that a specific section of the course is unnecessary or unwanted, and a possible change in structure might be in order. This change is possible only if the majority of the students agrees. Such a change can increase students' motivations and encourage them to participate more. Some courseware vendors add additional material to the back of the manuals for just such occasions. Sometimes the students might prefer an extended lab on a topic that the courseware does not cover well enough. Other times, the instructor might discard sections of the courseware because the material is dated and is not as valid at that time. In order to keep the learning atmosphere positive, the instructor must explain why a change in the course plan will take place. The instructor must announce the rationale for the change, and the students must agree to this change.

NOTE: *If you are preparing for the CTT exam, remember that instructors must explain the rationale for changing any course plan or course change that affects the learning process. (We discussed this concept in depth in Chapter 1.)*

The entire objective of this type of positive feedback is to help the students buy into the course. We want the students to know that we will discuss everything that they want to see covered to their satisfaction.

The interaction between the instructor and the students will help students believe that the instructor cares about their success in the class and that this class will be a good class for them.

---

[5]Original source: Andrew Zeff, ZTAC Inc. Copyright 2000.

Selling the Concept

In structured learning environments, instructors are constantly introducing new concepts to students. Students *must* understand why they should learn a new concept. The instructor needs to address the following items in order to ensure this understanding:

- Announce the motivation at the start of the concept.
- Focus the motivation on learner information.
- Give a brief explanation of specific motivations.
- Students could define their own motivations.
- Keep it structured.

When beginning a new concept, the trainer should indicate the start of the new material, explain the benefits of learning the new concept, solicit interaction from the students, explain and demonstrate the new concept in action, and have the students perform the new concept.

Announce Motivation at the Start of the Concept

One part of introducing a new concept is to tell the students how they will benefit from learning the next subject. Because we did an excellent job of getting the students to buy into the class previously, we want to continue this momentum with the students. Every single concept that we cover during a class must have some merit or value to the students. As mentioned previously, students often do not understand how they will actually benefit from the new information being presented to them. At times during a class, people tend to become complacent, and their internal stimuli tend to view the classroom as an unchanging setting. A student can easily begin to zone out from the classroom. Even if the students were initially interested in the course, they can still begin to phase out and daydream in the best of classes. The next subject becomes just the next subject. As a trainer, you want interaction and enthusiasm from your students throughout the entire course. You need the students' enthusiasm to build your own enthusiasm during the course and to keep motivation high.

Transitions from one subject to another are important. At this time, you should announce new motivations to wake up the class. Announcements usually link previous ideas to the next idea in the structure of the class. Tell the students how this next idea relates to the previous idea. Reinvigorate the class with positive incentives for learning the new information. Try to be specific at this point in the structure. The key is to hook the students into wanting to learn more and make the learning experience positive. Make sure that your motivation is effective to promote learning. As you announce the new topic and provide motivation, ask why the students think that this concept might be important, and praise them for their remarks. Be creative as you develop these concept transitions.

Types of Motivations

- Real-world scenarios to show benefits (before the automobile and school bus, we used to have to walk in the snow)
- Best-case scenarios
- Worst-case scenarios
- On-the-job benefits (helps to make their jobs easier, more rewarding, less tedious, more fun, more proactive, more successful, and so on)
- Unique benefits (few people know about this feature, and you can only perform the next task if you know about this concept)
- Fundamental information that is necessary for students to perform the work

Brief Explanation of Specific Motivations

Real-world scenarios are excellent tools for getting students interested in the discussion. Trainers have ample opportunities to show expertise in their field by giving examples of past jobs where they worked with the subject matter. Real-world situations that help the student understand a rule are often more readily accepted. For example, after explaining why hitting the wrong switch can create problems, also provide a real-world example to add emphasis and to provide a reality check:

> "In 1995, we were on a job outside New Orleans, Louisiana. Andy, a fellow engineer, accidentally hit switch D instead of switch B, and the entire plant nearly went up."

Students tend to remember a rule stated this way. The scenario really happened, it was interesting, and it kept the students' interest. What is interesting about using scenarios is that students are often more accepting of a rule when an instructor uses a real-world example. This example can help turn an abstract concept into a concrete, important piece of information. We discussed this concept in depth in Chapter 6, "Demonstrating Effective Presentation Skills."

Best-case scenarios get students interested in a concept by giving an example or demonstration of the concept in action and showing how successful the concept is. Usually, we promote student interest by using the students' own experiences and job situations in our examples. For the student who does not want to learn the concept because he or she never expects to use the information, we might need to explain that his or her job might change in the future, and the concept will become important later.

Worst-case scenarios can also create motivation. Showing what can happen in a worst-case example is fun as well as informative.

The trainer should explain or show the students how they will benefit on the job by learning these concepts. Point out that this new feature of the software will make their jobs easier:

> "So listen up—you will want to remember how to do this step, otherwise, you might have to stay at the job site for an additional eight hours. Oh, that is what you are doing now."

Unique benefits give the students the idea that they are lucky to be in the class at this time. Trainers often will highlight learned knowledge or recent seminars with a software vendor in order to generate interest with the students:

> "You won't hear about this feature anywhere else. If you hadn't attended this class, you would have missed hearing about this problem and ways to fix it."

Sometimes it is necessary to simply state that the new concept is an important and fundamental part of the course. In the procedural learning cycle, explain that step one is required to understand step two, and step two is necessary in order to perform step three, and so on. Also, explain that students need to understand this concept or perform this task upon returning to work after the training session.

Students Defining Their Own Motivations

In addition to the motivations that the instructor provides, students also develop their own motivations. Instructors should always involve students in this part of the process. The instructor can actually ask the students, "Why do think you might want to learn this?"

What happens next can be interesting. Most people will be happy to tell you what they think. Benefiting from the learning process is often a singular and personal experience. Everyone has ideas about why they want to learn. By finding out how the student interprets his or her own positive incentives, the instructor can then move forward and explain the concept to a more receptive class.

Knowing what actually interests the students about the subject at hand is a powerful tool for the trainer. We can now skew the information to the students' perspective. We can utilize the course materials and make them valid for this particular group of students in this particular class. The classroom becomes a more stimulating and momentous environment. Students tend to forget about the hours that they are spending in a training room and focus on the exciting information that they are learning.

A Motivational and Enthusiastic Class

Ultimately, people should be able to walk into a classroom and expect a well-structured, thought-provoking, positive learning experience. For trainers, the key to providing this kind of positive environment is to focus on the students as much as they focus on the material and to encourage students to learn in a variety of ways by performing the following actions:

- Promoting interaction
- Providing feedback and reinforcement in responses to:
  - Student questions
  - Student answers
- Maintaining high energy to promote enthusiasm
- Encouraging questions with praise and positive comments
- Stressing positive results, which leads to fewer problem students

Interaction　The first step in getting students to become more enthusiastic in the classroom is to include them in the discussion. A rule states that every two to three minutes, the instructor should engage the students. This step should occur as soon as possible in the class format. In the real world, we try to elicit interaction during the daily reviews that happen at the start of the class period. Interaction between the instructor and the students must happen early and often.

In other words, the instructor should utilize his or her questioning skills to include students. Because we are attempting to gain enthusiasm and attention from the students, we require verbal responses whenever possible. The goal of verbal interaction is to keep the students focused on the discussion, to gain feedback from the students, and to evaluate their learning performance. Instructor-led interaction requires a proper usage of Competencies 5, 6, and 7. Trainers should follow many questioning-skills models in order to get the students to participate during the class.

Also, people need to see the instructor close up from time to time. Many instructors remain at the front of the room and never stray far from the white board. This body language puts not only a physical barrier between the instructor and the students but might create a psychological barrier, as well. Trainers should walk through the room and engage students with a few seconds of eye contact. This contact puts both the trainer and the students at ease.

Reinforcement   Motivation and interaction with the students needs to be an ongoing process. You must always be conscious of your interactions with each student and reinforce their interest and motivation in the material. Monitor their attitudes, and encourage them when they are having difficulties.

Enthusiasm   Enthusiasm and trainers should be synonymous. Instructors must be enthusiastic about their students and the material. They only have one chance to get their students to understand the information, and this opportunity is exciting. Sometimes after teaching the same material repeatedly, an instructor might need to create more internal motivation. One common statement from instructors is as follows:

" . . . I get so bored with the material. What can I possibly get excited about?"

Remembering that the information is new to the students and seeing the light bulbs turn on during the training will help create more personal enthusiasm. Also, one never knows when a student will ask a fabulous question that no one has ever asked.

When considering your own motivation and enthusiasm in the classroom, think about your favorite instructors of the past. Ask yourself these questions:

- Was your instructor enthusiastic?
- Did your instructor look at you?
- Did your instructor move about the room?
- Did your instructor engage you in the learning environment?

- Did you think that your instructor cared about you during the class?
- How many times do you think your instructor taught that class before?
- Which of the competencies did your instructor use in the classroom?

Now, ask yourself the same questions while considering the worst instructors in your personal experience.

Questioning Skills   In the endless effort to make the class a positive and motivating experience, we must mention questioning skills (addressed in Chapters 7 and 8). Whenever we ask questions, we are trying to get verbal responses—any verbal responses. So many instructors today simply lecture in the classroom and do not engage the students. Students nowadays rarely expect the trainers to verbally engage them. If we ask a question and then get a verbal response, we need to reward the student for participating. In other words, we must verbally praise the student with a variety of responses, whether the answer given was right or wrong. These responses can include the following:

"Great answer," "That's exactly what I was looking for," or "Excellent comment!"

or

"Good try," "You're almost there!" or "Can someone else help Steve out here?"

These verbal rewards will enable other students to know that speaking up and answering questions is acceptable (without fear of reprisals).

Getting students to *ask* questions is a bit harder. The key is to reward the first few questions that occur in the class environment and to set the standard right at the start. Give verbal praises such as the following:

"Great question," or "I am glad that you asked."
"So you want to know what the quantum in quantum physics means? Interesting question. Perhaps we can discuss that at a break?"

Remember the rules about asking and answering questions. Instructors should walk towards the person who is asking a question. Establish eye contact while the student asks or answers the question. Try to repeat people's questions so that you and others can hear the questions. Keep the responses positive.

Many instructors work from a public-speaking model and end up giving a lecture instead of establishing an interactive session. They seem to ignore the fact that the entire setting of a classroom is for the students. Instructors must do whatever they can to provide a motivational, participatory, and learner-centered environment. Some time ago, an instructor had to train some service engineers on a mainframe computer system. The trainer could not get the class engaged in the learning process. He knew that he had to do something to save this class and get the students involved. One day, he walked in dressed from head to toe in a clown suit. The entire class rolled with laughter. They pulled off his red nose and became a participating, enthusiastic class. Remember, you must do everything you can to involve your students.

Instructor Competencies

As the instructor, you must master a variety of skills to effectively reinforce and motivate your students. Many of the competencies discussed in other chapters are necessary components of motivation:

- Analyzing course materials and learner information (Chapter 1) helps you fit your teaching style to the learners. Who are the learners? What do they need to learn? What is the best way to teach the material? Make any necessary adjustments to meet learners' needs.

- Establishing and maintaining instructor credibility (Chapter 3) is essential. Introduce yourself. Tell and/or show students that you know your stuff—that you have the expertise. Show them how the information applies to them in their jobs. Develop their trust, and develop their confidence in themselves (but do not ridicule them). Listen to students, give them feedback, and use the feedback that they give you. Exercise good judgment; be flexible, fair, and ethical; and keep your integrity.

- Managing the learning environment (Chapter 4) is also essential. Be organized, systematic, and effective. Set the tone for the course, and communicate your expectations for the class (feedback, behavior, group interaction, and so on). Tell learners what benefits the course will give them. Manage your time with the material (slow down the course or speed it up based on understanding). Manage the students (group dynamics/conflict resolution). Make sure that your presentation encourages and involves learners. Also, make sure that learners feel comfortable enough to ask questions and take risks (better now than on the job when the client is watching). Provide opportunities for learner success, and acknowledge these successes.

- Responding appropriately to learners' needs for clarification and feedback (Chapter 8) involves how and when should you respond to learners during instruction. Respond to learners by figuring out where they need help and demystifying what is confusing them. Respond in a sensitive way to the individual or group. Use a variety of types of feedback (including feedback from other students) that meets the needs of the learners and the situation. Provide feedback that challenges and supports them.

SUMMARY

In order to provide positive reinforcement and motivation, you must establish for the students why they need this instruction and what benefits they will receive from it. You must have a sense of excitement about the course content and its usefulness so that they will be motivated to learn the material. Offer unique perspectives on the subject and provide positive feedback and reinforcement. When the students leave your class, they should be able to go back to work with new skills and the confidence to use them.

So far, we have defined motivation. We have discussed why you should follow Competency 1, which involves gathering learner information prior to beginning class. We then went through the instructor, student, and course introductions. All of this information helps the students become more receptive to their own goals—increasing the students' knowledge and skills. Each step becomes imperative to the success of the class. By following these steps, the instructor is more informed for conveying new concepts and thought processes. The best part is that by finding out and meeting the students' needs at the start of the class, the probability that the students will become more engaging increases dramatically. If you get the students interested at the start of the class, then it is easier to maintain student interest throughout the entire course.

QUESTIONS

There might be multiple correct answers for some questions. The answers are located at the end of the chapter.

1. _____ are the focus of all motivations.
   a. The white board
   b. The students
   c. The instructor
   d. None of the above

2. In order to assist the students in the learning process, instructors must answer which two questions?

    a. Why do they *need* this instruction?
    b. Who will pay for their training?
    c. Why come to class at all?
    d. How will they will *benefit* from the material?

3. Which of the following are important in determining the best approach to motivating students?

    a. prior information about the students
    b. students' reasons for attending the class
    c. any predefined expectations for the course
    d. any ill-conceived notions about the course
    e. all of the above

4. The best time to motivate students is

    a. after the class has ended.
    b. before the class ever starts.
    c. at the introduction of a new concept.
    d. at the beginning of the class.

5. One of the most important aspects of providing positive reinforcement is

    a. focusing on a student's learning ability.
    b. focusing on the issues that are necessary to learn the concept.
    c. focusing on the excellent learning ability of the student's partner.
    d. focusing on the instructor's superior knowledge beyond the students.

6. Establishing _____ is necessary to gain the student's acceptance of the material and therefore creates a more positive learning environment.

    a. good grooming habits
    b. good moral backgrounds
    c. effective credibility
    d. effective halitosis control

7. Student introductions are of major importance to maintaining a positive learning environment (true or false).

8. Instructors should _____ attempt to "sell the class."

    a. always
    b. never
    c. sometimes
    d. none of the above

9. Among the things that instructors should look for during student introductions are:

   a. student expectations for the class
   b. that the students' expectations are realistic
   c. the students' prior experience with the subject matter
   d. the students' names
   e. students' burning issues with the subject matter
   f. all of the above

10. The proper response to unrealistic student incentives for taking a class might include the following:

    a. asking the student to leave the building
    b. suggesting more realistic incentives that the student might be able to apply to the course
    c. suggesting other material that might be deemed appropriate for the student
    d. asking the other students for their opinions of the unrealistic incentives being cited by fellow students

11. It is the instructor's _____ to maintain an enthusiastic approach to teaching the material to his or her students.

    a. job
    b. responsibility
    c. option
    d. none of the above
    e. both a and b

12. Getting student involvement by asking questions is

    a. irritating to the students.
    b. helpful in maintaining interest.
    c. a waste of the instructor's time.
    d. never done in the classroom as a rule.

ANSWERS

1. b
2. d
3. e
4. c and d

5. b
6. c
7. true
8. a
9. f
10. b
11. e
12. b

10

Using Instructional Methods Appropriately

Introduction

By the end of this chapter, you will be able to perform the following tasks:

- Implement a variety of instructional methods
  - Know their strengths and/or weaknesses
  - Determine their appropriate uses
- Decide when to use each method based on the following items:
  - Lesson objectives
  - Learner attributes

Competency 10 of the ibstpi Standards addresses the trainer's ability to appropriately use a variety of instructional methods. Each of the competencies that we have addressed have dealt with factors relating to the preparation and delivery of the course material and effective methods for interacting with students. This competency focuses on specific instructional methods that you should employ to assist students with comprehending the material. People used to widely believe that a teacher-centered approach was the ideal method of teaching. In other words, the teacher (the expert) shared his or her knowledge with the students through lectures, and the students simply took notes and absorbed the information. This learning environment was very passive. Research and experience show that students learn in a variety of ways that instructors can only address through a variety of methods. This situation shifts the learning environment to a student-centered approach that actively involves the students in the learning process. To instruct in this manner, you should use a variety of the instructional methods discussed in this chapter to meet the needs of all of your students.

Instructional Methods

One of the primary objectives of a technical training course is for the students to be able to apply a particular skill after the training ends. Recall the discussion about levels of learning in Chapter 7, "Demonstrating Effective Questioning Skills and Techniques." Application is the third level of learning, after knowledge and comprehension. In order to reach the application level, students need to be able to think about the topic and internalize it, rather than just memorizing what the instructor says. Think about the intended result of your lesson when deciding which instructional methods to utilize in your classes. The following list includes the methods that we will discuss:

- Lectures
- Demonstrations
- Guided learning
- Student teaching
- Group work
- Role play
- Simulations
- Case studies
- Games
- Independent practice
- Reflection

We will discuss each of these methods and look at examples of their use. We have described some of these methods in earlier chapters in order to illustrate other competencies. This section will summarize all of the methods.

Throughout the sections, we will discuss how you can apply these methods to the following two scenarios.

Scenario 1   You are teaching a course on how to use a spreadsheet to track student grades. The objective of this section is for the students to build a formula in a spreadsheet that will drop the three lowest grades for a particular student and then determine that student's grade-point average. They have already learned the basics of spreadsheets.

Scenario 2   You are teaching an introduction to computers course and are at the point in the class where you are describing the various components of a computer. The objective of this section is for the students to identify the components of a computer and understand their purpose. Some of these students have never seen a computer before.

As we discuss each of the instructional methods, keep in mind that there is not only one right way to teach a particular topic. The method that you choose will depend on a number of factors, including the type of students that you are teaching, the amount of time available, and the resources at your disposal.

Lecture

Chapter 6, "Demonstrating Effective Presentation Skills," discussed the mechanics of an effective presentation. We are not suggesting that presentations are the most effective and preferred method of instruction. Lectures are teacher centered, not student centered. If the only method that you use is a lecture, you will not be as effective a teacher as someone who employs a variety of instructional methods that are customized to meet the needs of a particular audience.

NOTE: *Do not just lecture during your CTT training video. Lectures alone will not convey your mastery of all of the required competencies.*

Having stated the down side of lectures, we want to say that they are still an effective means of instruction in the appropriate settings. A lecture is the quickest method of disseminating information to a group, and therefore, this format is often the preferred way to introduce a topic to the class. When you lecture, you need to keep two items in mind at all times: the lengths of the lecture and the amount of interaction with the students. Limit the length of a lecture to 45 minutes at the most, and preferably make them even shorter. An adult's attention span and concentration will deteriorate significantly with longer lectures. Do not allow your lecture to become a passive learning activity. Engage the students by calling on them, asking them questions, and involving them in the discussion. You can meld many of the other instruction methods in this section into the lecture in order to increase interactivity and make the methods more student centered.

Scenarios You can use lectures in both of the scenarios presented previously in this chapter. To effectively lecture on the material in either scenario, the instructor should follow the steps for preparing an effective presentation (discussed in Chapter 6), including appropriate visual aids and examples.

Summary Lectures are a tempting method for any instructor, because they enable the instructor to cover the material quickly and to be in control of the learning environment. To be effective, however, you must keep your lectures short and interactive. Timing is also important. Do not lecture immediately after lunch or at the end of the day, when the students' energy is low and they are easily distracted. Use lectures to introduce material and to summarize information taught through another instructional method.

Demonstrations

A demonstration is an expansion of a lecture. Most people have heard the saying, "A picture is worth a thousand words." This statement is especially true whenever you are teaching a concept to your students, such as a task or procedure. In a lecture, you are telling the students about something. In a demonstration, you are showing the concept to them. Replicating a task after having seen someone else do it versus just having the steps explained is much easier for a student.

Some demonstrations are easy to perform in a classroom, and others are not. For example, if you are teaching students how to format a floppy disk, all you need is a classroom equipped with a computer and a projector, and you can walk through the procedure with the students—showing them each step of the process. If you are teaching the students how to land an airplane, demonstrating the procedure is a little more difficult unless your classroom is the cockpit of an airplane. Depending on the resources available to you, however, there are ways to demonstrate most tasks. Videos are available on almost any topic and are a standard method for demonstrating concepts. Computers have made it possible to perform experiments and demonstrate procedures virtually. If you have flight-simulator software installed on the computer, you can demonstrate the steps for landing the airplane. Let's look at our two scenarios.

Scenario 1: Spreadsheet Formula The easiest method for demonstrating this task is to have a computer and a projector in the class so that you can build the formula for the students, showing them each step of the process and highlighting any potential problems that might arise. Instructors teach most computer skills in this way.

Scenario 2: Introduction to Computers Class One way to present the material is to create a presentation (lecture) that includes pictures and descriptions of each of the components. You can show the students what each item is and then discuss these items in detail. This method would work, but it is not too different from asking the students to read a book on the subject. The students are passive learners. A better way to teach the module is to bring in a computer, open it, and remove each component as you talk about it. You can then pass the component around the room so that each student can examine the item. This demonstration will remove some of the mystery about computers.

Summary   The strength of demonstrations is that, in addition to hearing about the topic, students can see and sometimes touch the objects. The major obstacle to employing demonstrations is that they sometimes require materials and setups that are difficult to bring into the classroom. If you make your demonstrations as hands-on as possible, they are a great way to include the student in the learning process.

Guided Learning

Guided learning refers to the process of assisting students as they work through a problem and figure out the answer for themselves. Your role in this process is to provide them with the tools that they need to solve the problem, assist them by answering their questions, and focus them whenever necessary. This method places the responsibility primarily on the learners' shoulders. The advantage is that a student who has worked through a problem, actively thinking about the factors involved, will internalize the information and remember the experience much more than an instructor simply telling the student the right answer. You can apply guided learning to both of these scenarios.

Scenario 1: Spreadsheet Formula   Creating formulas in a spreadsheet is easy when someone else is there to point you in the right direction. The problem occurs when you have to perform this task back in your office and no one is around to help you. By using guided learning, the students have an opportunity to work through a problem, where the instructor assists them with their problem-solving skills and helps them come up with the right answer.

The instructor's role in this situation is to teach the students about all of the resources available to them for searching for the right functions. First, you show the students how to use help to search for functions. Then, you show them the various categories into which the functions are divided. Next, you define the problem that they must solve. In this case, the students must create a formula that will drop the three lowest grades for a particular student and then determine the student's grade-point average.

At this point, you shift the responsibility onto the students. They must determine how to approach the problem. Ask them to think about the components of the problem. Prompt them for ideas about how they can create the formula. Try their ideas. If there are problems with a particular solution, ask them questions that will reveal the mistakes. Your goal is to assist them with discovering the right answer without doing the work for them.

Scenario 2: Introduction to Computers Class Because computers are constantly changing, components are also changing—and new ones emerge regularly. The students need to be able to identify the components for themselves. You can easily convert the demonstration discussed previously to a guided-learning experience in order to enhance this skill.

The first step in any guided-learning activity is to provide the students with the core knowledge that they will need to complete the activity. In this case, you could provide a handout that describes the various components so that they have a resource to which they can refer. The next step would be to open the computer and ask the students to identify each of the components. Remove a component—for example, a memory SIMM—and ask the students what the object is and what function it performs. When they are having problems, refer them to the documentation that you provided and ask directed questions that guide them in the right direction. Using this approach will teach them about the components and the general process for identifying any component.

Summary In order to use guided-learning activities, the instructor must master the effective questioning skills discussed in Chapter 7. The instructor must allow the students to work through the problem without immediately giving them the answer whenever they are stuck. The major strength of this method is that the students are actively involved in the learning process, and the instructor is simply providing them the information and direction they need to solve the problem. This skill will empower them to solve problems independently when they return to the workplace. One consideration with this method is that it will take more time than a lecture or demonstration. You cannot rush the students through this process if you want to be effective.

Student Teaching

One of the best methods for learning a subject inside and out is to teach it to others, because the teacher will want to be prepared for the questions that the students will ask and will need a solid understanding of the topic. You can use this technique to your advantage in the classroom. You implement this instructional method by assigning each student (or group of students) a topic from the lesson plan. Each group is responsible for preparing a short lesson for the rest of the class. Your role is to assist each group with learning the topic and preparing the lessons. Now, we will use the student teaching method in our scenarios.

Scenario 1: Spreadsheet Formula   The average formula would be one of several formulas that you would use in a student grade worksheet. To employ the student teaching method, you could develop a list of all of the types of formulas that a user might need and assign groups to be responsible for each of them. This lesson would then be one of several that the students present.

Scenario 2: Introduction to Computers Class   You could assign a particular component of the computer to each group and have them prepare a short lesson on its attributes and functions. The students would then present the lessons to their peers.

Summary   In order for student teaching to be successful, you must provide adequate time for the lesson preparations and the presentations. The skills discussed in Chapter 4, "Managing the Learning Environment," are crucial for creating the positive, safe environment that is necessary for the students to feel comfortable with this activity. The instructor must also make sure that he or she covers all of the appropriate information during the lessons. You can perform this task while helping the groups prepare and by asking probing questions during the lessons. The instructor must also make sure that the students realize that they are responsible for all of the material covered, not just for the topic that they presented.

This method can also be an effective way to expose a group to a variety of situations that relate to the subject matter. For example, you could ask each student to present a short lesson on how they will use the subject matter in their jobs. As with many of the instructional methods, a consideration with student teaching is that it can take a considerable amount of time and is not well suited for short training sessions.

Group Work

Working in groups is an effective instructional method and is often a component of other methods, such as student teaching (which we just discussed). When students work together, it offers them the opportunity to exchange ideas and concerns and to work through problems together. If you have a class with students of varying skill levels, you can organize them into groups that include advanced students and those who need extra help. The advanced students can assist the others, which strengthens their understanding of the material as well. Incorporating group work into our scenarios is easy.

Scenario 1: Spreadsheet Formula   In the student teacher example, we already created groups to study each formula and then to teach the rest of the class. Another way to use groups is to place the students in pairs and ask them to work through the problem themselves. Two minds are generally better then one, and this approach will increase their chance of success.

Scenario 2: Introduction to Computers Class   After you have described the computer and the terminology associated with its components, you can divide the class into several groups. Give each group several computer sales advertisements and ask them to compare and contrast the ads and write a recommendation about which system is the better deal. Then, have each group make a sales pitch to the class and defend their choice. This activity requires the students to understand the function of each component and be able to analyze the advertisements. This activity also teaches a skill that they will need the next time they shop for a computer.

Summary   Group work encourages teamwork and collaboration and promotes problem-solving skills. Students revealing their weaknesses and problems to other students is often less intimidating than revealing them to a teacher. If the course is longer than one day, you can also give group assignments for the students to complete outside of class. One concern with group work is that the students in the group will stray from the task and use it as a social period. To prevent this situation, the instructor should clearly define the purpose of the activity and monitor each group's progress to make sure that the group stays focused. If the groups are too large, students can be passive and let others do all of the work. You must also set a specific time limit for the activity, because this limit will also encourage concentration.

NOTE: *If you are preparing for the CTT video, you should show part of your group work on the video. Although you are limited to 20 minutes and might have to use your one camera stop during group work, show part of it to demonstrate this aspect of Competency 10.*

Role Play

Role playing is a method that involves the students acting out a real-life situation related to the topic of the course. For example, if the course was teaching students how to answer users' questions on a help line, the role play might involve two students: one as the caller with a problem, and the other as the help-desk operator. The instructor might give the student who is acting as the caller a script to follow or a problem to ask about. Role playing can be very controlled, with both participants reading from a script, or it can just be a scenario that the students can act out however they choose, depending on the purpose of the exercise. If the purpose is to illustrate a point or the right or wrong way to do something, then you should script the role playing. If you are having the participants experience a situation to see how they respond to it, you can make the script very open. Role playing gives the students an opportunity to experience a situation and teaches them how to respond to it.

When setting up a role-playing activity, you must establish a safe and positive learning environment. If not, students will be hesitant to participate for fear of being ridiculed or embarrassed. You can ask the students who are observing the role playing to take notes on any points relating to the current lesson. A sheet with questions can focus their attention on specific details. After the role playing is completed, you should "debrief" and discuss the issues that arose during the session. One caution concerning role playing is to make sure that the participants are willing. Do not force anyone to participate. This action would be counterproductive to the learning environment. The only exception to this rule is when the role playing is a requirement for completing the course. In some situations, such as the help-desk example, students might be required to participate in those exercises to prepare for the job of answering real callers' questions.

Role playing is ideal for training that deals with skills that are necessary for particular situations, such as customer service. Role playing might be useful in our scenarios, depending on the objectives of the class.

Scenario 1: Spreadsheet Formula   Once the students develop their grade book, you could test the functionality of the grade book with the following role-play activity. One participant could be the teacher, and another could be a student who wants to know how he or she is progressing in the course. The student asks what his or her final grade would be based on his or her performance on the remaining tests and projects. The teacher would use the grade book to enter various grades and show the student the effects that they would have on the final average. This scenario would also be a good introduction to the course to indicate the benefits of having an automated grade book. Instead of having the teacher use the spreadsheet, he or she could calculate all of the possible grade combinations by hand.

Scenario 2: Introduction to Computers Class   If one of the objectives for the class is to prepare the students to deal with salespeople when purchasing a computer, then you could use role playing to simulate a trip to the computer store. One student can be the knowledgeable salesperson, and another student can be the customer. The student could portray the salesperson as helpful or pushy, depending on how much you want to test the customer's knowledge.

Summary   Role playing can be an effective instructional method whenever you want students to experience a situation or need to prepare them to respond to emergency situations. Remember, too, that a positive learning environment is crucial to the success of these activities.

Simulations

A simulation is similar to role playing because students have the opportunity to experience a real-life situation. This technique is different because it does not require the students to act out a script or situation in front of the class. In the previous example, where students were learning to land an airplane, we could use flight simulators to enable the students to practice a skill in a safer environment until they perfect it. The best simulations elicit the emotions of the real situation and prepare the learners to successfully cope with the situation.

The recent advances in computer capabilities offer significant opportunities for simulations. Virtual-reality simulations now enable people to see, hear, and feel a simulated event. I recently attended a sales presentation for a software program that has been used to create a virtual environment that dental assistants use to practice cleaning teeth. By wearing special gloves and goggles, the students clean virtual teeth—and it feels like the real thing. Several years ago, we could only find this technology on "Star Trek" and in our imaginations. Science classes are also using simulations frequently to reproduce experiments that would not be possible for economic or safety reasons. If you are teaching a course on network management, it might be useful to have a simulation of a particular system problem that the students can try to solve.

Scenarios   The learning objectives of our first scenario do not lead to simulations. The second scenario would benefit from a simulation program that enabled students to assemble and disassemble a computer. The program could lead students through the steps, asking them to identify the various peripherals and testing their ability to set up a computer. If one of the objectives of the course was to learn basic file-management skills, we could use a simulation to practice formatting, copying, and deleting files. This practice would enable the students to try these procedures without the fear of deleting something that they should not.

Summary   Use simulations whenever students need to learn a skill or experience a situation that you cannot reproduce in class. The problem with simulations is that they sometimes require expensive or specialized equipment that is not always available to you or to your students.

Case Studies

Think of case studies as written simulations. Case studies are an effective tool for examining specific situations and encouraging students to determine the appropriate response. Case studies teach students how they can apply the knowledge that they are learning to the real world and how they can examine the right and wrong ways to do something. The results are similar to those of role playing and simulations but do not always require interaction or equipment. Instructors can give case studies to the students as homework or as supplemental reading. Instructors can also use them as a basis for generating discussions on a topic.

Scenario 1: Spreadsheet Formula   You can use case studies to present a variety of grading schemes that teachers use. They could range from simple grade books that just calculate test averages to complex systems that take into account attendance, homework, projects, quizzes, and exams. Each case study could be a problem for the students to solve or include the solution to assist the learner with developing his or her own grade book.

Scenario 2: Introduction to Computers Class   We have already used case studies with this scenario in the group work section. We handed out computer advertisements to groups to examine. We can use each of those ads as a case study for which the students must evaluate and summarize the strengths and weaknesses of each product.

Summary   You can use case studies in any lesson to connect the material to real-world situations. Give case studies as assignments or supplemental reading to reduce the time needed in class. You should include a list of questions to assist the students with examining and evaluating the case studies.

Games

Games can be an effective instructional method to stimulate and encourage learning and to review course material. You can also use games as icebreakers to relax the students. Many people enjoy and respond well to a challenge or competition.

One advantage of games is that they often make learners forget that they are learning something. For example, ever since Microsoft introduced the Windows operating system, the application has included several games that are effective tools for learning how to use the mouse. In virtually every computer class that I teach, there is at least one student who plays one of these games during a break. They do not consciously choose to play the games in order to improve their coordination with the mouse, but this learned skill is a natural byproduct of playing.

On the other hand, games are not always appropriate. You have to be careful when using games, because some audiences might see them as childish and a waste of time. You will have to get to know your learners and determine whether this method is suitable for them.

Scenarios   You can use a game in either of the scenarios as a mechanism for reviewing the material. One of my first experiences as a trainer involved teaching an introduction to computers course in which I always ended with a game of computer trivia based on the popular television show, "Jeopardy!" The game was a fun way to end the session and review the material. The students won small prizes (candy) for giving right answers.

Summary   Games, if presented properly, can be an effective instructional tool. Evaluate your audience and incorporate games into the lesson where appropriate to reduce stress and create a positive learning environment.

Independent Practice

Independent practice or lab sessions are one of the most common instructional methods included in almost every training class. After an instructor presents a procedure, he or she asks the students to work through exercises in order to practice the skills. The instructor's role in this method is to develop examples and exercises that address the topic just discussed and to provide the learners with the information necessary to complete the task. The instructor must also observe each student's progress and assist them whenever necessary.

NOTE: *You must master the evaluation skills discussed in Chapter 12 in order to be successful at this activity.*

If you discover that the students are having an overly difficult time with the exercises, you can switch to group work and use the same exercises.

Scenarios   Both scenarios can include time for independent practice. The spreadsheet class requires this practice in order for the learners to practice the skills taught in the course. In the introduction to computers class, the students could independently do research on the Web and find several deals on computers, then report back to the class with their findings.

Summary   The key to successful independent practice is to create exercises that specifically test the objectives of the course. If they do not, or if the instructor did not cover the knowledge necessary to complete the assignments, then the students will become frustrated and the exercise will not be productive.

Reflection

Reflection is an activity that enables the students to think about the material they have learned, to determine any questions they might have regarding the information, and see how the material will apply to their work. An example would be to take 10 minutes before the end of a lesson and ask each student to make a bulleted list of the items that they learned in the lesson (or provide this list for them). Then, ask them to make a list of the ways in which they will be able to use these skills in their jobs. This activity helps establish the relevance that the subject has to their lives and assists in the transference of these skills from the classroom to the real world. Students could also perform this activity at the beginning of the class to identify their preconceptions about the material that they will be learning.

Scenarios In either scenario, the instructor could set aside time at the midpoint of the class for a reflection activity. The student could think about what he or she has learned so far and write down the three most useful things that he or she has learned and the three things that he or she needs to know before the class ends. The instructor could collect this information and summarize it for the class. This exercise helps the students focus on and review the course material, and it gives the instructor valuable insight into the needs of the students.

Summary Reflection is an instructional method that you can use any time you want the students to stop and think about the material in the course. Reflection is a great way to follow-up other activities, such as role playing, where students have observed or participated in an activity and need to think about the information in order to properly synthesize their experiences.

Conclusion

Each of these instructional methods has its strengths and weaknesses. Your lessons should utilize multiple strategies. You will find that these methods overlap, and you can combine them to suit any situation with which you are faced. Once you have mastered each of these instructional methods, you will have the tools you need to teach any type of subject matter.

Choosing the Right Instructional Method

With so many instructional methods to choose from, what is the right one for a particular situation? The answer to this question is not simple. Choosing the right instructional method depends on a number of factors, including the following:

- Subject matter
- Learners

- Time required
- Available resources
- Other modules
- Time of day
- Your comfort level with the method

Each of these factors will vary from one class to the next. Let's consider each of the variables.

The subject matter will narrow down the instructional methods to those that are and are not appropriate. For example, role playing does not make sense as a choice for teaching a lesson on how to format a document on a word processor. Even if you came up with a script that involved the steps in the process, it would not be as effective as a demonstration, guided learning, group work, or student teaching. If the subject was learning to perform a task in a stressful environment, then role playing is a perfect choice for creating the stressful environment. For each lesson, think about the strengths and weaknesses of the instructional methods that you choose to use.

The attributes of the learners in the class also impact the way you teach the material. Recall the stereotype of the engineer. This type of student wants the facts without any extra fluff. A lecture or demonstration followed by individual practice might be the most appropriate choice for this type of student. You also need to consider the student's attention span. You should vary your instruction frequently. A particular module should not last longer than about 45 minutes. If it does, the students' minds will start to wander. Your analysis of the learners, Competency 1, should assist you with matching instructional methods to the learners.

The time that you have for a particular lesson will significantly impact your decision. The more interactivity involved in an instructional method, the longer it will usually last. If time is limited and there is no way to extend the class, then you should choose an instructional method that might be less interactive and that you can complete in the allotted time. Even if another method might be more effective if time allowed, the activity is not a good choice if it has to be rushed.

The resources at your disposal for a course often dictate the types of methods that you cannot choose. In a perfect world, the training room is equipped with all of the latest and greatest technology. In reality, this situation is seldom the case. The best method to train a skill might be to utilize a three-dimensional virtual-reality system, but this system is seldom available. Your analysis of the training site, Competency 2, will tell you what resources you can use.

You also need to take into account the instructional methods that you have used in other modules within the course and when you used them.

NOTE: *You should vary the instructional methods that you use throughout a course to keep the students stimulated and interested in the material.*

Some methods are appropriate for introducing a subject, while others are better for review. For example, it would never make sense to start a lesson with individual practice. For role playing to be successful, you first need to establish a safe and positive learning environment. A typical class might start with a brief lecture or demonstration to introduce the subject, followed by group work to explore the information. Through the group work, the class has a chance to get to know each other and relax. A role-playing activity might be appropriate next. The sequencing of the modules will have a significant impact on their success.

You should consider the time of day when selecting an instructional method. Many people are not used to sitting in classrooms for an entire day, and this situation will accentuate the normal periods of low energy that people experience throughout the day. For example, many people feel tired by the end of the morning or afternoon or immediately after lunch. These would be good times to select a method that includes activity.

Finally, your comfort level with an instructional method is an important factor when deciding what to use. If you are teaching a prepackaged course and it suggests using a particular game as an icebreaker, and if you do not feel comfortable running the game, then the learners will sense your feelings. This situation might jeopardize the lesson. Pick a different icebreaker with which you are more comfortable.

NOTE: *If an exercise is a required part of a training program, you must include it. If you do not feel that it is appropriate, consult the designers of the course before you make a change.*

Given all of these factors, you will find that even if you teach one topic your entire training career, you will need to occasionally vary the instructional methods that you use.

SUMMARY

Competency 10 addresses the specific instructional methods that you will incorporate into your curriculum. The most important point of this chapter is that you must use a variety of instructional methods to reach your students. Your choice of methods will depend on a variety of factors. These methods complement the skills in the rest of the competencies of the ibstpi Standards. You must be an effective communicator, presenter, and questioner to successfully employ these instructional methods. If you do not know these methods, you will not be able to teach effectively.

When you are planning your lessons, think of yourself as a chess master who must always plan many moves ahead and determine how each move will impact the following one. Your goal is to create an exciting lesson that uses the most effective instructional methods for each topic and that keeps the learners engaged throughout the course.

QUESTIONS

There might be multiple correct answer for some questions. The answers are located at the end of the chapter.

1. What factors affect your choice of instructional methods?
    a. type of student
    b. time available
    c. available resources
    d. course requirements
    e. All of the above

2. Which of the following instructional methods encourage the most student participation?
    a. demonstration
    b. lecture
    c. guided learning
    d. case study
    e. None of the above

3. An effective game includes the following components:
    a. It is fun.
    b. It reduces stress.
    c. It teaches a skill.
    d. It is not childish.
    e. All of the above

4. Which of the following are strengths of student teaching?
    a. Student teaching creates a passive learning environment.
    b. The students are motivated to learn their topic, so they are prepared for questions.
    c. Student teaching takes the focus off the instructor.
    d. Student teaching is effective in short classes with a tight time schedule.
    e. All of the above

5. Which of the following instructional methods would not be appropriate at the end of the day?
    a. a lecture
    b. a demonstration
    c. role playing
    d. a simulation
    e. All of the above

6. Which of the following are weaknesses of group work?
    a. Students can become passive and not participate.
    b. Group work is not appropriate for large audiences.
    c. Group work can turn into social time if the session is not well structured.
    d. Group work creates an active learning environment.
    e. All of the above

7. Which of the following instructional methods will most likely create a passive learning environment?
    a. a demonstration
    b. a lecture
    c. guided learning
    d. a case study
    e. None of the above

8. Which of the following are strengths of case studies?
   a. Case studies relate the subject matter to real-world situations.
   b. Case studies create an active learning environment.
   c. Case studies can be completed outside of class.
   d. Case studies can be directly related to the students' jobs.
   e. All of the above

9. Which of the following are strengths of guided learning?
   a. Guided learning provides the opportunity for students to work through their mistakes.
   b. Guided learning creates a passive learning environment.
   c. Guided learning takes less time than many other methods.
   d. Students must think through the solution themselves.
   e. None of the above

10. An effective lecture includes the following components:
    a. All of the material is covered in one long lecture so that students do not have to sit through multiple lectures.
    b. The lecture is after lunch, so the students have a chance to settle back in to the class.
    c. The lecture is short enough to keep the students' attention.
    d. Audience questions are included to keep the audience an active part of the learning process.
    e. All of the above

11. Which of the following instructional methods will provide the students with the best chance to master a hands-on skill?
    a. demonstrations
    b. lectures
    c. reflection
    d. simulations
    e. games

12. Which of the following instructional methods require the most amount of time?
    a. student teaching
    b. reflection
    c. demonstration
    d. lecture
    e. independent practice

13. Which of the following are weaknesses of role playing?

    a. Some students will not want to participate.
    b. Role playing creates a passive learning environment.
    c. Role playing does not teach specific skills.
    d. Role playing can create a stressful environment.
    e. All of the above

14. Which of the following instructional methods will be most effective for a large audience?

    a. group work
    b. demonstration
    c. simulations
    d. case study
    e. independent practice

15. Which of the following instructional methods will enable you to cover the most material in a given period of time?

    a. simulations
    b. student teaching
    c. lectures
    d. case studies
    e. guided learning

ANSWERS

1. e
2. c
3. e
4. b and c
5. a
6. a, b, and c
7. b
8. e
9. a and d
10. c and d

11. d
12. a
13. a and d
14. d
15. c

Using Media Effectively

Introduction

By the end of this chapter, you will be able to perform the following tasks:

- Select appropriate media
  - Be competent with a variety of media options
- Use media effectively
  - Use a variety of media to address the needs of the learners
  - Recognize strengths, weaknesses, and/or limitations

Competency 11 of the ibstpi Standards deals with the trainer's ability to effectively utilize media throughout the lesson. The term *media* refers to any resource that adds a visual, audio, or other sensory stimulation to the lesson. Chapter 5, "Demonstrating Effective Communication Skills," and Chapter 6, "Demonstrating Effective Presentation Skills," stressed the need to address all of the senses in your instruction. This chapter focuses on the options that you can use to add media to your lesson. A variety of tools are available to trainers to assist with their teaching, and the rapid improvements and increasing affordability of technology has increased this arsenal. As a trainer, you need to be familiar with these options and be able to select the most appropriate resource for a particular topic. You must also be competent in basic troubleshooting and safety considerations for each device. These skills will not only reduce your stress when you use the media but will also impact your credibility with the learners. Chapter 3, "Establishing and Maintaining Instructor Credibility," stressed that you need to be an expert in the subject matter. You also need to be proficient with the technology that you use. If you, the expert, have problems with the media, your students will see you as unprepared and possibly incompetent. The media that we discuss in this chapter are the tools of your trade, and you must know how to use them.

Selecting the Appropriate Media

With all of the media options available to you as a trainer, how do you select the most appropriate one for your lesson? This answer varies, depending on several factors. In Chapter 10, "Using Instructional Methods Appropriately," we listed the following variables when we discussed how to choose the right instructional method:

- subject matter
- learners

- time
- available resources
- relationship to other modules
- your comfort level with the method

Each of these variables can vary from one class to the next and will determine your choice of instructional method, which in turn will determine your media choice. Your media options are tied to the instructional methods that you use and to the level of understanding that you expect the students to reach. You will find that more than one choice will meet your needs. You must decide which one is best.

For example, if you are demonstrating a procedure, you could draw diagrams, use a computer simulation, or show a video of someone performing the procedure. When making this choice, you need to focus on the reasons for including the media. You might decide that you should use several media options together. The purpose of the media is as follows:

- To reinforce and illustrate key points of the lesson
- To keep the students' interest and attention
- To overcome any physical limitations of the room (acoustics, visibility, and so on)

Every form of media that you add to the lesson should address these three points. If they do not, then you do not need them.

When selecting the media, ask yourself the following questions:

a. What level of understanding am I expecting the students to reach?

b. What media option will highlight the important details?

c. What media option will show the most realism?

d. What media options have I already used?

e. What resources are available?

The answers to these questions will help you decide what to use. Consider the following scenario:

Recall the example of the Introduction to Computers course that we used in previous chapters. If you are trying to teach the students how a computer processes data, you have a variety of choices:

- Give the students handouts to study as you explain the process.
- Draw pictures on the board or overhead projector describing the flow of data from the input device to the processor and then to the output device.

- Create a computer animation describing the process and project it through a data projector.
- Create a movie depicting the process and play it on a television.
- Place each component of the computer on the visualizer as you discuss its role in the data flow.

Which of these would be the most useful?

Any of these options might work, but the best one should illustrate the details of the lesson and at the same time include the interactivity that can hold the students' attention. I would use three of the options. First, I would use a computer animation, enabling the students to view the flow of data in the computer. This animation enables you to show details inside the computer that students cannot observe just by looking at part of a computer. Then, I would show them a real computer and point out each component that relates to the process. This activity enables the students to make the connection between the theory and the real world. The instructor could also include handouts, which the students could refer back to for review. This scenario utilizes multiple types of media to assist with maintaining the students' attention and addressing their multiple learning styles. If you cannot create a computer animation, then create diagrams ahead of time that show the process. If you do not have a computer and a data projector available to you, the other options are viable and will work. A simple drawing on a board or overhead describing data flow can illustrate the point; however, it will not be as interesting or descriptive as the animation.

 NOTE: *The most important thing to keep in mind when selecting your media is to remember its dual purpose: illustrating the concept as clearly as possible and engaging the students.*

Using Instructional Media

Both high-tech and low-tech devices exist that can assist you with instructing your students. We discussed some of these items briefly in Chapter 2,

"Assuring Preparation of the Instructional Environment." In this chapter, we discuss tips and considerations for each type of media.

General Tips

The following tips apply to any type of media that you might use. As in every other competency, the keys to this competency are planning and preparation.

- Check on the availability of the equipment before the class.
- Test all of the equipment prior to class.
- Do not stand where you block the students' view of the media.
- Make sure that the information you display is clear, concise, and large enough for everyone to see.
- Use good graphical design (refer to Chapter 6).
- Keep your attention on the students, not on the media. (For example, when you use a board, do not write with your back to the students.)
- Use equipment that enables maximum lighting in the room. When the room is dark, people tend to sleep.
- Check the volume level for any audio device.
- Make sure that all projection devices are in focus.
- Provide handouts for the students to refer to for review.
- Vary the media throughout the lesson to stimulate the learners and maintain their attention.

Consider each of these tips when planning your lessons.

NOTE: *Have a contingency plan in case the media fails.*

Types of Media

Let's look at the following types of media that you commonly find in the classroom. This section discusses some tips and considerations for each:

- Course handouts
- Boards, flip charts, and overhead projectors
- Visualizer
- *Video Cassette Recorders* (VCRs)/slides/film
- Data projectors
- Computers
- The Internet
- Audio aids
- Laser pointers

Course Handouts

Course handouts are the one thing that each student will take with him or her when the course is over. The course developer should create a complete set of handouts that includes all of the material covered in the course. In addition to this documentation, the trainer should create supplemental handouts to highlight and clarify information.

Strengths

- You can use handouts with any size audience.
- Create handouts for your presentations so that the students can concentrate on what you are saying, not on taking notes.
- If a student is late or misses a section, the handouts will assist them with catching up.
- You can add handouts to any of the other media that we will discuss.

Tips

- Review the design suggestions for handouts in Chapter 6.
- If you are using a presentation program (such as PowerPoint), use the Handouts feature to give the students copies of the presentation. Select the option that includes space to write notes.
- Make the handouts clear and concise.
- Use a consistent style and format so that they are easy to follow.

■ Include images where appropriate.

■ Bring extra copies.

Considerations

■ Determine when to give the students the handouts. If you give the handouts to the students before the presentation, it might distract them from the discussion. If, however, the documentation will clarify the point that you are discussing, it might be useful for them to have during your presentation.

■ The quality of your handouts will affect your credibility. Make them look professional, and keep them up-to-date.

Boards, Flip Charts, and Overhead Projectors

Boards, flip charts, and overhead projectors are the most frequently used tools for writing in the classroom. You can find a black/white board in most classrooms. A flip chart, usually placed on an easel, is one of the simplest tools to utilize and is best for situations where notes or ideas need to be written down and referred to, such as during a brainstorming session. Overhead projectors offer this option, as well. You can also use them to display transparencies that you made prior to class. Figure 11-1 shows a typical board, flip chart, and overhead projector.

We discussed the general rules for creating visual aids in Chapter 6 and included appropriate font sizes, colors, and organization. You should follow these rules for any visual aid that you use. You need to make sure that the students can clearly see and read the material. If you make transparencies to use on the overhead, make sure that they follow these guidelines, as well. Check each of them before the class by displaying them and then viewing them from the back row.

Strengths

■ Boards and flip charts are best for small groups, because they are difficult to read from a distance. An overhead projector can project a large image if it can be moved farther away from the screen.

■ Neither the flip chart nor the black/white board utilizes technology that can fail during class. As long as you have adequate supplies of markers, chalk, or pens, you should not have a problem.

Chapter 11

Figure 11-1
Board, flip chart, and
overhead projector

■ These tools are the best option for creating information on-the-spot, such as during brainstorming sessions or group work.

■ Markers, pens, and chalk are available in a variety of colors, and you can use each of these devices to write notes and draw diagrams for the students.

■ You can hang flip charts around the room to remind students of prior comments.

■ You can refer to overhead transparencies repeatedly in order to stress a point.

Tips

■ When writing on a board, easel, or overhead, many people find that the text (or lines) that they write angle up or down. A tendency also exists to underestimate how much space is needed and squeezing in information. Both of these situations make it difficult for the student to read the information. You should practice using these visual aids and check your writing from the students' perspective to guarantee that your work is legible.

- If you have material that you have already prepared, cover up the information and reveal it as needed. This action will prevent the students from reading ahead and becoming distracted by the information.

- Label your transparencies and flip charts well so that you can find the right page when needed.

- With an easel, after you write on pages, you can either flip them over or tear them off and hang them around the room. This feature is useful for the students, because they can refer back to them at any time.

- Use a pen or pencil to point to items on an overhead transparency. You can leave the pen or pencil on the overhead while you interact with the audience. If you are nervous, rest the pen on the overhead rather then holding it in your shaking hand.

- When using an overhead, you should attach a piece of dark paper (or cardboard) to the projection lens housing that enables you to cover the lens. You can use this paper to shield the audience from the bright white light that shines each time you switch transparencies. Simply cover up the lens, change the transparency, and then uncover it when you are ready to proceed. You could also accomplish this task by turning off the overhead each time you change transparencies, but turning the overhead on and off repeatedly can significantly reduce the life of the bulbs.

- The farther back you move the overhead from the screen, the bigger the image becomes.

Considerations

- Seeing information on boards and flip charts from a distance is difficult. They are best suited for small classes.

- Check to make sure that the pens are the appropriate kind for the media. Many people have ruined whiteboards with permanent markers.

- When using an overhead projector, you might have to dim the lights for the students to be able to see the material. Make sure that you can darken the room if needed.

■ A concern when using an overhead is that the bulb might blow. Most overhead projectors hold two bulbs, so if one blows, you can move the slider over and the second bulb takes its place. Learn how to change the bulb in the overhead. This process is simple but sometimes requires a screwdriver to access the bulbs. Always make sure that both bulbs work before the class. Also make sure that you have enough transparencies on which to write.

Visualizer

A visualizer, or document camera, is a device that looks similar to an overhead projector but is much more sophisticated. Instead of a lens on the arm, like an overhead, a mounted camera points down to the light source. You must connect the camera to a data projector, monitor, or some other display unit. This device enables the visualizer to project any object (two-dimensional or three-dimensional) placed under it. A zoom option even exists. For example, you could place a hard drive under the visualizer and zoom in to display all of the details or place a technical drawing under it and zoom in on any section. You can also use the visualizer like an overhead to view transparencies. Use the zoom feature to overcome the problem of small fonts. This tool is wonderful for instruction. Figure 11-2 shows a typical visualizer.

Strengths

■ You can use the visualizer with any size audience, depending on the projection device that you use.

■ A visualizer is the only tool that enables the instructor to project three-dimensional objects in a live setting.

Tips

■ The visualizer is the best option when you want the students to examine the details of an object but cannot provide each of them with an object to examine, due to class size or cost.

■ The same light considerations as the data projector apply. Check the legibility of the projected image before class.

Figure 11-2
A visualizer

Considerations

- You control options on the visualizer through function keys. Study them before class so that you are competent in their use.
- You must connect the visualizer to a display device, such as a data projector.

VCRs/Slides/Film

Showing a video, film, or slides is a good method for supplementing the material in a lesson. You can use these media to demonstrate procedures or to set up case studies or role playing. Figure 11-3 shows a VCR.

Figure 11-3
A VCR

Strengths

■ You can use video, slides, or films with any size audience.

■ This media is one of the best ways to show real-life situations.

■ This media can take the spotlight off of the instructor, which adds variety to the session and gives the instructor a break.

Tips

- Preview the media ahead of time to identify the major points, issues, and follow-up questions.
- Tell the students what they will see in order to focus their attention on particular details.
- Give the students a list of questions to answer while viewing the media.
- Tell the students how long a video is so that they know what to expect.
- Provide handouts for review.
- Make the experience as interactive as possible. Stop the video and/or replay important sequences to highlight major points, have follow-up discussions, and clarify any questions/issues that arise.
- Cue the tape or film to the appropriate point beforehand to save class time.
- For slides, do not have empty slots in the slide tray that will blind the students with bright light between slides.

Considerations

- This media can be passive, and students will drift during long sessions.
- Seeing an image on a standard-size television from a distance is difficult. This media is best suited to small groups unless a large-screen TV is available.
- Production of these tools can take considerable time, effort, and money.
- If the VCR is playing but there is no picture on the TV, make sure that the TV is on the correct channel.
- If you are training in a foreign country, verify the format of the video (it can be different).

Data Projector

A data projector is a device that enables you to project output from a computer onto a screen. Several kinds of data projectors are available today, each of which utilizes a different technology. The most common ones now are *Liquid Crystal Display* (LCD) projectors. The earlier versions of these were formed as panels that rested on top of an overhead projector. They are now self-contained units, and some are as small as a laptop computer and are easily transported. Their brightness is measured in *American National Standards Institute* (ANSI) lumens, which is a standard unit of measure for light. Early models with ratings of 300–600 ANSI lumens required the lights to be dimmed considerably in order to see the image. Models are now available with ratings of more than 1500 ANSI lumens that work well in normal light conditions. Current data projectors enable you to project from a computer and other video sources. Figure 11-4 shows a typical data projector.

Strengths

- Data projectors can, depending on the model, accommodate any size audience.

- Data projectors offer the instructor a considerable amount of flexibility. Anything that you can do on a computer you can project for the students to see.

- Most projectors can also receive input from any video source, such as a VCR, which eliminates the need for multiple projection devices in the room.

Figure 11-4
A data projector

Tips

- Colors might look different when projected, compared to your computer monitor. If colors are important, such as in a graphics course, then check them ahead of time.

- Depending on the age of the data projector, it might not support resolution settings as high as your computer does—and you might have to lower the resolution setting on the computer to accommodate this situation. If you are connecting a laptop to a data projector, this action might cause a problem—because laptop display options are sometimes limited. Check the connections ahead of time to prevent last-minute surprises and headaches.

Considerations

- If you have to turn off the lights in order to adequately see the image, limit the length of the presentation so that the students are not in the dark for too long.

- The computer must be connected to the data projector and to the computer monitor in order to view the image in both places. Some projectors have a Y cable that connects the computer to both the data projector and the monitor. Other models require a cable from the computer to the projector and another one to connect the projector to the computer monitor.

- The distance between the computer and the projector might impact the signal quality. If the distance is too great, the signal might not be strong enough without adding a device to amplify it.

- Data projector bulbs do blow occasionally. This event is less common than overhead bulbs blowing, but the potential exists—and these bulbs are more difficult to replace. They also cost much more ($300 or greater), so it is less likely that you will have a spare one available. Have backup plans (handouts, transparencies, and so on).

- To prevent the bulbs from overheating, most data projectors have a standby mode that you should use to temporarily turn off the light without turning off the fan. Some projectors have a built-in delay that prevents the bulb from being turned off and then immediately on again.

- You can control data projectors, depending on the make, through function buttons or a remote. Learn how to focus the image and make necessary adjustments on the model that you are using.

Computers

We have discussed the use of computers for presentations, demonstrations, and simulations several times already in this book. Computers can be a powerful resource in your lesson. With the benefits, however, also come several risks. Computers are more complex than any media we have discussed so far. An in-depth discussion about troubleshooting problems is a subject for an entire book. You are not required to be a computer hardware expert in order to be a trainer (unless you are teaching the topic), but you should be familiar with the basics. In other words, you should be comfortable with setting up computers (for example, connecting the monitor, keyboard, and mouse to the Central Processing Unit, or CPU) and with the basic settings (for example, changing the display setting, managing files, and setting up printers). These skills will enable you to address most of the problems that can occur that you can correct immediately.

Strengths

- You can use computers with any size audience, depending on the quality of the data projector.
- You can use computers to incorporate color, motion, and sound into the presentation.
- Presentation software provides a consistent look and feel to the entire lecture.
- You can modify the presentation at any time.
- With the appropriate technology, you can deliver computer presentations to students at remote locations and provide the opportunity for distance learning.

Tips

- Always test the system ahead of time to verify that the system is working properly.
- Use the brightest LCD projector possible.
- Bring a backup copy of your files on a separate disk in case your computer crashes.
- If you are using someone else's computer, verify that the right software is installed.

Considerations

- Presentation software makes it easy to add multiple fonts, colors, graphics, and transitions. Do not let the technology overshadow the lesson, however.
- Some computer setups require a password. Find out the password ahead of time.
- Turn off screensavers so that they do not distract the students.
- When using a laptop, check the power management settings to make sure that the laptop does not shut down unexpectedly during the session.

The Internet

The Internet, and the information access that it offers, has become an important component of many jobs and is also becoming a part of many training sessions. Some might not consider the Internet instructional media, but many instructors use a computer to access it as a resource. Therefore, the Internet deserves some consideration here.

Strengths

- The Internet provides access to a wealth of real-time information.
- You can use Web pages as the presentation medium and make them accessible to the students for future reference.

Tips

- Always verify the sites that you plan to use in class, because they can change or disappear at any time.
- Web browsers enable the user to determine how much space is allocated to temporary storage (cache) of the pages that you visit. If you increase the size for this setting and then access the sites before class, they will load faster during the lesson.

Considerations

- Verify the speed of the connection at the training site and determine whether it is reasonable to rely on live Internet access.
- Do not rely on Internet access. At any given time, the Internet can be extremely slow or not available at all. Always have a backup plan.
- Remind the students that not everything on the Internet is true or valid. They should always verify the source of the information.

Audio Aids

If you are teaching a large audience or the acoustics in the training room are poor, you might find that you need a microphone. If this situation is the case, try to use a wireless microphone or a lavaliere (a small clip-on microphone). Figure 11-5 shows a standard microphone and a wireless microphone.

Strengths

- Audio aids enable large audiences to hear you clearly without you having to shout.

Figure 11-5
Microphones

Tips

- Turn off the microphone during breaks or private conversations.
- Carry spare batteries for the portable microphone.

Considerations

- The microphone amplifies every sound that you make (swallowing, coughing, chewing, and so on).

Laser Pointer

A laser pointer is a useful tool for directing the students' attention to a particular topic. They are now quite affordable and a good addition to any trainer's toolbox. Figure 11-6 shows typical laser pointers.

Strengths

- A laser pointer enables you to point to anything in the room without having to move to that object.

Figure 11-6
Laser pointers

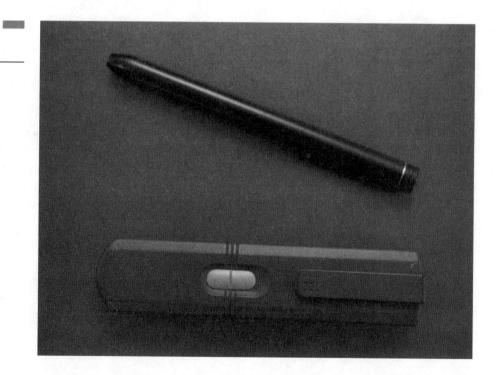

Tips

- Do not overuse the laser pointer. If you are always flashing it around the screen, the students will become distracted. Just use it to direct their attention to important points.

Considerations

- Be careful about where you point the laser. The laser can cause eye damage. Never use it to point to anything near students. The laser beam can also go through glass. Be careful.

The instructional media discussed here is not all-inclusive, but it does include the most commonly used tools.

NOTE: *The key to successfully using any media is to test it ahead of time and always have a backup plan.*

SUMMARY

Competency 11 requires you to be adept at incorporating media into your curriculum in order to facilitate student learning. Your media selection will depend heavily on the instructional methods that you select and the resources that you have available to you in the classroom. Regardless of whether you choose high-tech or low-tech options, you can still address the needs of the learners as long as you select media that will capture their attention and encourage interaction. How successful you are will depend on your familiarity with the media and the planning and preparation that you put into the lesson ahead of time.

QUESTIONS

There might be multiple correct answers for some questions. The answers are located at the end of the chapter.

1. Which of the following are reasons for using media in your lesson?
   a. To capture the students' attention
   b. To highlight a particular point
   c. To overcome inadequacies in the physical environment
   d. To demonstrate something that you could not bring into the classroom
   e. All of the above

2. What factors will assist you with determining the appropriate media to use?
   a. subject matter
   b. physical environment
   c. available resources
   d. your comfort level
   e. All of the above

3. Which of the following media equipment is least likely to have technical problems?
   a. computer
   b. overhead projector
   c. chalkboard
   d. visualizer
   e. VCR

4. Which of the following media equipment is most likely to have technical problems?
   a. computer
   b. overhead projector
   c. chalkboard
   d. visualizer
   e. VCR

5. What are the strengths of using the Internet?
   a. The Internet creates a lot of visual stimulation to keep students interested.
   b. Internet sites are always available.
   c. Everything on the Internet is true.
   d. You have instant access to a wealth of information.
   e. All of the above

6. What are the limitations of using a computer and a data projector?

    a. You might have to dim the lights in order to see the image clearly.

    b. Colors might not be exactly the same as on the computer.

    c. The distance between the computer and the projector is limited, so you might be not be able to move around the room.

    d. Technical knowledge is required.

    e. All of the above

7. Which of the following media equipment can you use to focus the students' attention on a particular object anywhere in the classroom?

    a. laser pointer

    b. microphone

    c. visualizer

    d. VCR

    e. All of the above

8. Which of the following devices enables you to zoom in on a three-dimensional object?

    a. an overhead projector

    b. a white board

    c. a visualizer

    d. a laser pointer

    e. All of the above

9. Which of the following devices enables you to redisplay class notes for later use?

    a. a white board

    b. a flip chart

    c. an overhead projector

    d. a data projector

    e. All of the above

10. When is the best time to give the students handouts?

    a. before the lesson

    b. during the lesson

    c. after the lesson

    d. It depends on the purpose of the handouts.

    e. Never use handouts.

11. What are the benefits of showing a video during a training session?

    a. Videos provide a break from other parts of the lesson.
    b. Videos can illustrate items that you cannot bring into the classroom.
    c. Videos take the focus off the instructor.
    d. Videos can be entertaining.
    e. All of the above

12. What can you use to facilitate a brainstorming session?

    a. an overhead projector
    b. a flip chart
    c. a computer/data projector
    d. a white board
    e. All of the above

13. What are the limitations of using a flip chart?

    a. Not conducive to large audiences
    b. Frequent technical problems
    c. You cannot prepare material ahead of time.
    d. The instructor must have legible handwriting.
    e. All of the above

14. If you are teaching a class with 100 students in a large lecture hall, which of the following media options would be appropriate?

    a. a computer and data projector
    b. a flip chart
    c. a blackboard
    d. a TV and VCR
    e. All of the above

15. If you are teaching a class with five students in a small classroom, which of the following media options would be appropriate?

    a. a computer and data projector
    b. a flip chart
    c. a blackboard
    d. a TV and VCR
    E. All of the above

ANSWERS

1. e

2. e

3. c

4. a

5. a and d

6. e

7. a

8. c

9. b and c

10. d

11. e

12. e

13. a and d

14. a

15. e

Evaluating Learner Performance

Introduction

By the end of this chapter, you will be able to perform the following tasks:

- Clearly communicate the lesson objectives
  - Define the lesson objectives
  - Define the evaluation criteria
- Utilize a variety of evaluation techniques to evaluate and monitor learner performance
  - Formal evaluation
  - Informal Evaluation
  - Testing

Competency 12 of the ibstpi Standards deals with the trainer's ability to effectively evaluate each learner's performance. Evaluating student performance is an important skill that all trainers must master. Evaluation must occur throughout the course so that the instructor always knows how far the students have progressed. Without evaluation, the instructor is working in the dark and has no way of knowing how successful the instruction is or whether the students are mastering the objectives of the course. The students also need to be aware of the course objectives and the standards with which the instructor will measure their evaluation. Formal methods of evaluation, such as tests and quizzes, are necessary for any course that leads to a grade or certification. Because these events occur at the end of the course, the instructor must also rely on informal evaluation tools for assessing student progress throughout the session. These tools enable the instructor to provide constructive feedback to each student so that the students are aware of their progress and can address their weak areas. Evaluation is the only way to determine whether the instruction has been effective. This chapter addresses the essential components of evaluation.

Course Objectives and Evaluation

Many sections throughout this book have stressed the importance of proper planning in determining the success of a course, which is measured by the success of the students in meeting the course objectives. During the planning process, you must identify the instruments that you will use to determine the students' level of understanding. Does the course lead to certification? If so, there is most likely an exam that the students need to take at the end of the course. Is the exam hands-on, multiple choice, short answer, or all of the above? The answers to these questions will determine the objectives of your course. The course objectives will then determine the skills and level of mastery upon which you will base the evaluations. Once you have clearly defined the course objectives, you will be able to build evaluation mechanisms into the course that address each of the course objectives.

You *must* define the course objectives well from the start so that both you and the students will understand exactly what you expect from each other. To perform this task properly, you need to start each session with a discussion regarding the necessary level of understanding for the particular topic. Remember the levels of understanding that we discussed in Chapter 7, "Demonstrating Effective Questioning Skills and Techniques"? The students should know from the start what level they will need to obtain in order to successfully complete the course.

Consider the format of each chapter in this book. Each chapter begins by stating the objectives of the chapter. To become a *Certified Technical Trainer* (CTT), you have to complete a multiple-choice exam testing your knowledge of the 14 ibstpi Standards and demonstrate that you can apply these skills by taping a training session. You can pass the multiple-choice exam by studying this book, but without applying the knowledge and practicing the competencies, you will not be able to demonstrate the required skills in the video. Each of the 14 competencies includes distinguishing characteristics that tell you exactly what you must be able to do.

Discuss with the students the skills that they must master and how you will address these skills at the start of the training session. Each time you begin a new topic, address the specific objectives of the lesson. This action will help the students focus on the necessary information from each lesson and know what level of mastery is necessary to attain the objective of the lesson. When the course is completed, finish with a review of the required material and discuss any next steps that the students should take in preparation for exams or subsequent courses. By identifying and discussing the course objectives throughout the course, you will be able to create appropriate assessment tools, and the students will always know what you expect of them.

Evaluation

A variety of formal and informal methods are available for monitoring and evaluating a student's progress. For this book, we define formal evaluations as tests or quizzes that are scheduled events during or after the course. We define informal evaluations as other activities that you can use to evaluate students' progress. Formal evaluations are required for certification and sometimes are incorporated into other courses in order to judge performance. Informal evaluations are ongoing and should be a component of every course.

When developing the course, you need to incorporate assessment strategies into the course so that you can always be cognizant of how the students are doing. You can then determine the adjustments that you have to make to the pace and instructional methods. The following sections discuss in detail the environment that is necessary for accurate evaluations and the various methods of evaluation at your disposal.

Environment

Imagine being a student in a class where the instructor constantly rushes through the material and acts aggravated every time a student asks a question. Would you feel comfortable speaking during class and possibly showing your ignorance on a particular topic? I certainly would not. As long as I keep my mouth shut, the instructor has no idea that I am having a problem with the material.

To accurately assess student performance on an ongoing basis, you need to develop a positive learning environment where students feel comfortable taking risks (showing their lack of understanding of a topic). We addressed this subject in depth in previous chapters, but we should reiterate our points. If you do not develop a positive learning environment, you will have a difficult time evaluating the students. The students will not feel comfortable asking and answering questions. They will not want to take the chance that they will be wrong and look like fools. If the students are not responsive, it will be impossible to determine their level of understanding with any of the informal methods discussed in this chapter.

NOTE: *Your first step in evaluating the students is to develop a positive, supportive, and interactive learning environment.*

Formal Methods of Evaluation

First, we will discuss formal evaluations. The types of questions that we will discuss can also apply to informal evaluations. One of the most common methods for evaluating students is to give tests or quizzes. Depending on the type of course that you are teaching, this activity might or might not be possible. If the course is not tied to any certification and there is no requirement for all of the students to leave the course with a specific skill set, then you probably will not include a formal test at the end. *We are not saying that you should not evaluate them*; rather, you will just use options that are less formal than tests or quizzes. If the course does require an evaluation at the end, the course developers might provide it, or you might have to create the test yourself. You can use the types of questions that we describe as follows in a variety of situations to address many of your evaluation needs.

NOTE: *Make sure that you demonstrate methods of evaluating the learners when you prepare your video for CTT certification. You do not need to show the entire evaluation process in the video, but the process must be evident to your students. You might find it appropriate to use your one allowable after the evaluation begins.*

You can design a test in many ways to evaluate student progress. Tests can include any or all of the following types of questions:

- True/false
- Matching
- Multiple choice
- Short answer
- Essay questions

■ Scenarios

■ Simulations

Each of these question types has its strengths and weaknesses. Some are better for evaluating memorization skills, whereas others test the ability to apply the knowledge. By combining a variety of types of questions, you will be able to successfully assess each student's knowledge and understanding of the topic. Remember the techniques discussed in Chapter 7 regarding effective questioning skills, and apply those techniques when you evaluate the students.

True/False   In Chapter 7, we discussed open-ended and closed questions. True/false questions are closed, because they ask questions for which the answer is only true or false (or yes or no). Only one right answer exists. We display several examples of true/false questions in Figure 12-1.

The first two bullets ask the same question: one as a statement, and the other as a question. Only one correct answer exists. The third bullet asks a general-knowledge question that will determine the students' understanding of the features and capabilities of databases. The fourth bullet is an example of a knowledge question that is not well suited for this format. Either answer can be correct, depending on the background of the user and the content of the course. This situation highlights one of the drawbacks of

Figure 12-1
True or false
questions

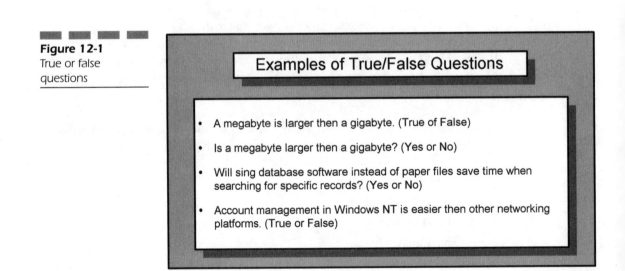

Examples of True/False Questions

- A megabyte is larger then a gigabyte. (True of False)

- Is a megabyte larger then a gigabyte? (Yes or No)

- Will sing database software instead of paper files save time when searching for specific records? (Yes or No)

- Account management in Windows NT is easier then other networking platforms. (True or False) true/false questions: the question needs to have a definitive answer. If the question does not, then you should use another question type.

The second disadvantage of this question type is that if the student has no idea what the correct answer is, he or she still has a 50 percent chance of guessing it. Everyone has probably seen at least one movie in which the hero is trying to diffuse a bomb and must choose between the red wire and the green wire. The hero never seems to be able to remember which one to cut but luckily always guesses the right one at the last minute. The same result could occur with true/false questions. You must also use other question types to ensure an accurate evaluation.

Despite these disadvantages, this approach is one method for quickly assessing a student's understanding of a topic. Students need little time to complete these questions, because a lengthy explanation is not necessary (just one-word answers). These questions also do not require a significant amount of time to grade. They can determine a broad understanding or focus on minute details. Because there are only two possible answers, these questions are good to use in group settings to quickly assess the class's understanding. Starting and ending training sessions with these questions will quickly survey a group's comfort level with a particular topic.

Matching   Matching questions are a good tool for testing vocabulary or relations between various words or concepts. Figure 12-2 shows an example of matching questions.

These questions have the same strengths and weaknesses as true/false questions. They can quickly evaluate knowledge and memorization when only one right answer exists. In the example, this type of question determines the student's understanding of the different uses of the applications in an office suite program. Instructors can also correct these questions quickly.

The disadvantage of using matching questions is that they do not offer the students a chance to explain or qualify their answer. A student might have a good understanding of the topic but not remember the matching word. This student would not perform well on the question, which might not indicate his or her true level of understanding. The other issue is that the chance of guessing the correct answer increases because all of the possible answers are visible.

Multiple-Choice Questions   You commonly find multiple-choice questions in many of the certification exams (such as the CTT), because they can

Figure 12-2
Examples of
matching questions

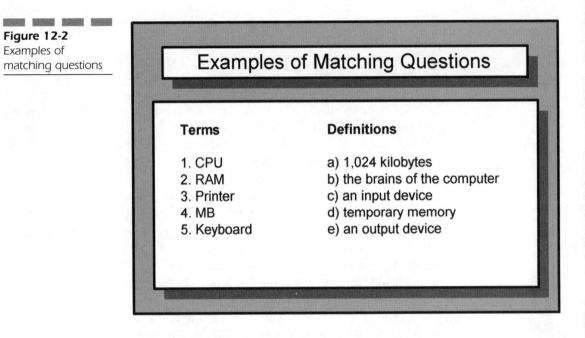

Examples of Matching Questions

Terms	Definitions
1. CPU	a) 1,024 kilobytes
2. RAM	b) the brains of the computer
3. Printer	c) an input device
4. MB	d) temporary memory
5. Keyboard	e) an output device

evaluate a variety of learning levels and are quick to grade. Figure 12-3 shows an example of several multiple-choice questions.

Multiple-choice questions can test vocabulary, concepts, and application skills (such as the order in which you must perform a task). The difficulty level of these questions depends on how they are designed. If a multiple-choice question has four distinct possible answers and only one choice is acceptable, then the student knows that one of them must be correct and automatically has a 25 percent chance of guessing the correct answer. If he or she can eliminate one or two of the possible answers, the odds go up considerably. This situation is not necessarily a negative; rather, it is just the nature of this type of question. If you allow multiple answers, then the difficulty increases significantly. Furthermore, adding the choice "None of the above" creates the hardest questions. Some instructors design multiple-choice questions so that there are several possible answers, and the student must choose the most correct answer. With all of these variations, the multiple-choice question becomes a flexible evaluation tool.

The true/false, matching, and multiple-choice question formats all share the advantage of instructors being able to grade them quickly and computer testing systems easily delivering them.

Figure 12-3
Examples of multiple-
choice questions

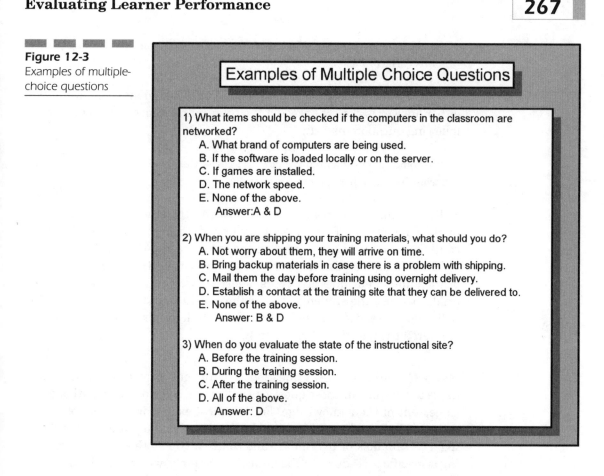

Examples of Multiple Choice Questions

1) What items should be checked if the computers in the classroom are networked?
    A. What brand of computers are being used.
    B. If the software is loaded locally or on the server.
    C. If games are installed.
    D. The network speed.
    E. None of the above.
      Answer:A & D

2) When you are shipping your training materials, what should you do?
    A. Not worry about them, they will arrive on time.
    B. Bring backup materials in case there is a problem with shipping.
    C. Mail them the day before training using overnight delivery.
    D. Establish a contact at the training site that they can be delivered to.
    E. None of the above.
      Answer: B & D

3) When do you evaluate the state of the instructional site?
    A. Before the training session.
    B. During the training session.
    C. After the training session.
    D. All of the above.
      Answer: D

Short-Answer Questions Short-answer questions require the student to supply the answer from memory. These questions can be as simple as a statement missing a word that the student must supply. The following statement is an example:

> The temporary memory space that a computer loads applications into is called _____.

This format is different than the previous question types because it does not give the students any choices from which to select. Of the four question types discussed thus far, short-answer questions are the first that offer the student a chance to explain the answer. Recall the true/false example that stated:

Account management in Windows NT is easier then other networking platforms (True or False).

This true/false question is not good, because a student could argue that either answer is correct based on the frame of reference. You could ask the following question instead:

Is account management in Windows NT easier than in other networking platforms (Yes or No)? Explain your answer.

By including a short-answer requirement, the student has a chance to qualify the answer. This opportunity provides the instructor with significantly more information regarding the student's knowledge.

The primary disadvantage of a short-answer question also applies to all of the subsequent question types: short-answer questions take longer to grade, because the students answer the questions in their own words. You will have to read each answer carefully to determine whether students answered the question appropriately.

Essay Questions   Essay questions are the most time consuming for students to answer, but these questions will reveal the most information about the extent of their knowledge. For technical exams, instructors often use essay questions when asking students to describe the process for performing a certain task or to compare and contrast two methods for accomplishing a specific procedure. In the matching example, which asked students to pick the appropriate software application for specific tasks, we could have asked the question in this format, as well. Look at the following example.

Describe the various applications found in the Microsoft Office suite and discuss which office tasks are most appropriate for each one.

The question is more difficult as an essay, because the students have to think of the various applications and associated tasks without any examples to jog their memory. When designing a test, you have to decide which type of question is most appropriate based on the objectives of the course. If students will have to return to their department and recommend more efficient ways of doing business by using an office suite program, they should be able to answer the essay questions. If instead they will have to use the office suite effectively when a project comes up, the matching question should suffice. The difference is that the matching questions enable them to work with existing examples, whereas the essay question draws on their knowledge of the programs and asks them to think of new ways to use it.

> **NOTE:** *Remember to always match the question type to the course objectives.*

Scenarios   Scenarios, rather than questions, are appropriate in a particular context. You can use a scenario to focus on any of the question types listed, but scenarios most often appear in essay questions. Asking students to respond to scenarios is one of the best methods for checking whether they can apply their knowledge to a situation. This technique is useful for skills-based courses, which include most technical courses.

Consider the following examples:

Scenario Example 1   You are the office manager for your department and have to determine more efficient ways to accomplish tasks by using computers. Given a list of tasks, select the most appropriate software application that could be used to complete the task.

Scenario Example 2   You are asked to develop customer-service policies for your department. What key issues should you consider? Do existing departmental policies foster good customer service?

Scenario Example 3   You are answering calls at the company's help desk, and someone asks the following question: "I have data in my spreadsheet that I am trying to sort and it is just not working; how do I sort it?" What additional information do you need to know, and what are the instructions that you would give to the caller?

Scenario Example 4   You are the systems manager for a company that has more than 200 employees. You are in the process of setting up a network drive so that employees can share documents. What are the security issues regarding shared network drives, and what precautions should you take to protect against them?

Each of these scenarios puts the question in a specific context so that the student knows how to focus his or her answer. You could add Scenario 1 to the matching question example to provide a situation where the scenario might actually arise. Scenarios 2 and 3 require the student to use technical knowledge and apply it to a specific situation.

NOTE: *Being able to apply skills to a specific task is the goal of most technical courses. Using scenarios to frame a question or exercise is one of the best ways to evaluate this skill.*

Simulations All of the question types described test the student's knowledge but do not prove that the student can actually perform the task. People can buy books that will teach the steps to building a computer. If they study hard enough and memorize everything in the book, they will most likely be able to answer a written test on the topic, but they will unlikely be proficient at actually building computers. Every technical course includes a lab component, because hands-on practice is necessary in order to master a skill. Using simulations or hands-on exercises, such as the one depicted in Figure 12-4, is the most effective way to evaluate a student's ability to perform the necessary procedures.

Incorporating simulations, or hands-on exercises, into the test is a crucial element of technical training. In every computer software course that I have taught that requires testing, hands-on tests have contributed to a significant portion of the grade. This method is the only one that positively tests the students' abilities to apply the material that they have learned.

Consider the CTT exam process. You are required to take the written exam to prove that you have the required knowledge, but you are also required to submit a video of your training to prove that you can apply the knowledge. Knowing the information in technical courses is not sufficient; students must also be able to apply their knowledge to real-world situations.

NOTE: *You should always use simulations to test hands-on skills.*

The Right Questions

The right type of question depends on your objectives, which determine what the student should be able to do at the end of the course. Before you

Figure 12-4
Example of
simulations, or
hands-on exercises

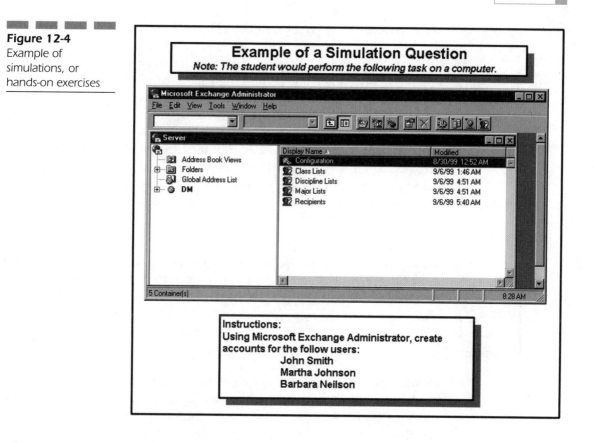

can choose the right types of questions, you have to decide what you are trying to evaluate. Recall the levels of learning discussed in Chapter 7. Is the
goal of the course for the students to be able to apply the skills to existing
problems or to evaluate existing practices and determine the appropriate
tools for the task?

For example, when teaching a course on word processing, you might set
an objective for the students to type or edit a report with the appropriate
features of the word processor. If you establish this objective, would the following question be appropriate?

"List three methods for changing the font size of the text."

I would argue that it is not appropriate, because the student would not
have to know every method for changing the font to meet the objective of

the course (which is typing a report). They are only required to accomplish the task, which means that one method is good enough.

When I teach an application course to students who are new to computers, the many options for performing each task often overwhelm them. I always start the class by explaining that there are several ways to do everything and that they are only responsible for learning one method. I will show them several techniques, but if they find them confusing, they should focus on one way and stick with it until they are more comfortable with the program. Then, they can focus on more efficient methods. You have to make sure that you set the proper expectations at the beginning of the course so that the students know which information is required and which information is supplemental.

NOTE: *Questions must always match the course objectives, which you must always clearly convey to the students.*

When you have to generate your own evaluation instrument, always try to place the questions in the proper context by using scenarios to focus the students. Remember, the goal of most technical training courses is to teach a skill that the students will apply on the job. Therefore, design tests that will evaluate this ability. All of the question types described here will work, depending on the situation and context.

Administering Exams

Formal certification courses sometimes require you to administer exams. When you administer an exam, you need to make sure that the testing environment adheres to any requirements set by the organization that offers the exam. The requirements can concern any of the following:

- Student space
- Computer equipment
- Time limitations
- Proctors

Before the training session, when you perform the site survey, you need to guarantee that the room arrangement is acceptable for administering tests. If each student must have four feet separating him or her from other students, bring a tape measure. Check whether the computers meet the minimum standard required for the exam. Determine whether the Internet connection is fast enough. You need to address the physical environment before the class begins, because afterward, it might be too late.

If the test has a time limit (which most do), make sure that the students know about it—and make sure that you have a clock available to track the time. A proctor might also be required, possibly one who has required credentials. Make sure that you address each of these issues. If you fail to adhere to one of the requirements, it might disqualify the exam results—which means that a student might not pass an exam because of your oversight.

Another issue that you have to consider is cheating. Although we like to think that no one would cheat in our courses, we need be aware of the possibility and limit the potential for any problems. To safeguard against any inappropriate behavior, you should arrange the testing environment so that students are not tempted to seek assistance. You should also try to eliminate any other distractions that the facilities might present, such as windows or doors.

NOTE: *You want to create an environment that is conducive to student success.*

Informal Evaluation

Throughout this book, we have discussed the need to assess the students' progress and level of understanding at various points throughout the course. Informal evaluation refers to any method used to determine their progress. The term *informal* means that you do not give the students a test or a quiz. You build activities into the lesson that assist you with evaluating the students' progress, and you make observations throughout the lectures, discussions, and activities that help you determine the success of each student.

NOTE: *Informal evaluations should not interrupt the flow of instruction. They are observations that you make throughout the lessons.*

To be successful at informal evaluations, you must master the questioning skills discussed in Chapter 7. You also need to be able to interpret body language, which we discussed in Chapter 5. Without these skills, you will not be able to determine whether a student is confused, lost, or actually understands everything. The key to ongoing evaluations is to constantly observe the students throughout the training session. When you introduce new material, look for their reactions. Use the various question types discussed in the formal evaluation section to test their knowledge. The training session has to be interactive for you to be able to accurately evaluate their progress, so continually ask them questions and solicit feedback.

One goal when designing the course outline should be to include components that assist you in evaluating the students' progress. The following activities can be useful for determining the students' progress:

- Exercises/lab work
- Small-group work (presentations)
- Self-assessment

Exercises and Lab Work   Every technical course should include hands-on exercises during which the students practice the skills they are learning. Each time you teach a new skill, you should include exercises as a component of the lesson. I have attended training sessions in which the instructor assigned a project and then left the room to attend to something else while the students worked on the project. The instructor is missing one of the best opportunities for evaluating the students' progress.

NOTE: *Observing and assisting the students as they work through the exercises will enable you to spot instantly any problems they might be having with the material.*

One caution when assisting students is to not assist them too much. If you do not let them work through the problems, then you will have a harder time identifying their strengths and weaknesses. Remember that the material is new to them, and it will take them some time to work through it. Your eagerness to assist them will prevent them from reaching the proper conclusion themselves, which they will have to do when they return to their jobs.

Conversely, you should not sit at the front of the room and wait for your students to ask for assistance. Many will be hesitant to bother you even if you have developed a positive learning environment. Assisting and evaluating students as they work through problems is a skill that will improve as you gain experience.

NOTE: Remember, the video that you produce for the CTT certification must show assessment strategies. If time does not allow for a complete assessment, at least show part of the assessment activity. At this point, you might want to use your one stop.

Small-Group Work   You can use small groups to assist you with the evaluation process. By having the students work together on exercises and lab problems, you encourage communication. Whenever you divide the class into small groups for activities, they will tend to discuss any problems that they might be having with the material. You should encourage this communication and give them an opportunity to share these problems at the end of the activity. Build these sessions into your lessons and encourage students to answer each other's questions and take note of any common problems they are having. This activity will enable you to clear up any issues before you move on to the next lesson.

Self-Assessment   Having the students assess their own abilities is another useful method of evaluation. Previous chapters have mentioned performing comfort-level checks during the course to quickly assess the students' attitudes toward the new material. If you include a skills checklist at the end of each section of the course, you can quickly survey the class by asking the students to evaluate themselves on each of the items. Realize that self-evaluation is not always the most accurate, because people often overestimate or underestimate their skills, but it will help you determine how well they think they are doing. Comparing their opinion with your other observations also assists you with your overall evaluation of each student's progress.

Feedback

Evaluating students is an ongoing process, which means that you need to constantly monitor their performance throughout the presentations, labs, and other activities. For the evaluations to be of any use to the students, you must provide them with feedback based on your observations. This feedback will help them identify their strengths and weaknesses and work to overcome any problems. Refer to Chapter 8, "Responding Appropriately to Learners' Needs for Clarification or Feedback," for an in-depth discussion of appropriate feedback techniques.

NOTE: *Use the informal evaluations to provide the students with appropriate feedback so that they can prepare for the formal evaluations (for example, the certification exams).*

Instructor Competencies

As the instructor, you must master a variety of skills to evaluate your students effectively and react to the evaluations appropriately. All of the skills discussed in this book are necessary components of evaluation:

- Preparation of the course material and learner information (Chapter 1) involves preparing for formal and informal evaluations.

- Preparing the instructional site (Chapter 2) is necessary to meet any testing requirements.

- Establishing and maintaining your credibility (Chapter 3) is essential for creating a positive learning environment, which makes informal evaluation possible.

- Management of the learning environment (Chapter 4) is crucial for maintaining order.

- Using communication skills (Chapter 5) to read verbal and nonverbal messages is a required component of evaluations.

- Effectively presenting the material (Chapter 6) will determine how well the students perform on the evaluations.

■ Questioning skills (Chapter 7) are imperative for evaluating the students.

■ Feedback skills (Chapter 8) enable you to give the students constructive criticism.

■ Positive reinforcement and motivational incentives (Chapter 9) will assist you with encouraging the students to improve upon their weaknesses.

■ Properly using instructional methods (Chapter 10) will enable you to address the weaknesses that you identify.

■ Effective use of media (Chapter 11) will enhance the instruction and thereby improve student performance.

All of these skills are inter-related, and you must master each of them to be able to teach effectively. Evaluation is an integral part of instruction.

Evaluating Your Evaluations

Once you evaluate your students, you must be able to justify and defend your decisions. If students question their grades, you must be able to explain your evaluation. There are two situations that students can point to that might undermine your evaluations. The first is the legitimacy of the tests. This situation brings us back to the issue of clearly stating, and regularly restating, the course objectives and basing your evaluation tools directly on them. If you always perform this procedure, then students can never make the argument that they were not aware of the material on which they would be tested. The second issue is the frequency of observations. If you only observed the student once throughout the course, the student could argue that you saw only the one success and not all of the successes. Your evaluations need to be based on multiple observations in order to adequately defend your decisions.

NOTE: *To justify your evaluation procedures, always base them on clearly stated course objectives—and evaluate the students frequently throughout the course.*

SUMMARY

Instructors must learn to use evaluations to determine student performance and to identify any areas of the lesson that must be reinforced. Formal evaluations are a component of many technical courses that lead to certification. The instructor must learn to use informal evaluations throughout the course, without interfering with the instruction. This chapter addressed the various types of methods used in both formal and informal evaluations and where they are most effective. Course objectives and evaluations are inter-related, and the instructor must keep the students informed of the goal of each lesson and of their progress throughout the course. Always seek to evaluate the students' performance in each section of the course. This information is essential for you to appropriately address students' needs throughout the course and for the students to succeed.

QUESTIONS

There might be multiple correct answers for some questions. The answers are located at the end of the chapter.

1. Why should you evaluate student performance?
   a. It is required for the certification.
   b. To create a stressful environment
   c. To determine student progress throughout the course
   d. All of the above
   e. None of the above

2. Which of the following is an example of a formal evaluation?
   a. a self-test
   b. a certification exam
   c. a peer review
   d. a pre/post test
   e. None of the above

3. Which of the following is an example of an informal evaluation?
   a. reading the student's body language
   b. a pre/post test
   c. a peer review
   d. question and answer sessions
   e. All of the above

4. Which of the following must occur for the students to be successful?

   a. establishment of a positive learning environment
   b. clearly defined course objectives
   c. adequate training materials
   d. All of the above
   e. None of the above

5. When would you use a multiple-choice question?

   a. To test students' abilities to apply their skills
   b. To simplify the grading process
   c. To test the students' knowledge of a topic
   d. All of the above

6. When would you use a short-answer question?

   a. To create an open-ended question
   b. To simplify the grading process
   c. To give the students the opportunity to explain their answers
   d. None of the above

7. When would you use an essay question?

   a. To simplify the grading process
   b. To pose a scenario to the students
   c. To ask a question regarding the process (steps) for performing a task
   d. To test the students' writing skills

8. When would you use a scenario in a question?

   a. To place the question in a particular context
   b. To focus the question and answer
   c. To test specific skills
   d. All of the above
   e. None of the above

9. Which of the following items should you be concerned with when administering an exam?

   a. the lighting in the room
   b. the requirements of the certification group
   c. cheating
   d. possible distractions
   e. All of the above

10. When should you perform informal evaluations?

    a. Never

    b. At the beginning of each session

    c. At the end of each session

    d. Throughout the session

    e. After the session is over

11. Why should you use informal evaluations?

    a. To determine the students' understanding throughout the course

    b. To test the students for certification

    c. To provide an opportunity for the students to assess themselves

    d. All of the above

    e. None of the above

12. What must you communicate to the students throughout the course for the evaluations to be successful?

    a. The time of day

    b. The type of evaluation to be used

    c. How the course will relate to their jobs

    d. The objectives of each lesson

    e. All of the above

13. What types of questions should you use to test memorization of terms?

    a. short-answer questions

    b. true/false questions

    c. essay questions

    d. matching questions

    e. multiple-choice questions

14. What types of questions should you use to test concepts?

    a. short-answer questions

    b. true/false questions

    c. essay questions

    d. matching questions

    e. multiple-choice questions

15. What types of questions should you use to test general knowledge?

    a. short-answer questions

    b. true/false questions

    c. essay questions

    d. matching questions

    e. multiple-choice questions

16. What types of questions should you use to test relationships?

    a. short-answer questions
    b. true/false questions
    c. essay questions
    d. matching questions
    e. multiple-choice questions

17. What types of questions should you use when there might be multiple answers?

    a. short-answer questions
    b. true/false questions
    c. essay questions
    d. matching questions
    e. multiple-choice questions

18. Which of the following instructor skills are necessary to be an effective evaluator?

    a. Understanding nonverbal signals
    b. Understanding verbal signals
    c. Effective listening skills
    d. Effective questioning skills
    e. All of the above

19. Which of the following items could lead to inaccurate evaluations?

    a. frequent evaluations
    b. a poor learning environment
    c. an inappropriate pace
    d. small-group work
    e. All of the above

20. What is a disadvantage of only using a written test to evaluate student skills?

    a. The students will be bored.
    b. The students might not be able to apply their knowledge.
    c. The test will not be challenging enough.
    d. All of the above
    e. None of the above

21. When should you perform formal evaluations?

    a. before the course begins
    b. during each lesson
    c. at the completion of the course
    d. never

22. What needs to be included in the course outline in order to assess the students effectively?

    a. icebreakers, in order to establish a positive learning environment
    b. an initial assessment of student skills
    c. adequate time for evaluation after each session
    d. review exercises at the end of each section for self-review and evaluation
    e. All of the above

23. Why would you have the students perform self-assessments?

    a. To take up time in a class that is moving too quickly
    b. To assist them with recognizing their strengths
    c. To have them do your work for you
    d. To help them identify weaknesses without embarrassment

24. How are group activities useful for assessment?

    a. Students might be more open with each other.
    b. Students can learn from other students.
    c. You can quickly assess the overall class performance.
    d. They are less threatening then individual evaluations.
    e. All of the above

25. When should you give students feedback regarding their progress?

    a. Never
    b. Each time you observe issues that need to be addressed
    c. At the end of each session
    d. Every 15 minutes
    e. None of the above

ANSWERS

1. a and c
2. b and d
3. a, c, and d
4. d
5. b and c
6. a and c
7. b and c

8. d

9. e

10. b, c, and d

11. a and c

12. b and d

13. d and e

14. a and c

15. a, b, d, and e

16. d

17. a, c, and e

18. e

19. b and c

20. b

21. a and c

22. e

23. b and d

24. e

25. b and c

Evaluating Delivery of Instruction

Introduction

By the end of this chapter, you will be able to perform the following tasks:

- Determine the success of the lesson based on multiple criteria:
  - Student success
  - Instructional design
  - Learning environment
- Utilize a variety of methods to evaluate the lesson:
  - Criteria to evaluate
  - Types of evaluation questions
  - Methods of evaluation

Competency 13 of the ibstpi Standards deals with the trainer's ability to effectively evaluate the delivery of instruction. The question that trainers should ask themselves at the completion of the course is, "Have all of the objectives of the course been met?" In other words, were the students successful in completing the course and mastering the material? If the students did not succeed, then you must determine why.

NOTE: *The purpose of evaluating all aspects of the course is to identify any weaknesses so that you can correct them for the next sessions.*

If you fail to identify the problems in a course, the students will continue to fail. This chapter discusses the items that you must evaluate in order to determine the success of the course. You will also learn several methods of evaluation that will assist you with gathering the data.

NOTE: *When preparing the CTT video, you will find that Competency 13 is assessed primarily on the Video Documentation Form. There should be visible evidence in the video, however, of the instructor's evaluation of his or her delivery of instruction. For example, if the CTT candidate writes on his or her form that objectives were met because learners were able to answer questions that the trainer posed, then this claim should be evident in the video.*

The Circle of Training

Think about each of the topics discussed so far in this book. First, we gathered information about the course, students, and training facilities. Then, we designed the course—keeping in mind the objectives and the audience. Then, we discussed delivery skills. The previous chapter covered evaluating the students. Finally, we turn back to the course design and evaluate the instructional design and delivery of the course. The process then returns to the beginning as we prepare to teach the course again. The preparation of the course is a cyclical process, depicted in Figure 13-1.

This process means that you are continually evaluating your courses to identify any weaknesses and correct them before the next training session. To be successful, you need to effectively evaluate the decisions you made during the course (concerning delivery methods, content, pace, and so on). You then need to interpret the evaluations and act on them if there are any problems.

NOTE: *Each time you teach the course, you build on your previous experiences and improve the session.*

Figure 13-1
Development circle

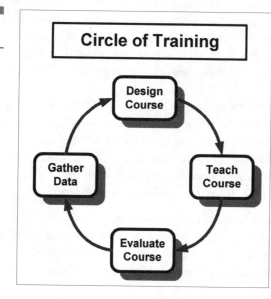

Items to Evaluate

To effectively evaluate the course, you must first identify the factors that can affect its outcome. The following list indicates the general categories into which we can group all of the factors:

- The student
- Instructional design
- Instructor decisions
- Course materials
- Environment

Each of the items will have an impact on the success of the delivery; therefore, you must determine methods for evaluating each of them in order to identify any potential problems.

The Student

The success of the students in mastering the objectives of the course is the most telling indicator of how successful the course was. There are students who succeed despite the worst possible instruction, and there are students who fail regardless of how well you do—but the overall success of the class should be an important clue as to how well you designed and delivered the course. Therefore, you *must* have a means of measuring student success. To completely understand why a particular student succeeds or fails, you should consider student issues that are outside your control (including the students' backgrounds, prior experiences, and interest in the material). You must factor all of these issues into your conclusions when evaluating your course.

Chapter 12, "Evaluating Learner Performance," covered a variety of formal and informal evaluation mechanisms that you can employ to determine student success. Once you have the results of these evaluations, you then need to decide what to do with them. First, determine whether there were any factors outside your control that might have affected the success of any of the students. Imagine the following scenario:

> You are teaching a five-day course on network management that covers the process of installing and managing a server. At the end of the course, the students are required to take an examination including written questions and hands-on exercises. There are 15 students in the course. When you review the

results of the exams, you discover that 10 students passed and five did not. In other words, one-third of the class failed.

What should you do? Do you throw out the entire course and redesign it from scratch, or do you just accept the fact that some students are not cut out for network management? Do you decide that you are not the right person to teach this type of class, because you obviously did not do a good job this time? The answer to all of these questions is no.

NOTE: *You always need to evaluate the factors that might have affected student performance.*

Your goal is to discover what caused the difficulties and determine whether you could have done anything better in order to improve the situation. When reviewing the scenario, ask yourself several questions about the students to determine the cause of their failure:

a. Did the students have the prerequisites for the course?

b. Did the students miss any of the classes?

c. Did the students arrive late or leave early?

d. Did the students do all of the exercises?

e. Did the students participate in class?

f. Did the students show interest in the material?

g. Did the students ask questions?

Based on the answers to these questions, you should be able to determine where the problems occurred. The answers will assist you with determining how to remedy the problem for future courses.

If the answer to Question a is no, then you might determine that the instruction was sound but the registration procedures might need to be evaluated. You should find out why the students were able to register for the course. If they do not have the prerequisite knowledge, then they are bound to fail the class. One option would be to develop a test (possibly a self-test) that potential students could take to determine whether they meet the minimum requirements for the course. The other item to evaluate is whether you clearly defined the prerequisites and objectives of the course at the beginning so that the students knew the challenge they would face.

Questions b and c determine whether the students missed any of the instruction. If this absence trend matches the material that they failed on the exam, then you have discovered the reason for their failure. Your solution for the future could be to emphasize more greatly the importance of attendance and share statistics of past students who had poor attendance.

The rest of the questions target the attitude, participation, and attentiveness of the students during class. Their answers might indicate the need to work harder on developing a positive learning environment or to encourage questions and risk taking. You also might need to emphasize the relevance of the material to their jobs in order to increase interest in the material.

The success of the students will be a significant factor in evaluating the course, but you need to make sure that you understand the reasons why the students failed. By discovering the reasons, you will better understand the issues that you need to address in order to improve the course.

Instructional Design

The instructional design of the course is the most significant factor in determining the success of the instruction. The choices you make in regard to the methods of instruction employed in the course are directly related to student success. Each of the instructional methods discussed in Chapter 10 has its place in a course. You learned that each has its strengths and that you should incorporate a variety of methods into a course. If you lectured during the entire course without including any student interaction, students are bound to be bored, lose interest, and most likely fail the course. There is no way to access student success without interaction.

NOTE: *When you evaluate your delivery, you need to pay close attention to each of the activities included in the course and recall how successful the activities were.*

Ideally, you should keep notes throughout the course, documenting strengths and weaknesses. This record enables you to easily evaluate each section. You should ask yourself the following questions at the end of each activity:

a. What was the objective of the activity?

b. Did the students achieve the objective?

c. Was there any confusion regarding the objective of the activity?

d. Did each student participate in the activity?

e. Did anything unexpected occur during the activity?

f. Was there anything that could have been improved?

g. What would you change the next time you teach this lesson?

Each of these questions will assist you with pinpointing any areas in which improvements could be made. If you keep a notebook handy and get in the habit of assessing each learning activity, you will be well prepared when you re-evaluate the lesson and look for ways to improve the course.

Instructor Decisions

When the class begins, you have an outline that you plan to follow. Invariably, something unexpected happens and you have to deviate from that outline. While preparing for the course, you should have developed contingency plans to account for most issues. After each course, you must evaluate how well you reacted to the situations that arose and the effects that your modifications had on the course. Consider the following scenarios:

Scenario A You are teaching an Introduction to Spreadsheets course. You discover that your students are having a difficult time understanding the financial spreadsheet that you are creating because they are getting confused with the formulas in the example. You do a quick poll and determine that all of the students are teachers, so you change the example to a grade book. The example is one that they can relate to, and they quickly grasp the new material.

Scenario B You are teaching an introductory e-mail course, during which you instruct the students how to log on to the system for the first time, change the passwords, and use the basic features of the e-mail system. The course is set to begin at 1 P.M., but two of the eight students have not arrived. You wait for five minutes and then begin without them. The first part of the course is the most difficult, because each student must log on and determine a new password. This procedure often requires individual assistance for each student and normally takes about 10 minutes. You finally get everyone into the system, and you start the lesson—at which time the last two students arrive, apologizing profusely. They ask whether they can still join the class. This day is the only day that they can make it. You decide to let them join the class and try to quickly get them logged in. The process takes an additional 10 minutes because one of them has never used a computer before.

In each of these scenarios, the instructor was presented with an unexpected situation and reacted to it. Scenario A had a happy ending, because the instructor discovered a problem with the example and refocused the lesson by using an example to which all of the students could relate. In Scenario B, however, the students who arrived on time had to wait 10 minutes for the late students, which meant that the instructor had to rush through the material in order to finish on time. You had little time for questions, and student comprehension suffered. Continuing with the lesson and catching up the tardy students at the break would have been better. This way, you do not punish the class because of the two students' late arrival.

NOTE: *Every time you teach a class, something unexpected could happen that will require you to modify your original plans.*

After each lesson, evaluate your decisions and learn from them. The longer you teach, the more comfortable you will be with the unexpected—because you will have experience dealing with situations.

Course Materials

The quality of the course materials that you use in the training session will have a significant impact on the students' results and satisfaction. The course materials include the training manuals, your presentation materials, any media that you use, and any supplemental resources to which you refer. Depending on the type of course you are teaching, there might be required course materials already developed, or you might have to develop them from scratch. Either way, you should evaluate them at the end of each course and decide whether you can improve them.

The training manual should be clear and concise, including all of the necessary instructions for each task. When you evaluate the manual, look at issues such as readability, appropriate graphics, and consistent format. Are all of the exercises explained completely, or is there missing information that the students are assumed to know? If you are teaching a course developed by others, check to see whether the instructions are generic. You might have to include additional information in order to assist the students. The following scenario shows an example of this type of problem:

Scenario You are teaching a course on file management, and the training manual uses the C: drive (hard drive) as the starting point for all directory structures. The manual instructs the students to create a directory on the C: drive called *data*, which they will use to store all of their files. The company for which you are teaching the course, however, has a network drive (letter P:) for all data. In fact, each time the computers are restarted, the hard drives are wiped of any files that are not part of the standard setup.

In this situation, you are not teaching the students the information that they need to know. If they are new to the concepts of file management and drive letters, it might be difficult for them to make the leap from using the C: drive in class to the P: drive when they return to work. You will find that you will have a lot of unhappy students after the computers restart.

NOTE: In your evaluation of the course materials, you should recognize any omissions or generic references that might cause problems and remedy them by including supplemental documentation that is specific to the students in the course.

The presentation materials and the media that you use can also be significant factors in student success. Items in this category include overhead transparencies, slides, computer presentations, posters, and any other materials that you use. You should also consider the equipment that you will use to display the material, such as overhead projectors, *Liquid Crystal Display* (LCD) projectors, and slide projectors. Ask yourself the following questions in order to evaluate the equipment:

a. Was the information on the slides/overhead transparencies adequate and appropriate?

b. Were the students able to read the material clearly (font size, color, layout, and so on)?

c. Was the information organized well?

d. Was the projector/overhead bright enough for the room conditions?

e. Was there anything that I could have used if it were available?

Without adequate course materials, the students will have difficulty following the material and your presentations.

NOTE: *After each course, evaluate your material through self-assessment and student feedback.*

Environment

We stressed the importance of the learning environment frequently throughout this book, and you cannot overlook this factor when evaluating the session. Make note of environmental issues about which the students complain. This procedure will assist you when you perform the pre-session site evaluation for your next course. Overlooking items that will distract students (or disregarding them as minor inconveniences that the students should be able to ignore) is easy.

NOTE: *Remember that some students might not want to be at the training session, and any distraction will prevent them from concentrating on the material.*

You should consider the following areas in your evaluations:

- Lighting
- Acoustics
- Seating (comfort and location)
- Distracting items in the room

- Temperature
- Line of sight
- Accessibility for physically challenged students

These are the same items that you evaluated before the beginning of the session. By re-evaluating them immediately afterward, you will learn from the students' perspectives.

Methods of Evaluation

Now that we have looked at the items that you should evaluate in order to determine the success of the course, we will discuss the methods that you can use to gather feedback. There are several audiences from whom you should seek feedback, including yourself, the students, and possibly the students' employer(s).

Who Should Provide Feedback?

All instructors should strive for perfection when teaching a course, but they also must realize that things will go wrong. Their job is to evaluate the problems and prepare for them in the future. In other words, your self-analysis will often be the most critical evaluation, because you will know each thing that went wrong—even if the students did not notice.

The students' perceptions of each of the factors listed here are significant. They will indicate whether or not they feel comfortable with the material and the instructional methods that you employed. They will also be able to identify any weaknesses that you might not have recognized.

If a company sent the students to the course in order to learn a specific skill set that they will need back at the workplace, it is useful to include the employers in your evaluation process, as well. Immediately after the session (or even before it begins), you should discuss this evaluation with the managers and arrange a time to meet with them after the course ends. The actual evaluation should occur after the employees have had a chance to return to their jobs and apply the skills that you have taught. This data will be the most telling indicator of the students' success in achieving the objectives of the course.

How to Obtain Feedback

You will gather two types of data when evaluating your course: quantitative and qualitative. Quantitative data is information that you can use to generate statistics on the course. Any closed questions will fall under the category of quantitative. Examples of these questions include yes/no questions and ratings questions. Figure 13-2 shows several examples of yes/no questions, and Figure 13-3 shows several examples of ratings questions.

The advantage of gathering qualitative data is that it is easy to summarize, and it enables you to generate statistics on your courses. For example, it would be nice to be able to report to the employer that 95 percent of the students said "yes" when asked if they felt that the training was worthwhile. Statistics are useful for the evaluation of individual courses and the

Figure 13-2
An example of yes/no questions

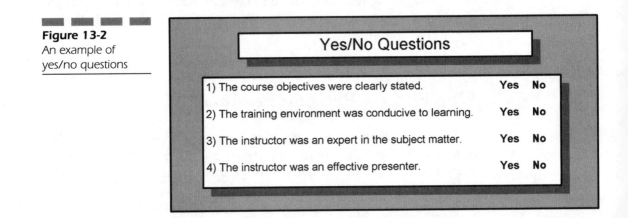

Figure 13-3
An example of ratings questions

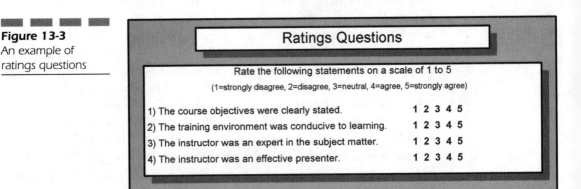

entire training program. Another advantage of this question type is that the student can respond to it with a single word or by circling an answer. The disadvantage of quantitative evaluations is that they limit the students' responses.

Qualitative questions are open-ended questions that give students the opportunity to explain their opinions on a particular topic.

NOTE: *The most valuable information to you, the trainer, are the comments and suggestions that students give when answering qualitative questions.*

Many students will tell you exactly how they feel regarding the course. The major advantage of qualitative questions is that they enable you to gather this type of detailed information. Figure 13-4 shows several examples of qualitative questions.

A disadvantage of qualitative questions is that it is difficult to summarize the students' answers. You can derive common ideas and themes, but it is often impossible to evaluate these answers statistically. Another disadvantage is that these questions require the student to spend more time answering them, and it takes you more time to read the comments.

Based on the strengths and limitations of quantitative and qualitative questions, you need to determine what is appropriate for your course and

Figure 13-4
Examples of
qualitative questions

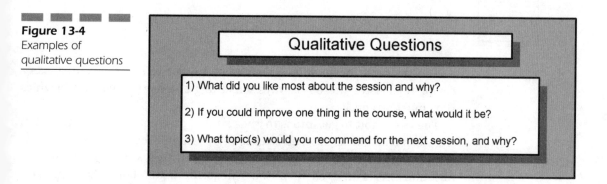

Qualitative Questions

1) What did you like most about the session and why?

2) If you could improve one thing in the course, what would it be?

3) What topic(s) would you recommend for the next session, and why?

for the audience. You need to consider how long the evaluation can be if you expect the students to complete it willingly. You also need to decide when to give the evaluation. If you have the students fill out the evaluations before they leave the class, the return rate should be 100 percent—and their memories of the course will be the freshest. Most students are ready to leave when the course ends, however—especially in technical courses where they have been studying complex theories and applications. This situation might lead to brevity in their answers. To solve this problem, you might ask them to take the surveys with them and mail them to you when they are complete; however, this procedure significantly reduces the return rate. For the quantitative questions, this approach would cause a problem with the validity of the statistics, because the number will represent only a small portion of the class. For the qualitative questions, you might only get responses from students who really felt they had something to say and who took the time to complete the evaluations. One solution to this problem is to have the students complete a short evaluation with quantitative questions immediately at the end of the course, then have them return a longer evaluation with qualitative data at a future date. Your decisions regarding the evaluations will depend on the amount of information that you need to gather.

For self-evaluation, you can use a variety of methods for gathering feedback on your course. One of the best ways is to keep a notebook with you at all times that you use to record any situations upon which you feel that you need to improve.

NOTE: *The problem with notes is that many trainers never take the time to read them after the course has ended.*

The trainers always intend to take notes, but unless the course was a complete disaster, there is always something else more important to which they must attend.

The best habit to get into is to review the course notes immediately after the class ends (or as soon as reasonably possible). You need to review the course while it is still fresh in your mind. You then want to ask yourself questions regarding each of the categories listed here. An organized approach to this review is to create a course evaluation sheet with all of the necessary questions and use it for each course. Keep these evaluations in a file for future review. By working through the questions and reflecting on the notes you took during the course, you will be able to identify and track all of the weaknesses that you observed.

Another option that you can use, if necessary, is to follow up with the students after the course with a phone call, e-mail message, or mailing. This follow-up solicits any data that was not gathered at the end of class and gives the students the chance to comment further on the material once they have had the chance to apply it on their own.

Interpreting the Data

Once you have gathered all of the data, you need to interpret it. At this stage, one thing to remember is that all trainers must have thick skins.

NOTE: *Do not take each negative evaluation personally.*

You also need to realize that many students do not like to be critical of the instructor in writing and will often give positive feedback—even if they were not completely satisfied with the course. Therefore, you should pay more attention to the negative comments than to the positive ones. If students take the time to make negative comments, then they definitely had problems with the course.

A colleague once attended a training session about effective presentation skills. Unfortunately, the trainers did not apply any of the skills about which they were talking. They had poor body language, used filler words (such as "umm" and "okay") frequently, and used poorly designed visual aids. Many of the other students wrote positive comments on their evaluation forms because the content of the course was useful to them. My colleague, who has many years of training experience, was so appalled at the fact that the instructors were not "practicing what they were preaching" that he gave them an extremely negative evaluation including many extensive comments. They probably learned more from his evaluation than they did from all of the others.

NOTE: *Look at any negative feedback that you receive and determine whether it is an honest assessment of the course. Use this information to improve the next session.*

Creating the Evaluation

Once you have decided the most appropriate types of questions, you need to create evaluation instruments that will effectively gather the following information:

- Student evaluation of the course
- Student evaluation of the facility
- Student evaluation of the instructor

Depending on the nature of the course, you might be required to generate reports on any of the evaluation items discussed. You must create evaluation forms that will address this need. This section includes several sample questions for each area that you can use in your evaluations. All of the quantitative questions ask the student to rate the item on a scale of 1 to 5, with 1 being "strongly disagree" and 5 being "strongly agree." These questions can be rephrased as yes/no questions, as well. The qualitative questions solicit more detailed information, however. Examples of both types of questions are included for each evaluation category.

Student Evaluation of the Course

Quantitative Examples

The course met my expectations	1 2 3 4 5
The course objectives were clearly stated	1 2 3 4 5
The exercises and activities were relevant to the objectives	1 2 3 4 5
The course was well organized	1 2 3 4 5

Qualitative Examples

What did you like most about the course?

What did you like least?

How do you think you will be able to apply this material at your workplace?

What recommendations do you have for improving the course?

Student Evaluation of the Facility

Quantitative Examples

The room layout was appropriate for the course activities	1 2 3 4 5
The furniture was comfortable	1 2 3 4 5
The training center is conveniently located	1 2 3 4 5
The acoustics were satisfactory	1 2 3 4 5

Qualitative Examples

Was there anything about the facilities that was unsatisfactory? If so, what?

What are the strengths and weaknesses of the training facility?

With regard to the training facility, is there anything that you would improve?

Was the technology adequate for the needs of this course? If not, why?

Student Evaluation of the Instructor

Quantitative Examples

The instructor was well prepared and organized	1 2 3 4 5
The instructor stimulated my interest in the material	1 2 3 4 5
The instructor was an effective teacher	1 2 3 4 5
I would recommend this instructor to others	1 2 3 4 5

Qualitative Examples

What is the instructor's greatest strength?

What is the instructor's greatest weakness?

Could the instructor have done anything to improve the course?

How did the instructor build your confidence in the material?

Preparing for the Next Session

After you have evaluated the course, you have completed the circle of training shown in Figure 13-1. You have returned to the beginning and will start the cycle again as you prepare for the next time you teach the course. Many trainers see the developmental process as a straight line, rather than a cyclical process. Once you develop the course, it never changes. For you to be a successful and skilled trainer, you need to return to the beginning of the circle. The process might not take as long the second time because the initial development is already in place, but you must take the time to evaluate the course. At this point, you reap the benefits of the evaluation process and learn from the mistakes that you made in the previous session. Each time you teach a course, you strive to improve it.

SUMMARY

The ability to evaluate a training session is a required skill for a trainer. You must be able to recognize the strengths and weaknesses of your courses and learn from your mistakes. The data that you use to evaluate your courses will come from observations by yourself, the students, and the students' employers. The circle of training never ends. You must always be aware of the impact of each of your decisions throughout the preparation and delivery of a course and use this knowledge to improve the session the next time you offer it.

QUESTIONS

There might be multiple correct answers for some questions. The answers are located at the end of the chapter.

1. Why should you evaluate the delivery of instruction?
   a. To determine problems with the course structure
   b. To identify instructor weaknesses
   c. To identify the strengths of the course
   d. To determine why students succeeded or failed
   e. All of the above

2. When should you evaluate the delivery of instruction?

    a. throughout the session

    b. never

    c. at the end of the session

    d. every third time you teach the course

3. What instructional design issues should you evaluate?

    a. the pace of the course

    b. the course outline

    c. the course materials

    d. course objectives

    e. All of the above

4. What will assist you in determining the appropriate instructional modifications that you should make during the course?

    a. the informal evaluations of the students

    b. the demands of the overbearing students

    c. preplanning of alternate learning activities

    d. All of the above

5. What course material issues should you evaluate?

    a. the layout of the course manual

    b. the appropriateness of the examples and exercises

    c. the depth of the material

    d. All of the above

6. What categories should be on every student's course evaluation?

    a. instructor competencies

    b. food

    c. course objective

    d. learning environment

    e. All of the above

7. From whom should you seek feedback regarding the course?

    a. the students

    b. yourself

    c. the students' employer(s)

    d. All of the above

    e. None of the above

8. Which of the following questions are quantitative?

   a. How many types of floppy disks are there?
   b. What are the strengths and weaknesses of operating system X?
   c. Should you give everyone system privileges?
   d. Why do people create computer viruses?
   e. Did you like this course?

9. What strategy can you use to maximize your self-analysis of the course?

   a. Set aside a day each month to evaluate each course.
   b. Rely on your memory to keep track of problems.
   c. Keep a notebook for documenting each problem as it arises.
   d. None of the above

10. Which of the following questions are qualitative?

    a. What is the meaning of life?
    b. What is the best time of day for surfing the Internet?
    c. Why is a *Graphical User Interface* (GUI) environment better then a text-based environment?
    d. Is a GUI environment better then a text-based environment?
    e. All of the above

11. Why should you solicit feedback from the employer?

    a. You should not.
    b. They pay for the training.
    c. They can tell you whether the students are successful in applying the skills at work.
    d. To spy on the students
    e. All of the above

12. What must you communicate to the students throughout the course in order for the course to be successful?

    a. the time
    b. that you are an expert in the field and they should listen to you
    c. the course objectives
    d. the difficulty of the material
    e. All of the above

13. What should you do if you discover that a majority of the class did not comprehend the material?

    a. Give up on teaching.

    b. Re-evaluate the students' backgrounds.

    c. Accept that some classes will fail.

    d. Evaluate the course structure.

    e. None of the above

14. What information would assist you in determining why a student did not pass the course?

    a. the student's interest in the material

    b. the student's age

    c. the student's technical background

    d. the student's marital status

    e. None of the above

15. How do you evaluate the instructional design of the course?

    a. student evaluation results

    b. self-evaluation throughout the course

    c. the student success rate

    d. All of the above

    e. None of the above

16. What should you do if you discover that the required course material does not adequately cover a particular topic?

    a. Do not use it.

    b. Create supplemental material to cover the topic.

    c. Skip that section of the course.

    d. Use it "as is," because that is the way the vendor designed it.

    e. All of the above

17. What are the advantages of qualitative questions?

    a. easy to grade

    b. Students have the opportunity to explain their answers.

    c. easily automated

    d. You can ask questions of greater depth and complexity.

    e. All of the above

18. What are the advantages of quantitative questions?

    a. easy to grade
    b. effective for testing facts
    c. easily automated
    d. easy to analyze the results statistically
    e. All of the above

19. When is the best time to have students fill out a course evaluation?

    a. before the class
    b. never
    c. throughout the course
    d. immediately after the course ends
    e. one week after the course ends

20. What question should every instructor ask at the end of a training session?

    a. Did everyone in the class like me?
    b. Were the course objectives met?
    c. Why do I do this?
    d. What can I improve for the next time?

21. What information can student evaluations provide when evaluating the course?

    a. evaluation of the room
    b. evaluation of the instructor
    c. evaluation of the course material
    d. evaluation of the overall course
    e. All of the above

22. What strategies can you use to assist with evaluating the course?

    a. Keep notes throughout the course.
    b. Create an effective post-training evaluation.
    c. Constantly use informal evaluations to determine student success.
    d. All of the above

23. When is deviating from the lesson plan the correct decision?

    a. Whenever a student is lost and falling behind
    b. If the entire class is having difficulty with a topic
    c. When a topic is not interesting to the students
    d. When a lesson takes too long and you are short on time
    e. All of the above

24. Why should every evaluation form include quantitative questions?

    a. They enable you to evaluate the course results statistically.
    b. They are easier to answer.
    c. Quantitative questions are easier for students to understand.
    d. All of the above
    e. None of the above

25. What should you do when you receive a negative evaluation?

    a. Ask yourself how you failed.
    b. Evaluate it, and do not take it personally.
    c. Ignore it.
    d. Call the students and demand to know why they did not like you.
    e. All of the above

ANSWERS

    1. e

    2. a and c

    3. e

    4. a and c

    5. d

    6. a, c, and d

    7. d

    8. a, c, and e

    9. c

    10. a and c

    11. b and c

    12. c

    13. b and d

    14. a and c

    15. d

    16. b

    17. b and d

    18. e

19. d

20. b and d

21. e

22. d

23. b and d

24. a

25. b

Report
Evaluation
Information

Introduction

By the end of this chapter, you will be able to perform the following tasks:

- Evaluate appropriate components of instruction
  - Students
  - Instructor
  - Lesson
  - Instructional material
- Report evaluation information to appropriate groups
  - Students
  - Employer(s)
  - Training organization

Competency 14 of the ibstpi Standards deals with the trainer's ability to evaluate the various components of the lesson. This chapter highlights the items that you must be prepared to report on at the end of a course. This process is the final step in the training process, and you can use this evaluation as a resource to improve future sessions. The key to successfully reporting all of the pertinent information is to find out what reports are required before the training sessions and document the information that you will need throughout the session. Many of the previous chapters discussed methods and strategies for evaluating the students, your performance, and the success of the overall course. This chapter summarizes the types of reports that you might have to prepare and the groups that might require information from you.

NOTE: *Always remember this administrative detail, because it will assist you with becoming a better trainer and will address the needs of all of the groups involved in the training process.*

Reports to Prepare

The final step for any course is to make sure that you adhere to all of the follow-up procedures. Although the specific details might vary for each course, the general procedures will remain the same. The following list highlights the issues that you should address after the course:

- Performance of the students
- Performance of the instructor
- Satisfaction of the students
- Satisfaction of the instructor
- Revision suggestions
- Demographics of students

Your analysis of these items will be based on your observations throughout the course and the evaluations from the students. The purpose of following up on these items is to assist the students with their educational process and to identify anything that you should do in order to improve the course for future students. You should perform these steps as soon as the class is over so all of the information is fresh in your mind.

Performance of the Students

We discussed the process of evaluating student understanding of the topic in Chapter 12, "Evaluating Learner Performance." Several audiences will be interested in the results of the course. If the students are required to take an exam at the end of the training sessions, then you might be required to submit the results to their employer—especially if the employer paid for the training session. If the exam was part of a certification process, then you must also submit the results to the organization that handles the certifications.

At this time, you should also submit any negative feedback regarding problem students to their employer and to yours. You want to defend against any negative comments that students might make about you and/or your training company.

Performance of the Instructor

In Chapter 13, "Evaluating Delivery of Instruction," we covered in detail the process of evaluating yourself. This evaluation should always include the results of the students' evaluation of you and the course. You should use this information to assist you with identifying your strengths and weaknesses and to help you grow as a trainer. The information is also useful for documenting your training successes. These evaluations can assist you with advancing your career and defending yourself if your abilities are ever in question. One thing to remember when reviewing evaluations is that you should never take the comments personally. Every trainer receives negative evaluations; you just need to make sure that you learn from them.

Satisfaction of Students

The evaluation that the students fill out should have questions regarding their satisfaction with the various facets of the course. The three general categories that you should address are the overall course, the instructor, and the learning environment. You need to make note of any negative comments and determine whether they identify a problem that is correctable.

Satisfaction of the Instructor

Throughout the course, you should be taking notes on a number of items that can affect the success of the course. The following list summarizes the most important ones:

- The course structure
- The physical environment
- The students

If you found anything lacking in any of these areas, make sure you note it. From your evaluations of the course, determine whether you should change anything.

Revision Suggestions

Remember to summarize any issues that you discovered regarding the course materials so that you can make suggestions to the author/publisher. Make note of any material that was incorrect or confusing to the students. Also, be sure to comment on typographical errors, book layout, and design. An example might be the use of poorly designed illustrations. A fellow trainer recently wrote to the publisher of the training manual because all of the screen captures had the mouse pointer placed in a location that obstructed the view of the important information. The publisher was glad to hear the comment and fixed the problem in the next edition. You do not have to accept the mistakes that you discover in the material you are given. The publishers want to hear your comments so that they can improve the material.

Demographics of Students

The backgrounds of the students in the course will be useful when evaluating the success of the course and in determining marketing strategies for future courses. This data should include basic information such as students' names, companies, and addresses, any prior experience with the material, and courses of interest in the future. The purpose of collecting this information is to help you determine the background of the class, which might indicate why certain issues arose during the class, and to make sure you have all of the necessary information that you might need to submit to the various groups.

Submitting the Reports

For each course, you need to determine who should receive the evaluation information. This situation will depend on the nature of the course, who you work for, and who the students are. In general, the groups that might be interested in the course are as follows:

- Students
- Employers of students (if they paid for the course)
- Vendor/creator of course material
- Certification organization
- Training center management
- Training center sales department

Each of these groups has an interest in the result of the course and might require some (or all) of these various reports.

Students

If you have promised to send the students any information after the class, make sure that you send it. Forgetting these details once the class has ended is easy, because many times you will have a new course to immediately start working on. Do not forget to address any commitments that you made to the students. Following through will show the students that you do care about their success and will encourage them to attend future training sessions.

Employers of the Students

The employer will want to know whether the employees attended the entire course and how well they did. Employee training is an expensive endeavor, and the company will want to know that it is getting its money's worth. When creating this report, make sure that you find out ahead of time exactly what information the company wants to know. If your course included a final exam, then it is easy to evaluate the students' performance (possibly leading toward certification). If you do not have a qualitative method for determining their comprehension, be careful of sending qualitative evaluations. They are more difficult to defend if the students disagree.

NOTE: *If you know ahead of time that the employer requires an evaluation of each student's skills, then create a pretest and posttest so that you can report this information accurately.*

Always determine before the class what information is required and acquire any special forms that you should use to submit this information.

Vendor/Creator of the Course Material

As previously mentioned, the vendor/creator of the course material wants to know and should be told about any problems with the course materials. Elicit the students' help with this task. I have attended several training sessions where the instructor told the students at the beginning of the course that anyone who discovers an error in the text will win a door prize. This activity makes a game of it and increases the chances that problems will be detected and reported. The vendor also needs to know about any suggestions you have regarding the flow of the material and the relevance of the examples and exercises.

Certification Organization

If the course leads toward certification, then the certifying organization might need information regarding the students. Determine ahead of time any necessary forms that you will need for submitting the names and any parameters that you must follow when submitting them.

Another issue that the certification organization might be interested in is the quality of the course material that you used. Whereas some certification courses require you to use course materials created by a single vendor, others certify materials from multiple vendors. For example, there are several vendors producing manuals that have Microsoft's seal of approval as training guides for the Microsoft Office User Specialist exams. If you determine that the course materials you are using are inadequate, you should notify the certification organization so that it can address the issue.

Training Center Management

The company or educational institution that offers the training session might need all of the information discussed here. Determine this situation ahead of time and have all of the proper forms with you. I once taught a session (as a consultant) for a local company, and two days after the course, I discovered registration sheets and evaluation forms in my mailbox. When I reported to them that the information had arrived late and I did not collect all of the necessary information, they had a difficult time obtaining it. The organization that had contracted the session did not want to provide each student's Social Security number without the students' knowledge, and few of the evaluations that were sent out were ever returned. In this case, I made the mistake of assuming that all of the proper forms would be ready at the training location, and the company assumed that I already had the paperwork. This experience taught me that I should always call before the session to double check any administrative details.

The management of the training center also needs to know about any concerns with the physical environment so that it can address these concerns for future training sessions. Let them know about issues such as inadequate equipment, poor acoustics, or limited parking. Even if you believe that the problem cannot be solved, report the problem so that it is on record.

Training Center Sales Department

The sales department will want to know the demographic information of each student. This information will help it follow-up with the students and inform them of future training options. If the students are in the process of becoming certified, then the sales department will be able to create a training program specific to their needs. Ask the sales department what information it will find useful.

The following checklist will assist you in remembering what to evaluate and who should receive an evaluation:

Evaluation Information Checklist

Report on the following items:

- Students
  - Attendance
  - Skill level
  - Progress
  - Interest in certification
  - Satisfaction with the course
- Instructor (based on student evaluations)
  - Knowledge of material
  - Training abilities
  - Course management
  - Course structure
  - Satisfaction with the course
- Course material
  - Accuracy
  - Ease of use

- ▪ Relevance of examples
- ▪ Graphic design and layout
- ■ Learning environment
  - ▪ Physical environment
  - ▪ Logistical issues
- ■ Send reports to the following groups (as necessary):
  - ▪ Students
  - ▪ Employers of students (if they paid for the course)
  - ▪ Vendor/creator of course material
  - ▪ Certification organization
  - ▪ Training center management
  - ▪ Training center department

Evaluating and Justifying Reports

Every report that you create needs to have supporting data to which you can refer if required. Therefore, you *must* document pertinent information as it arises throughout the course. Many groups might use the reports that you generate for a course, and you need to make sure that you can verify and back up the information that you are sending.

SUMMARY

The success of future courses depends on your use of course evaluations. The problem with course evaluations is that they are often not followed up on. The instructors are so busy teaching courses that they do not take the time to properly use the information that is found in the evaluations. One way to prevent this situation from happening is to get into the habit of taking care of the administrative details immediately after the class ends. Include time in every course for the follow-up procedures.

Student evaluations of the overall course will be of interest to you and to a number of other groups. After each course, you should evaluate how successful it was and determine whether you can do anything to improve the course. The developers of the course also need to know about any problems.

If you found inaccurate information or poorly organized sections, you should report them. Ask the students if they found the course material easy to follow. Consider every facet of the course, and ask yourself how you can improve it. Summarize this information and submit it to the author of the training material.

At the end of the course, you should have evaluations for several different areas: the overall course, student progress, and the instructor. You need to determine what reporting procedures you are required to follow based on the organization for which you are teaching, the students' employers, and (where applicable) the organization that is offering the certification. Each group has a vested interest in the success of the course, and your job is to let them know why the course was or was not successful.

QUESTIONS

There might be multiple correct answers for some questions. The answers are located at the end of the chapter.

1. Who might need to receive reports at the end of the course?

   a. Students
   b. Course developers
   c. Training center management
   d. Certification boards
   e. All of the above

2. What must be included in student performance evaluations?

   a. Gender
   b. Attendance
   c. Performance evaluation
   d. Attitude
   e. All of the above

3. What details should you address in a report to the vendor/instructional designer?

   a. Student evaluation of the course material
   b. Names of students
   c. Number of students
   d. Suggested revisions

4. What details should you address in a report to the certification organization?

     a. Student name

     b. Attendance

     c. Exam score(s)

     d. Proctor's name

     e. All of the above

5. What details should you address in a report to the training center sales department?

     a. Suggested course revisions

     b. Number of students

     c. Student demographics

     d. Student evaluation of physical environment

     e. All of the above

6. What details should you address in a report to the training center management department?

     a. Student evaluations

     b. Suggested courseware revisions

     c. Instructor evaluations

     d. Evaluation of the training facilities

     e. None of the above

7. What can you do to simplify the reporting process?

     a. Ask students to send evaluations directly to the various areas.

     b. Do the reports immediately.

     c. Keep good documentation.

     d. All of the above

     e. None of the above

8. What should you address in the report concerning the instructor (based on student evaluations)?

     a. Appearance

     b. Knowledge of the material

     c. Presentation skills

     d. Course-management skills

     e. All of the above

9. When should you complete the reports?

    a. Never

    b. Before the day of the training session

    c. The morning of the training session

    d. Immediately after the training session

10. What is the purpose of generating the reports?

    a. To create another administrative task for the trainer

    b. To document any issues regarding the course

    c. To look over the trainer's shoulder

    d. To assist the sales force with registering students for future courses

    e. To accommodate all groups that have a role in the training process

ANSWERS

1. e

2. b and c

3. a and d

4. e

5. b and c

6. a, c, and d

7. b and c

8. e

9. d

10. b, d, and e

15

Next Steps: The Certified Technical Trainer (CTT) and Other Certifications

Next Steps

Practice! Practice ! Practice!

Each chapter of this book focused on one of the 14 competencies of the ibstpi Standards. By this time, you should realize that each of these competencies overlaps with the others, and you must master them all in order to become an effective trainer. The following list summarizes the 14 competencies that we have discussed:

14 Instructor Competencies of the ibstpi Standards

1. Analyzing course materials and learner information
2. Assuring preparation of the instructional site
3. Establishing and maintaining instructor credibility
4. Managing the learning environment
5. Demonstrating effective communication skills
6. Demonstrating effective presentation skills
7. Demonstrating effective questioning skills and techniques
8. Responding appropriately to learners' needs for clarification or feedback
9. Providing positive reinforcement and motivational incentives
10. Using instructional methods appropriately
11. Using media effectively
12. Evaluating learner performance
13. Evaluating delivery of instruction
14. Reporting evaluation information

If you have studied each of the chapters and understand the concepts, then it is now time to practice what you have learned. Each training session that you teach will offer you the opportunity to improve your skills as a trainer. Use the checklists found in many of the chapters to make sure that you are checking all of the necessary items prior to the course, preparing for all foreseeable issues, and creating the most effective instructional environment possible.

Once you have mastered the skills in this book, you should strongly consider (if you have not already), obtaining the CTT certification, which will legitimize your skills in the eyes of your clients.

Certified Technical Trainer (CTT)

The 14 ibstpi competencies that we have discussed throughout the book are the core of the CTT certification. The CTT Candidate Handbook of Information describes the certification as follows:

The Chauncey Group International® (The Chauncey Group®), a subsidiary of *Educational Testing Service®* (ETS®), developed the *Certified Technical Trainer* (CTT) Program to help define and establish professional standards throughout the training industry. The CTT certificate is a cross-industry credential providing recognition that a technical instructor has attained a standard of excellence in the training industry.

The CTT examinations are based on the competencies for instructors defined by the *International Board of Standards for Training, Performance and Instruction* (ibstpi) in the widely recognized Instructor Competencies: The Standards, Volume I (The Standards)—referred to in this candidate handbook as the ibstpi Standards. The CTT program is designed to measure the mastery of core instructor competencies—those decisions, actions, and behaviors that competent instructors must demonstrate to complete an instructional assignment successfully. (See Instructor Competencies: The Standards, Volume I, page 2.)

A committee of training experts determined the scope and content of the CTT examinations. The examination questions for the computerized knowledge test are designed to assess the level of knowledge acquired by trainers through their professional experience and their knowledge of the ibstpi Standards. Specifications for the performance videotape, also developed by the test committee, provide the framework for evaluating a trainer's ability to apply the instructional skills described in the ibstpi Standards.

This cross-industry certification is available to all training professionals. The CTT Program was initially created through the collaborative efforts of the *Computer Education Management Association* (CEdMA) and the *Information Technology Training Association, Inc.* (ITTA) to eliminate redundancies among various instructor certification programs in computer training and education. While it is significant that the computer industry is the first to endorse the CTT Program, the wider impact is that the certification can be applied to all industries that provide technical training and education. To earn the CTT designation—for topics such as software, technical, scientific, mechanical, and professional development—the candidate must pass both a computer-based test that assesses knowledge of the ibstpi Standards and a performance assessment in which the candidate demonstrates the skills described in the ibstpi Standards.[1]

The CTT certification is a cross-industry credential that signifies that the trainer has mastered the 14 instructor competencies addressed in this book. This certification is not vendor specific. Candidates who successfully complete the examination process will be recognized as competent technical trainers.

Vendor Certifications

Other vendor-specific trainer certifications require you to master the same skill set as CTT. Some of these certifications even enable you to use the CTT certification to fulfill their training requirements. For example, Novell offers this option for its *Certified Novell Instructor* (CNI) certification.

Presentation Skills Requirement

Once a *Certified Novell Instructor* (CNI) candidate's application has been accepted, the next step is to have an evaluation completed of their technical and presentation skills. Novell offers two options for this requirement.

CTT Certification

One option is to obtain the software industry endorsed *Certified Technical Trainer* (CTT) certification. This certification created by the Chauncey Group using input from major certification vendors including Novell, Adobe, Autodesk, Netscape, Microsoft, and Oracle meets the presentation skills requirement for the instructor certification programs offered by each of these vendors . . .

---

[1]Original source: *The CTT Candidate Handbook of Information*, The Chauncey Group International, `http://www.chauncey.com/`, May 2000.

Instructor Performance Evaluation

The second option is to attend and pass an *Instructor Performance Evaluation* (IPE) at a one of Novell's corporate training locations around the world. The IPE lasts for two days. The first day consists of an orientation of Novell's instructor programs and policies. After lunch on the first day, the candidate is assigned a topic from one of Novell's courses to present to the evaluator on the second day. Candidates are able to choose from a limited number of courses but will not know which topic they will present until it is assigned to them on the first day. They will spend the remaining part of the first day installing a NetWare server, workstation client and preparing their presentation. On the second day, each of the candidates will give a one-hour presentation to the instructor and other candidates. The presentation is videotaped for the evaluator's reference.

You may register for an IPE after you have been accepted into the CNI program.

To register for an IPE in the U.S., call 1-800-233-3382, option 4, or 1-801-861-3382, option 4. Candidates outside of the U.S. may register through their Novell instructor program contact.

Novell recommends that candidates download and become familiar with the document entitled Teaching Effectively for Novell and read the following Web page—Instructor Performance Evaluation `http://education.novell.com/certinfo/ipe.htm`. These will help you to prepare for your IPE. These documents are available to download from the Web at `http://education.novell.com/cni/`.[2]

Microsoft also accepts the CTT certification as an option for proving your training skills, as described in the following quote:

If you are an experienced technical trainer:

Option 1: Prove that you are an experienced technical trainer by including with your MCT application your instructor completion certificate from any of the following vendors:

- Novell
- Lotus
- Santa Cruz Operation
- Banyan Vines

---

[2]Original source: *Novell Certified Instructor's Program Guide*, Novell, `http://education.novell.com/cni/`, March 2000.

- Cisco Systems
- Sun Microsystems

Option 2: Become a *Certified Technical Trainer* (CTT). The CTT program was designed to certify technical presentation skills of technical trainers. Include with your MCT application your CTT completion certificate. For more information on the Certified Technical Trainer Program, contact the Chauncey Group International.[3]

In order to become an Adobe Certified Training Provider, the instructors must also prove their competency as trainers.

In addition to certification, instructors must also satisfy a one-time verification of instructor skills by submitting one of the following:

- Certified Technical Trainer Certificate of Mastery
- Valid teaching credential
- Valid *Microsoft Certified Trainer* (MCT), *Certified Lotus Instructor* (CLI), or *Certified Novell Instructor* (CNI) credential[4]

Novell, Microsoft and Adobe are examples of the process that most IT vendors have established for IT certifications that you must obtain in order to be an authorized trainer for their product. These certifications require specific knowledge of their product and evidence of your skill as a trainer. If your career plans include technical training in business and industry, then the certification is an extremely beneficial goal toward which you should work. You might choose to obtain a specific vendor certification or elect the CTT certification, which is the cross-industry standard. Your choice will depend on your long-term career goals.

CTT Certification Process

The process for CTT certification includes two parts. The first part is a computer-based test:

---

[3]Original source: *Microsoft Certified Trainer 2000 Guide*, Microsoft, http://www.microsoft.com/mct/, May 2000.

[4]Original source: *Adobe Solutions Network: Certified Training Provider Program*, Adobe, http://partners.adobe.com/asn/training/main.html, June 2000.

The computer-based CTT knowledge examination consists of 105 multiple-choice questions based on the 14 ibstpi competencies. Candidates have one hour and 45 minutes to complete the examination and answer several biographical questions. An additional 15 minutes is allowed for a short pre-test tutorial and an exit evaluation.[5]

The second part of the process is a performance assessment video:

The CTT performance assessment is based on a 20-minute videotape submitted by candidates of an actual instructional performance. The videotape is reviewed by professionals trained to evaluate the instructor's performance according to the ibstpi Standards. In addition to the videotape, the candidate must also complete a written Videotape Documentation Form to provide additional information about the instructional performance.[6]

The complete process for becoming certified is outlined in the CTT Candidate Handbook of Information, which is included in the appendix of this book and on the Chauncey Group International Web site at http://www.chauncey.com/. If you are interested in obtaining this certification, read the entire bulletin that contains a detailed description of the process, all necessary forms, and advice for working through the process.

The CTT certification will set you apart from other trainers and will verify your training abilities.

SUMMARY

The role of a trainer is an exciting one, but it can also be extremely nerve-wracking when the unexpected happens and things do not go as planned. If you are well prepared, you will be able to face these challenges with confidence. We can divide the competencies addressed throughout this book into three areas: preparation, implementation, and follow-up. Recall the circle of

---

[5]Original source: *The CTT Candidate Handbook of Information*, The Chauncey Group International, http://www.chauncey.com/, May 2000.

[6]Original source: *The CTT Candidate Handbook of Information*, The Chauncey Group International, http://www.chauncey.com/, May 2000.

training, which included an ongoing cycle of data collection, course development, delivery, and evaluation. Each of these areas encompasses many of the competencies, and all of them are crucial to your success as a trainer. If you concentrate on developing your skills and seek to improve each course every time you teach it, you will continually grow as a trainer.

Good luck.

# APPENDIX

CANDIDATE HANDBOOK OF INFORMATION

MAY 2000 – July 2001

THE CHAUNCEY GROUP INTERNATIONAL®

A subsidiary of Educational Testing Service®

ACKNOWLEDGEMENTS

The Chauncey Group International® (Chauncey Group®) and Educational Testing Service® (ETS®) would like to acknowledge the contributions of the many members of the Computer Education Management Association (CEdMA) and the Information Technology Training Association, Inc. (ITTA) who were involved with the design and development of the Certified Technical Trainer program.

We would also like to express our gratitude to the following individuals who donated time and professional commitment to provide their colleagues in the training profession with a global mark of excellence.

Lucent Technologies, Pat Bayers, Ed.D., *Quality Director, Learning and Performance Center*
Adobe Systems Incorporated, Barrie Barrett, *Channel Manager*
Autodesk Inc., Wayne Hodgins, *Technical Director, Customer Education and Training*
Bellcore, Jane Perlmutter, *Executive Director, Bellcore TEC*
Friesen, Kaye and Associates, Michael Nolan, *President*
IBM, Patricia J. Douglas, Ph.D., *Certification and Testing Consultant, Education and Training Division*
ITTA, Inc., Doug McBride, *Executive Director*
Lockheed Martin Energy Systems, Stewart Chason, *Training, Staff Development*
Lotus Development Corporation, Cindy Bailen, *Senior Education Specialist, Consulting Services Group*
Microsoft Corporation, Dan Hurwyn, *Subject Matter Expert, MCT*
    and Anne Marie McSweeney, *Certification Program Manager*
Netscape Communications Corporation, Tina Beach, *Manager, Partner Education Programs*
Novell,Inc., Bill Lowrey, *NTI Manager, Western Region Education,*
    and David Marler, *Manager, Instructional Certification Program*
Oracle Corporation, Nancy Hall, Director, Core Technology
    and Rob Pedigo, Manager, Certification Programs
ibstpi, Peter Dean, *(University of Tennessee);* Dennis C. Fields, *(St. Cloud State University);* Rita C. Richey, *(Wayne State University)* and Diane Wagner, Consultant Management & Education

Additionally, we would like to thank the American Society for Training and Development (ASTD) for participating in the test review process.

CONTACTING THE CERTIFIED TECHNICAL TRAINER (CTT) PROGRAM
If you need to contact the CTT Program, write to:

CTT Program
The Chauncey Group International
PO Box 6541
Princeton, NJ 08541-6541

Candidates may also:

call **800-258-4914** or

fax **609-720-6550** or

reach us via our internet address, www.chauncey.com, or e-mail address, **cttp@chauncey.com.** Be sure to include in your signature line your name and address information. We will respond to your inquiries as quickly as possible.

TABLE OF CONTENTS

TABLE OF CONTENTS (continued)

SPECIAL PROGRAM ANNOUNCEMENT

Certified Technical Trainer (CTT)
& Certified Professional Development Trainer (CPDT)

The CTT Program was initially created through the collaborative efforts of the Information Technology Training Association, Inc. (ITTA) and the Computer Education Management Association (CedMA). This original Certification Task Force unanimously agreed to base this certification program on the 14 Core Competencies defined by the International Board of Standards for Training, Performance and Instruction (ibstpi). In addition to demonstrating content expertise, trainers must meet a professional standard of excellence in training based on measurement of an individual's mastery of fundamental instructor knowledge and classroom performance. While it was the computer industry that initially endorsed the need for instructor certification, it became obvious that this certification should be applied to all industries that provide training and education. Although the content delivered is important, the instructional skills that are applied to the training determine this standard of excellence.

The CPDT Program was created as a parallel program based on the same 14 Core Competencies of CTT for those trainers outside of any technical training industry. After three years of operation, The Chauncey Group International has determined that no significant differences between CPDT and CTT exist, and therefore, with minor customization of requirements for CTT and identification of the content directly on the certificate received by the candidate, the establishment of the single designation, CTT, has been completed.

The scoring process considers the ways a trainer's performance meets the goal of any of the Core Competencies within the delivery of a particular content topic. For example, trainers in highly specialized scientific or technical areas may use very short lectures to deliver particularly detailed information accompanied by a learner-completed handout (Competencies 10 and 11). Another example would show that trainers in different parts of the world, where cultural differences impact training, explain how these language differences influence the manner in which the lesson was revised (Competency 1) and how the learners' behavior may not have met expectations in the review of the session (Competency 13).

Beginning September 1, 2000, all trainer certifications will be recognized under the CTT designation, with acknowledgements of the industry for which the CTT candidate indicates as his or her specialty. CTT is successful as a standard of excellence in the training industry and, by infusing CPDT into CTT, will expand its role into the future.

INTRODUCTION

Who Benefits from the CTT?

The Chauncey Group International® (The Chauncey Group®), a subsidiary of Educational Testing Service® (ETS®), developed the Certified Technical Trainer (CTT) Program to help define and establish professional standards throughout the training industry. The CTT certificate is a cross-industry credential providing recognition that a technical instructor has attained a standard of excellence in the training industry.

The CTT examinations are based on the competencies for instructors defined by the International Board of Standards for Training, Performance and Instruction (ibstpi) in the widely recognized *Instructor Competencies: The Standards, Volume I* (*The Standards*)—referred to in this candidate handbook as the *ibstpi Standards.* The CTT program is designed to measure the mastery of core instructor competencies—those decisions, actions, and behaviors that competent instructors must demonstrate to complete an instructional assignment successfully. (See *Instructor Competencies: The Standards, Volume I*, page 2.)

A committee of training experts determined the scope and content of the CTT examinations. The examination questions for the computerized knowledge test are designed to assess the level of knowledge acquired by trainers through their professional experience and their knowledge of the *ibstpi Standards.* Specifications for the performance videotape, also developed by the test committee, provide the framework for evaluating a trainer's ability to apply the instructional skills described in the *ibstpi Standards.*

This cross-industry certification is available to all training professionals. The CTT Program was initially created through the collaborative efforts of the Computer Education Management Association (CEdMA) and the Information Technology Training Association, Inc. (ITTA) to eliminate redundancies among various instructor certification programs in computer training and education. While it is significant that the computer industry is the first to endorse the CTT Program, the wider impact is that the certification can be applied to all industries that provide technical training and education. To earn the CTT designation—for topics such as software, technical, scientific, mechanical, and professional development—the candidate must pass both a computer-based test that assesses knowledge of the *ibstpi Standards* and a performance assessment in which the candidate demonstrates the skills described in the *ibstpi Standards.*

Trainers in the software, industrial/manufacturing, insurance, telecommunications, and health care industries took part in the beta stage of the CTT Program. This diverse population has helped assure that the test content is appropriate and meaningful to a wide variety of cross-industry trainers.

A Word about The Chauncey Group International

The Chauncey Group International, a subsidiary of Educational Testing Service (ETS), is the leading provider of certification and licensing examinations for professionals, business and government. With more than 25 years of experience in designing, developing and administering occupational, licensure, certification and professional assessment, The Chauncey Group has helped customers define competencies and measure those competencies effectively and fairly. The Chauncey Group administered certification and licensure programs to almost two million candidates via paper-and-pencil, computer-based, and internet-based testing programs in 82 countries over the past year. The Chauncey Group is headquartered in Princeton, New Jersey with offices in Washington, D.C. and Paris, France.

In servicing customers, The Chauncey Group draws upon its dedicated staff, its vast experience and demonstrated expertise in measurement and research, its unique relationship with ETS, expertise in computer-based testing, and a relationship with its test delivery partner, Prometric.

EXAMINATION PREPARATION MATERIAL

What is available?

The following preparation materials can help candidates prepare for the two–part CTT examination:

- The book, *Instructor Competencies: The Standards—Volume I*

ibstpi Standards – The *ibstpi Standards* is designed for trainers and provides an authoritative listing of competencies considered to be essential for effective training delivery. To help prepare for the CTT Examination, candidates should be thoroughly familiar with the 14 competencies described in **Instructor Competencies: The Standards, Volume I,** also known as the *ibstpi Standards.*

These standards provide a strong and credible base for developing certification assessments. The mission of the ibstpi Board is to promote high standards of professional practice in the areas of training, performance, and instruction. (Priced at $17.95 per copy.)

- The videotape, *Creating a Successful Videotape for the CTT Performance Assessment*

This videotape illustrates the variety of ways technical trainers have successfully met the *ibstpi Standards* for CTT certification. The examples shown on the videotape were selected from successful submissions by trainers seeking CTT certification and include commentary by a narrator describing the competency being demonstrated. In contrast to the successful examples displayed, the videotape includes several negative sequences to illustrate the kinds of techniques that have not helped trainers earn CTT status. (Priced at $25.95 per videotape.)

- The *Videotape Scoring Guide* found on pages 27 to 32 of this handbook.

This scoring guide presents the standards and criteria used by CTT performance assessment scoring judges. Candidates should familiarize themselves with this scoring guide so they can understand how their videotaped performance will be assessed.

How to order the book and videotape

Since the examination is based on the *ibstpi Standards*, candidates are encouraged to obtain copies of and carefully study all available CTT examination preparation materials. Information about how to order the book and the videotape can be found in the back of this handbook. When placing an order, please include the completed order form. **All sales are final.**

ABOUT THE EXAMINATION: AN OVERVIEW

The Computer-Based Test

The computer-based CTT knowledge examination consists of 105 multiple-choice questions based on the 14 ibstpi competencies. Candidates have one hour and 45 minutes to complete the examination and answer several biographical questions. An additional 15 minutes is allowed for a short pre-test tutorial and an exit evaluation. See page 12 of this handbook for registration information.

The Performance Assessment

The CTT performance assessment is based on a 20-minute videotape submitted by candidates of an actual instructional performance. The videotape is reviewed by professionals trained to evaluate the instructor's performance according to the *ibstpi Standards*. In addition to the videotape, the candidate must also complete and submit the written Videotape Documentation Form (see pages 40 to 42) to provide additional information about the instructional performance.

How much does it cost to take the CTT examination?

The total cost of the CTT examination is $300.00. (The fee for taking the computer-based examination is $150.00. The fee for the performance assessment videotape is $150.00.) All fees apply for first-time test takers and retesters.

UNDERSTANDING THE COMPETENCIES ASSESSED

The tables on the next four pages provide details on the content measured by both the knowledge and the performance assessment.

Competencies Sample Performances	Assessed in the Computer-based Knowledge Test*	Assessed in the Video Performance Test**
Competency One: Analyze Course Materials and Learner Information	**_(11–13%)_**	**_(2-4 points)_**
Review materials and audience information and identify areas where adjustments may be needed.	✓	✓
Make minor adjustments to learning materials.	✓	
Judge the appropriateness and adequacy of any adjustment.	✓	
State a rationale for the judgment and the adjustment.	✓	
Make appropriate adjustments to learning materials when needed.		✓
Competency Two: Assure Preparation of the Instructional Site	**_(4–6%)_**	
Confirm logistical arrangements.	✓	
Confirm the physical arrangement of the instructional site, materials, equipment, and furniture.	✓	
Control the physical environment.	✓	
Plan ways to minimize distractions.	✓	
Assure proper disposition of equipment, materials, and furniture.	✓	
Judge how well logistical and physical arrangements support the instruction.	✓	
State a rationale for decisions regarding logistics and physical environment.	✓	
Competency Three: Establish and Maintain Instructor Credibility	**_(4–6%)_**	**_(2-4 points)_**
Judge the degree to which credibility is an issue or distraction at any time during instruction.	✓	
State a rationale for the judgment and the actions taken to establish, maintain and re-establish credibility in a particular situation or in general.	✓	
Demonstrate content expertise.		✓
Demonstrate acceptable personal conduct.		✓
Demonstrate acceptable social practices.		✓
Provide a model for professional and interpersonal behavior.		✓
Demonstrate flexibility in response to learner needs and interests.		✓

Competencies Sample Performances	Assessed in the Computer-based Knowledge Test*	Assessed in the Video Performance Test**
Environment	*(11–13%)*	*(2-4 points)*
Select initial presentation strategies.	✓	
Involve learners in establishing an appropriate level of learner comfort.	✓	✓
Adapt delivery to account for learner characteristics.	✓	✓
Manage time available for course.	✓	✓
Provide opportunities for learner success.	✓	
Manage group interactions and participation.	✓	✓
Resolve learner behavior problems.	✓	✓
Judge whether the learning environment facilitates successful performance.	✓	
State a rationale for the judgment.	✓	
Competency Five: **Demonstrate Effective Communication Skills**	*(4–6%)*	*(2-4 points)*
Use appropriate verbal and non-verbal language.	✓	✓
Adapt verbal and non-verbal messages to learners' needs.	✓	✓
Use frames of reference familiar to the learners.	✓	✓
Determine whether learners understand messages.	✓	✓
State a rationale for the judgment.	✓	
Competency Six: **Demonstrate Effective Presentation Skills**	*(4–6%)*	*(2-4 points)*
Judge the effectiveness of a presentation.	✓	
State a rationale for the judgment.	✓	
Use the voice effectively.		✓
Use eye contact effectively.		✓
Use gestures, silence, movement, posture, space, and props effectively.		✓
Organize content effectively.		✓
Use anecdotes, stories, analogies, and humor effectively.		✓
Competency Seven: **Demonstrate Effective Questioning Skills and Techniques**	*(6–8%)*	*(2-4 points)*
Judge the adequacy of instructional questions.	✓	
State a rationale for the judgment.	✓	
Use appropriate question types and levels.		✓
Direct questions appropriately.		✓
Use active listening techniques.		✓
Repeat, rephrase, or restructure questions.		✓
Provide opportunity and adequate time for learners to state questions, comments, and concerns and respond to questions.		✓
Competency Eight: **Respond Appropriately to**		

Competencies Sample Performances	*Assessed in the Computer-based Knowledge Test**	*Assessed in the Video Performance Test***
Learners' Needs for Clarification or Feedback	*(6–8%)*	*(2-4 points)*
Identify learners with clarification and feedback needs.		✓
Determine when and how to respond.	✓	✓
Judge the adequacy of feedback and responses.	✓	
State a rationale for the judgment.	✓	
Provide prompt, timely, and specific feedback.		✓
Competency Nine: Provide Positive Reinforcement and Motivational Incentives	*(4–6%)*	*(2-4 points)*
Match learning outcomes to learner and organizational needs and goals.	✓	✓
Use introductory activities appropriate to developing learner motivation.	✓	✓
Plan and deliberately use feedback and reinforcement during instruction.	✓	✓
Judge the adequacy and appropriateness of motivational strategies used during instruction and adjust as necessary.	✓	
State a rationale for the judgment.	✓	
Competency Ten: Use Instructional Methods Appropriately	*(11–13%)*	*(2-4 points)*
Implement a variety of standard instructional methods.	✓	✓
Manage the group dynamics associated with each method.	✓	✓
Employ instructional techniques appropriate to methods and instructional situations prescribed.	✓	✓
Judge the appropriateness and effectiveness of methods and techniques.	✓	
State a rationale for the judgment.	✓	
Competency Eleven: Use Media Effectively	*(4–6%)*	*(2-4 points)*
Use media and hardware properly.	✓	✓
Troubleshoot minor hardware and other simple problems.	✓	✓
Substitute for, add to, switch, or create media as required.	✓	✓
Judge the effectiveness of the use of media.	✓	
State a rationale for the judgement.	✓	

Competencies Sample Performances	Assessed in the Computer-based Knowledge Test*	Assessed in the Video Performance Test**
Administer examinations and instruments.	✓	
Evaluate attainment of end-of-course objectives.	✓	
Judge the adequacy of the evaluation.	✓	
State a rationale for the judgment.	✓	
Competency Thirteen: **Evaluate Delivery of Instruction**	*(6–8%)*	*(2-4 points)*
Evaluate the instructional design, as modified, during delivery.	✓	✓
Evaluate the instructor's performance as it relates to the instructional design.	✓	✓
Evaluate the effects of other variables, including the instructional environment, on learner accomplishments.	✓	
Judge how well a course works for a particular group of learners in a particular situation.	✓	
State a rationale for the judgment.	✓	
Competency Fourteen: **Report Evaluation Information**	*(4–6%)*	
Prepare to report post-course summary and evaluation.	✓	
Report the evaluation and end-of-course information.	✓	
Recommend revisions and changes to existing materials and provide suggestions for new programs and activities.	✓	
Report information about learning and physical environments.	✓	
Judge the adequacy, appropriateness, and timeliness of reports to instructional designers and appropriate management.	✓	
State a rationale for both the information included in evaluation and summary reports and the audiences to receive that information.	✓	

*The percentages indicated in this column represent the relative weight of each topic in the knowledge test. The total number of questions in the test is 105.

**A score of 1 in any of the competencies will result in an automatic fail. A candidate will receive a score of 1 if and only if he or she demonstrates a behavior that contradicts the competency. For example, if the trainer uses inappropriate and offensive language, Competency 3 would be scored as a 1.

THE COMPUTER-BASED TEST

Strategies for Taking the Computer-Based Test

For the CTT computer-based test, only correct answers contribute to the candidate's score. This means that there is no penalty for incorrect answers. It is to the candidate's advantage to try to answer every question. If a candidate is unsure of the correct answer to a question, he or she should try to rule out one or two of the answer choices and then guess from among the remaining choices.

The computer allows candidates to mark questions for later review. Useful advice to candidates is to go through the entire examination once, answering those questions that can be answered immediately and marking the other questions for later review. After going through the entire examination, candidates may spend the remaining time answering the questions marked earlier.

Registering for the Computer-Based Test

How does the candidate register for the computer-based test **by phone**?

1. Call the CTT Registration desk at Prometric—**(800) 727-8490**.
2. The registration staff will ask for the candidate's name, telephone number, preferred date and time of testing, and the test center requested.
3. Before candidates can be officially registered and scheduled for the examination, payment must be received in full. Candidates may arrange payment over the telephone with a MasterCard, VISA, or American Express credit card. Payment of the examination fee may also be made by personal check, voucher, or money order. Be prepared to provide the registration staff with the preferred payment information. Please be sure to ask for the examination registration number, make a note of it, and bring it on the examination day. **Note:** If candidates choose to pay by personal check, Prometric **must** receive the check before the scheduled day and time of the examination. Prometric staff will provide candidates with a registration number that must appear on the payment check. Candidates should allow five business days to pass after sending in their checks. Then they should call Prometric to confirm the arrival of the registration payment and to schedule the day and time of the computer-based examination. If the candidate's preferred date or time is unavailable, candidates will be offered an alternative as close to the first choice as possible. Candidates should be prepared with alternative dates and times when they call.
4. Candidates should make a note of when and where they have been scheduled for the **examination.** If they are scheduling **at least two to three weeks prior to the examination date, candidates will receive confirmation of the appointment through the mail.** Otherwise, no confirmation of the appointment will be sent. Candidates should be sure to ask for directions to the test center if they need them.
5. Candidates may test anytime. Testing centers are usually open Monday through Saturday. Please note that operating hours may vary by test center.
6. Call Prometric one to two days prior to the examination day to confirm the appointment.
7. Plan for the testing session to last 2 hours.

How does the candidate register for the computer-based test **online**?

1. Select your area of certification from the drop-down menu and click "Go".
2. Enter your User Name and Password (PIN). If this is your first time registering for a test with Prometric, you will need to complete the new user form.
3. Click "Submit Login" to continue scheduling for your specific exam.

THE COMPUTER-BASED TEST (continued)

Special Testing Arrangements—Americans with Disabilities Act

What if the candidate needs special help?

Candidates seeking special testing arrangements under the Americans with Disabilities Act of 1990 must call the CTT Program staff at The Chauncey Group **prior to registering** for the examination. Formal written requests and documentation are required. Documentation should be in the form of a letter on the official letterhead of a licensed or certified professional qualified to diagnose and treat special conditions. A description of the special accommodation(s) requested should be included. Candidates' requests, along with the documentation, will be reviewed to determine if the accommodation is warranted. **The Chauncey Group staff will assist in the registration process.** There is no extra charge to the candidate for making these special arrangements.

Changing or Cancelling Computer–Based Test Appointments

What if the candidate needs to reschedule or cancel an appointment**?**

If candidates need to reschedule or cancel the appointment, candidates must do so by noon two business days before the appointment. Call the Prometric toll-free number **(800) 727-8490. If candidates fail to arrive for the appointment without giving at least two business days notice, candidates will forfeit ALL examination fees.**

Candidates who need to reschedule an examination appointment because of a medical emergency may mail a written request and official documentation such as a doctor's letter to the CTT Program at The Chauncey Group International. Requests must be made within the two-week period following the scheduled examination date.

Receipts

If a computer-based test administration is cancelled due to weather conditions, the test centers will announce, whenever possible, the cancellation on local radio stations. If cancellation is necessary, candidates will be rescheduled without penalty for another appointment. **No cash refunds will be granted.**

Computer-delivered Test
To obtain a receipt for the computer-based test portion of the CTT exam, candidates should contact Prometric's Client Inquiry Department at **1-800-806-EXAM**. To obtain a duplicate copy of your official CTT computer-based exam score report or an additional copy of your CTT certificate, candidates should contact The Chauncey Group customer service line at **800-258-4914**. There will be a $15 fee for duplicate score reports and a $20 fee for duplicate certificates.

THE COMPUTER-BASED TEST continued

The Performance Assessment
To obtain a receipt for the video portion of the CTT exam, candidates should indicate their request by marking the receipt needed box on the Video Performance Submission Form – Form A, located on page 37 of this handbook. Form A is the first of three forms that must be sent to The Chauncey Group along with the videotape, embossed photo and $150.00 payment. Candidates should indicate if they want the receipt faxed to them or sent in the mail. The Chauncey Group will generate a receipt on company letterhead indicating the amount paid.

Retest Policy

What does the candidate do if he or she fails the examination and wants to take it again?

Candidates must wait 30 days before a first retest and must wait at least 180 days for all subsequent retests. This means that during the first year of testing, candidates are permitted to retest twice or to receive a maximum of three test sessions. The Chauncey Group encourages candidates who do not pass the computer-based examination to use this time to review all material but focusing on the content areas in which they received low diagnostic ratings.

When calling to register for a retest, the test personnel (Prometric staff) should ask candidates if they are taking the examination for the first time or if they are retesting. If it is a retest, the candidate will need to provide the date(s) of the previous testing session(s) and the location of the testing center(s).

Candidates who do not abide by these retesting regulations or fail to disclose previous testing information to the test center personnel properly will have their new scores cancelled and will forfeit their computer-based exam fee.

On the Day of the Computer-Based Test

IMPORTANT! Please read carefully.

1. Candidates should plan to arrive at the test center at least 30 minutes before the scheduled examination time. If arrival is 30 minutes after the scheduled appointment, candidates may be required to forfeit the appointment. If the appointment is forfeited, candidates will be required to register and pay the fee again. **Candidates will forfeit the original fee.**

2. Friends or relatives who accompany candidates to the test center will not be permitted to wait in the test center or contact candidates during the examination.

3. Candidates must present a photo identification that includes the candidate's signature, along with a second form of signature identification. Test center personnel have the discretion of not admitting individuals who present insufficient documentation.

4. Candidates will be asked to sign in at the center. Signatures will be compared to those on the identification documents. Candidates will be asked to sign their name every time they enter or leave the examination area.

THE COMPUTER-BASED TEST continued

5. Candidates will be required to leave personal belongings outside the examination room. Secured storage will be provided. However, the two forms of identification presented at sign-in should be with candidates at all times. If candidates leave the examination room for any reason, candidates will be required to show the test administrator their identification to be readmitted to the room. Storage spaces are small, so plan accordingly. Do not take large bags, textbooks, notebooks, etc. to the test center. Test centers assume no responsibility for candidates' personal belongings.

6. The test administrator will give candidates a brief orientation and will then escort candidates to a computer terminal. Candidates must remain in their testing seat during the examination, except when authorized by a test center staff member to leave.

7. Candidates must raise their hands to notify the test center administrator if help is needed, for example, if they have a problem with the computer or need to take a break.

8. Candidates will have up to one hour and 45 minutes to complete the CTT examination and biographical questions. Additional time—a total of 15 minutes—will be provided for a short tutorial at the beginning of the examination and completion of an exit evaluation questionnaire. **There will be no scheduled breaks**.

9. The clock will continue to run and not be turned off for unplanned, unscheduled breaks. If a power outage occurs, the examination will resume at the point where the interruption occurred once the power is restored.

10. After finishing the examination, candidates will be asked to complete a brief computer-delivered questionnaire about the testing experience.

11. After candidates have completed the questionnaire, the test administrator will dismiss candidates.

Note: On rare occasions, technical problems may require rescheduling of a candidate's examination. In these situations, no additional fee will be required for rescheduling.

Identification Requirements

When candidates register for the examination appointment and whenever candidates contact The Chauncey Group for assistance, they should be sure to use the same form of their name. Candidates must not change the spelling or the order of their names.

Candidates will be required to present two forms of signature identification upon arrival at the test center. Candidates will not be admitted to the examination without the proper identification. Both pieces of identification must be signed, and one must have a recent photograph of the candidate. Examples of acceptable forms of primary identification (which must include a signature and photograph) are:
- a current driver's license
- an employee identification (ID) card
- a state identification (ID) card
- a current (valid) passport

THE COMPUTER-BASED TEST continued

Secondary forms of identification must include a signature. Examples of acceptable forms of secondary identification include:

- valid credit cards
- bank automated-teller machine cards
- check-cashing cards
- a citizenship card

Authenticity Measures

Security of the test and the testing environment is important for maintaining the validity of the CTT Examination Program.

- To maintain high credibility of the certification program and to protect the integrity of successful candidate examination scores, all candidates must bring a color photo with them to the testing center to be reviewed and embossed by Prometric test center staff. The photo should be full-color, at least passport size, and clear enough to perform an identification match with the videotape. This photo must accompany the videotaped submission as an authenticity measure. (See page 36.)

- Candidates will be observed at all times while taking the examination. This observation will include direct observation by test center staff as well as videotape and audio monitoring of the examination session.

Test Center Regulations

To ensure that all candidates' results are earned under comparable conditions and represent fair and accurate measurement, it is necessary to maintain a standardized testing environment. The following regulations are strictly enforced:

Grounds for Dismissal

The examination scores of a candidate who engages in misconduct will be cancelled. A candidate who does not heed an administrator's warning to discontinue inappropriate behavior may be dismissed from the test center. The Chauncey Group, in its sole discretion, may choose to cancel the examination scores of candidates if there is substantial evidence that misconduct has occurred. The following behaviors are considered to be misconduct.

- Giving or receiving assistance of any kind
- Using any unauthorized aids
- Attempting to take the examination for someone else, or having the examination taken for you
- Failing to follow examination regulations or the instructions of the test administrator
- Creating a disturbance of any kind
- Removing or attempting to remove examination questions and/or responses (in any format) or notes about the examination from the examination room
- Tampering with the operation of the computer or attempting to use it for any function other than taking the examination

Prometric Regional Service Centers

The registration process varies by region. To register for the CTT Examination, candidates will need to contact the Prometric Regional Service Center. This listing provides the Regional Service Center numbers where the examination is available. The Regional Service Center will assist candidates by either registering candidates or providing candidates with information about where to register.

USA
Prometric Minneapolis, MN
Regional Service Center
Registration Telephone Number: 1-800-727-8490
Canada, Puerto Rico, United States

FRANCE
Prometric Paris
Regional Service Center
Registration Telephone Number: 33-1-4289-3122
France & DOM-TOM (French Islands, Martinique, Guadeloupe), Ivory Coast, Morocco, Portugal, Spain

AUSTRALIA
Prometric Sydney
Regional Service Center
Australia (1-800-806-944), China (10800-3538), Fiji, Guam (001-61-800-277583), Hong Kong (800-8444), India, Indonesia (001-800-61606), Malaysia (800–0508), New Zealand (0800-44-1689), Pakistan, Philippines (102-718-0061-02161), Singapore (800-616-1132)

GERMANY
Prometric Dusseldorf
Regional Service Center
Registration Telephone Number: 49-2159-9233-50
Austria (0660-8582), Belgium (0800-1-7414), Croatia, Czech Republic, Germany (0130-83-97-08), Hungary, Italy (1-6787-8441), Latvia, Luxembourg, Netherlands (06-022-7584), Poland, Romania, Russia, Slovakia, Slovenia, Switzerland (155-6966), Ukraine

ENGLAND
Prometric, London
Regional Service Center
Registration Telephone Number: 44–181–607–9090
Bahrain, Botswana, Denmark, Egypt, Finland, Greece, Ireland (1-800-626-104), Israel, Kenya, Kuwait, Norway, Oman, Saudi Arabia, South Africa, Sweden, Turkey, United Arab Emirates, United Kingdom (08-00-592-873), Zimbabwe

JAPAN
Prometric Tokyo
Regional Service Center
Registration Telephone Number: 813-3269-9620
Japan 0120-387737

- Name
- Prometric Identification Number—a Prometric ID Number will be assigned if the candidate has not tested with Prometric previously
- Telephone Number (Home and Work)
- Mailing Address
- Billing Address (if needed)

- Exam Number: 9S0-001
- Exam Name: Certified Technical Trainer Examination
- Method of Payment
  -cash or personal checks (certain locations only)
  -credit cards (American Express, Visa or MasterCard)

Candidates must pay for the examination prior to testing. Scheduling may be arranged up to six weeks in advance. (In certain countries in Asia, payment is made at the test site on the day of testing.)

PRACTICE QUESTIONS

Practice Questions for the CTT Knowledge Test

The following four questions are similar in format and content to the questions of the CTT knowledge test. These questions are intended for practice, that is, to allow you to become familiar with the way the questions are asked. Read each question; select an answer and then check your response with the explanations beginning on page 46.

Question 1
During a group discussion, a learner asks how the content being discussed would apply to a situation in the learner's workplace. Which of the following is the best solution for the instructor to handle the situation?

a) Tell the learner how the content applies to a more generic situation.
b) Ask the learner how the content might apply in the workplace.
c) Ask the class members to discuss how the content applies in their situation.
d) Gather more information on the situation and then provide a response.

Question 2
For this question, decide whether the action makes it likely or unlikely that the trainer will achieve the goal. Select the best statement of the reason that the action is likely or unlikely to accomplish the goal.

GOAL: To reinforce the key points of a large group discussion that just took place.
ACTION: Ask one or more of the learners to summarize the discussion.

a) LIKELY, because the learners are actively involved in the summary.
b) LIKELY, because the instructor will not add bias to the summary.
c) UNLIKELY, because the learners may emphasize minor points in their summary.
d) UNLIKELY, because the instructor loses control of the key points to be included.

Question 3
An instructor would use which of the following forms of eye contact to put a learner at ease?

a) Establishing direct eye contact with each learner as often as possible
b) Maintaining eye contact with learners who seem most engaged in the presentation
c) Limiting eye contact to avoid intimidating the learners
d) Glancing around the group frequently to make sure everyone is engaged

Question 4
An instructor wants to capture ideas during a large group discussion for later reference in a training session, but acknowledges that handwriting on a chart is a problem. The best approach to this problem is to

a) divide the large group into smaller groups and have each group chart their ideas and report back
b) ask for a volunteer with good flip chart skills to write the group's ideas on a flip chart during the discussion
c) write the group's ideas on a transparency and project them on the available overhead projector
d) provide the learners with a simple form to jot down the group's ideas during the discussion

THE PERFORMANCE ASSESSMENT

As of February 2, 1997, all CTT candidates must successfully complete the computer-based test prior to submitting a performance videotape for scoring. Once notified of a passing score, candidates have up to **three** months to submit the performance assessment videotape component of their examination. For example, if a candidate passes the computer-based examination on May 2, 2000, The Chauncey Group must receive the performance videotape by August 2, 2000, or the computer-based score will be invalidated. If candidates need a time extension to submit the videotape, they should e-mail their requests to cttp@chauncey.com or fax a written request to CTT Program, The Chauncey Group, 664 Rosedale Road, Princeton, NJ 08540, fax (609-720-6550). State the reason(s) for the request as specifically as possible. All reasonable requests will be granted (for example, scheduling of the training session to be used for the videotape submission).

Certification candidates who pass the computer-based test but are unsuccessful in passing the performance assessment videotape requirement <u>will have an additional three months</u> to submit a second videotape and still maintain their successful computer-based score.

Preparing the Performance Assessment Videotape Submission

The CTT Program allows considerable flexibility as to the kind of training that is videotaped, the way in which it is presented, and the kinds of media or instructional strategies used, so long as the session lets candidates fully demonstrate the required 12 ibstpi competencies. Candidates should become thoroughly familiar with the *ibstpi Instructor Competencies: The Standards, Volume 1* as well as the CTT Videotape Scoring Guide to help plan the instructional module. (See pages 27 to 32 of this handbook.)

Because this is an unedited showcase performance, candidates will need to plan the videotape carefully. Filming any 20-minute slice of instruction *will not* necessarily provide evidence of candidates' ability to perform the required skills.

Outlining the presentation and rehearsing it several times before videotaping will help in creating a successful videotape. Another possibility is to videotape several presentations and choose the best, critiquing the performance on the basis of the CTT Videotape Scoring Guide.

As candidates critique their performance, they should use the CTT Videotape Scoring Guide to consider how well the videotape reflects upon their ability to perform the following required skills.

THE PERFORMANCE ASSESSMENT (continued)

1. Performing all of the required skills for each competency

Many of the presentation skills described in *The Standards* are interrelated. Even though candidates will be assessed on each competency, the same behavior could provide evidence for a number of competencies. For example, when candidates "Demonstrate Effective Questioning Skills and Techniques," candidates may also be showing that candidates "Respond Appropriately to Learners' Needs for Clarification." For a successful videotape, it is important that candidates plan a seamless, integrated module rather than one that abruptly switches from one competency to another.

*Remember: Just a statement in the Videotape Documentation Form testifying that candidates involved the learners in group activities in a training segment not shown on videotape cannot substitute for showing the actual interaction.

2. Engaging (not merely talking at) the learners - - student-centered learning

The Standards emphasize interactive, student-centered learning. The scoring judges are therefore looking not only at how well candidates understand the material but, more importantly, how well candidates help the learners understand the material. If candidates instruct primarily by lecture or demonstration, it is critical to incorporate strategies designed to engage the learners and, at the same time, let candidates know how well they are learning the material.

3. Keeping the learners focused on the subject

The most successful videotapes include a brief introduction that tells the learners and the performance scoring judges what will be covered in the next 20 minutes. To satisfy the requirements for organization and motivation, candidates will need to provide a kind of road map that keeps the instruction—and the learning—on track. The road map can be visual or verbal, obvious or subtle.

Do not feel that you need to rush through a module to reach closure. It may be sufficient to summarize what the learners have covered to that point or better yet ask the learners to recapitulate what they have learned.

4. Providing real training

One question likely to arise concerns authenticity: "Should trainers plant certain kinds of behavior or questions within the class so that you can provide evidence of how they respond?" The answer is a definitive no. Be assured that the evaluators are looking for the big picture with each competency. For example, if the class provides no evidence of behavior problems that the trainer has to resolve, then, of course, the trainer will not be expected to give evidence for that skill within Competency 4: Manage The Learning Environment. **However, if a videotape shows no interaction between the instructor and the class, then the trainer cannot meet the requirements for Competency 7: Demonstrate Effective Questioning Skills and Techniques.**

THE PERFORMANCE ASSESSMENT (continued)

Planning the Videotaped Performance

The CTT videotaped performance assessment provides candidates with the opportunity to showcase their skills in technical training according to 12 of the 14 ibstpi competencies. (See the tables starting on page 8 of this bulletin.)

Plan the videotaped performance session carefully. Be sure to consider the following to prepare for a successful submission.

Content
Because the CTT certification is recognized in many industries, it is important for the program to establish and maintain consistent and credible standards. The instructional content of the videotape should be clearly professional in nature and be of sufficient complexity to provide the depth and scope for scoring judges to assess the performance adequately in each of the competencies.

- Content that is too simplistic or self-evident will not allow candidates to adequately and realistically demonstrate proficiency in several of the competencies, such as Competency 8: Respond Appropriately to Learners' Needs for Clarification or Feedback.

- Content that is not rooted in actual business and professional topics (for example, how to care for houseplants) will not provide the appropriate evidence of Competency 3: Establish and Maintain Instructor Credibility.

Structure
The performance-based examination must show candidates demonstrating all 12 assessed ibstpi competencies (see *Instructor Competencies: The Standards—Volume I* and *The Videotape Scoring Guide*). The instructional module should be complete, with a clear beginning, middle, and end. The module, of course, may be a portion within a longer class, but it should have its own instructional objective(s). If it is part of a larger class, be sure to provide information about how this segment fits into the larger class. **Only one trainer should provide instruction per videotape**.

Setting
For the training event, choose a quiet, well-lit site that allows a videotape camera to record voices clearly and to show media or other instructional materials that candidates use, and that captures candidates' movements, and class interactions.

Class size
A minimum of **five** adult learners **must** appear on the videotape. The camera should occasionally pan the room so the scoring judges can confirm the learners' presence and interactions.

Authenticity
The learning situation, to the extent possible, should be authentic. The participants actually should be learning new knowledge and skills. Highly artificial or contrived situations could reduce the instructor's credibility as required for Competency 3: Establish and Maintain Instructor Credibility.

THE PERFORMANCE ASSESSMENT (continued)

Duration
The entire videotape should not exceed 20 minutes. After 22 minutes, the scoring judges will not continue watching. The videotape can be somewhat briefer, but fewer than 17 or 18 minutes may not allow candidates sufficient time to demonstrate the required competencies fully.

Editing
No editing of the videotape is allowed. The CTT program defines **editing** as cutting and splicing of tape. However, candidates may stop and restart the videotape <u>one time</u> during the videotape segment to allow learners sufficient time to practice a new skill. Under very specialized circumstances, a second stop may be accepted. For example, in the professional development topics where exercises require additional time, a second stop would be permitted. Be sure that enough of the activity is visible before the tape is stopped and resume filming as the practice session comes to a close to show how the transition occurs from one activity to the next. The videotaped instruction module **must** be presented in the sequence in which it was given.

Skills
The videotape and accompanying documentation need to provide clear evidence of the candidate's ability to perform skills in the 12 ibstpi competencies listed on pages 8 to 11. Evidence for Competencies 1: Analyze Course Materials and Learner Information and 13: Evaluate Delivery of Instruction, will most likely appear in the responses on the Videotape Documentation Form.

Review
Using the Videotape Scoring Guide found on pages 27 to 32 of this handbook, view and score the videotape before mailing it in for official scoring. Check to make sure that all of the competencies will be evident to the viewer (the scoring judges). Are the learners visible? Are the visual aids clear and visible? Is the picture clear? Is the sound clear?

Have a friend or colleague view and score the videotape.

Candidates should view and critique the videotape before mailing it in for official scoring.

Submitting the Video in the Appropriate Format

Listed below are some guidelines to follow when creating the videotape. Videotapes must show approximately 20 minutes of instruction. The scoring judges will not watch more than 22 minutes. All instruction must be in English.

Format
Cassette size: Only VHS tapes will be accepted. It is not possible for our scoring judges to have the equipment necessary to accommodate every alternative size.

THE PERFORMANCE ASSESSMENT (continued)

Standard
**NTSC standard (the standard used in the U.S.) is the preferred standard. Videotapes that
are** sent in other formats such as PAL will experience a delay in processing. If the submission is in
another format, please state in the Videotape Documentation Form which standard was used.

Equipment
Using the best videotaping equipment will help ensure that the videotape turns out well. The
training site or school might have videotape equipment designed for this specific purpose and
might be able to provide someone who has good working knowledge of videotaping who can assist
with the taping. However, candidates may need to use personal equipment. Many hand-held
cameras can produce the quality that is needed.

Tips for Filming a Successful Videotape

- Use a new, unused videotape for this submission.
- Use a tripod. A wobbly videotape will distract the viewer.
- Graphics, blackboard writing, etc., should be clear and legible. Writing legible to the human
  eye may not be legible to the camera's eye. Be careful of glare from chalkboards or whiteboards. Use markers on nonglossy paper taped to the board.
- Use only one camera. Positioning the camera at the side of the classroom will enable
  candidates to capture the learners as well as the candidate.
- If moving the camera during taping, set the zoom lens to its widest setting. This will reduce the
  shakiness of the picture.
- More light will improve the picture quality. Candidates may want to use a camera light to
  enhance the quality of the submission. However, do not shoot into the light source. For
  example, if the blinds are open, shoot with the windows behind the camera.
- Sound presents one of the most difficult issues for videotaping. It may be very difficult to hear
  the trainer and the learners. What is discernible to the human ear in person may not be so on
  videotape.
- Test the sensitivity of the microphone by doing a few practice tapings. Instruct class members
  to speak up. Candidates may want to attach a separate external microphone to help produce
  better-quality sound.
- Candidates may want to turn off any fans, air conditioners, or laboratory equipment.
  Candidates may need to sacrifice light from a window source if taping near the windows picks
  up outside noises, particularly from traffic. Using an external microphone (not the microphone
  on the camera) will help reduce extraneous noises that will mark the quality of the videotape.
- Make sure that the camera is running before instruction commences. A few seconds' delay in
  the beginning can cause the loss of important information.

Note: **Candidates should always keep a backup of the videotape submitted.** Although
videotapes are rarely lost or damaged, it is important that candidates have a backup to submit in
the event that loss or damage does occur. The Chauncey Group will NOT return videotaped
submissions to candidates.

THE PERFORMANCE ASSESSMENT (continued)

Preparing the Videotape Documentation Forms

As a precaution, candidates are advised to make several copies of the Videotape Documentation Form (Form C on pages 40 to 42 of this handbook) so they can freely plan and revise the answers before writing the final version to submit with the videotape. The scoring judges need the Videotape Documentation Form to assess Competencies 1: Analyze Course Materials and Learner Information and 13: Evaluate Delivery of Instruction.

Please remember to submit the Videotape Performance Submission Form (Form A) and the Videotape Release Form (Form B) also. **Videotapes will NOT be evaluated if all three forms do not accompany them.**

Submitting the Videotape and Documentation Forms

The following five items must accompany the videotape submission:

1. A VHS videotape that shows candidates instructing a group of adults.

2. The Videotape Performance Submission Form — Form A, located on page 37 of this handbook.

3. The Videotape Release Form — Form B, located on page 39 of this handbook — with signatures from everyone in the class.

4. The Videotape Documentation Form — Form C, located on pages 40 to 42 of this handbook — in which candidates answer questions about the instruction and the group candidates are instructing.

5. Color photo embossed by Prometric test center staff.

6. A check or money order for $150.00 made payable to **The Chauncey Group International**, *or* the credit card authorization form—located in the back of this handbook—completed and signed, to cover the test fee for the videotape performance assessment portion of the examination.

Candidates may submit the 20-minute performance videotape at any time. Send to:

Certified Technical Trainer Program
The Chauncey Group International
664 Rosedale Road
Princeton, NJ 08540- 2218 USA

See pages 35 and 36 for videotape checklists.

THE PERFORMANCE ASSESSMENT (continued)

How are the Videotapes and Documentation Forms Scored?

Scoring judges are used to evaluate the videotapes and the Videotape Documentation Forms. Each looks for clear evidence of each competency and awards a score based on the definitions provide on pages 27 to 32 of this handbook. They will not be counting the number of times a candidate does something. Instead, they will be judging, overall, how well the candidate performs the set of skills in each competency and how the needs of the specific lesson are met in relationship to the competencies.

Performance on each competency is assessed on a four-point scale:

> 4 Outstanding
> 3 Successful
> 2 Limited
> 1 Seriously Deficient

The specific criteria that describe how each of the four score points link directly to competency descriptions appear in the *Videotape Scoring Guide* beginning on page 27 of this handbook and in the *ibstpi Standards.*

A score of 1 (Seriously Deficient) on any of the 12 competencies being assessed on the videotape or on the Videotape Documentation Form will cause an automatic failure for the performance assessment. Depending upon the outcome from the first scoring judge, your tape may be scored by multiple scoring judges, each viewing and assessing a videotaped performance individually and independently of each other.

Who Scores the Videotapes and the Videotape Documentation Forms?

To qualify as CTT scoring judges, three requirements must be met:

1. They must be experienced instructors or professional trainers and have demonstrated their competency by having earned CTT themselves.

2. They must attend initial CTT scoring workshops to be thoroughly trained on *The ibstpi Standards,* and they must attend recalibration sessions throughout the year.

3. They must demonstrate that they can score sample CTT videotapes and Videotape Documentation Forms accurately and fairly, according to the standards set by the CTT Committee.

As a group, the CTT scoring judges are ethnically diverse, include both men and women, and have a variety of instructional backgrounds.

Statistical analysts continually monitor the scoring reliability of all the scoring judges. Any scoring judge who is not scoring reliably will receive additional training. However, because of the importance of CTT certification, if a scoring judge cannot maintain the high scoring standard required for this program, he or she will not be allowed to continue in the capacity as a CTT scoring judge.

THE PERFORMANCE ASSESSMENT (continued)

Quality Control

Evidence suggests that the most successful submissions are of the highest quality. We encourage all candidates to take quality control measures prior to mailing their videotaped performance to us. See pages 35 and 36 for suggestions and checklists.

What if the candidate fails the videotape assessment?

Certification candidates who are unsuccessful in completing the performance requirement will have an additional three months to submit a second videotaped performance and still maintain their successful computer-based score. Submission requirements for videotape performance assessment retests are the same as for first time submissions:

- Send the videotape along with the completed Videotape Performance Submission (Form A), Videotape Release Form (Form B), Videotape Documentation Form (Form C) and a check or money order for the performance examination fee of $150.00 made payable to The Chauncey Group International.

- If a candidate desires confirmation of scoring of a submitted video, the Chauncey Group will provide an independent review provided the request is submitted within 30 days of the score report. To request such a review, send your formal request in writing accompanied by a check for $65. Include in the letter the following information: name, date of submission, score report date and candidate ID.

Recertification

All Certified Technical Trainers are required to recertify every five years through a performance assessment videotape submission. Within the sixth year of certification, submit a videotaped performance for assessment (a candidate certified in the year 2000, must be recertified by 2005). This recertification submission must meet the same requirements and criteria as mandated for first-time candidates. Please indicate in writing and on the videotape that the submission is for recertification. Submission requirements for recertification are the same as for first time submissions except that the submission for recertification must be date stamped (on the video presentation):

- Send the videotape along with the completed Videotape Performance Submission Form (Form A), Videotape Release Form (Form B), Videotape Documentation Form (Form C) and a check or money order for the performance examination fee—$150.00—made payable to The Chauncey Group International.

Failure to comply with the recertification requirement will invalidate both components of the candidate's certification and candidates will need to retest in both areas for reinstatement. All fees will apply.

VIDEOTAPE SCORING GUIDE
Part A – ibstpi Competencies Assessed on Videotape

COMPETENCY — *Skills assessed on the videotape*	4 – OUTSTANDING — Performs all or most of the skills in a highly effective way	3 – SUCCESSFUL — Performs all or most of the skills in an appropriate way — *IS CLEARLY CREDIBLE*	2 – LIMITED — Performs all or most of the skills in a limited way — *HAS LIMITED CREDIBILITY*	1 – SERIOUSLY DEFICIENT — Performs all or most of the skills negatively, if at all — *LACKS CREDIBILITY*
III. Establish and Maintain Instructor Credibility				For example …
Demonstrate…. content expertise	Is extremely well informed about the subject and its applications	Is well informed about the subject and its applications	Is informed about the subject and its applications, but may give vague information, seem tentative, or be tied to notes	Misinforms or confuses the class
acceptable personal conduct acceptable social practices	Displays exemplary interpersonal skills, appropriate to various professional settings	Displays positive interpersonal skills, appropriate to various professional settings	Displays little ability to promote learning through the use of interpersonal skills	Seems extremely nervous or Hesitant
Provide model for professional and interpersonal behavior	Creates an atmosphere of mutual respect and confidence	Creates a positive learning environment		Is highly distracting in behavior or appearance
Demonstrate flexibility in response to learner needs/interests	Demonstrates exceptional open-mindedness and flexibility, and is supportive of the learners	Demonstrates open-mindedness, and flexibility, and is supportive of the learners	Displays self-confidence but makes little effort to establish learner confidence	Makes frequent and/or seriously offensive comments or dismisses learners' views
IV. Manage the Learning Environment	*MANAGES EXCEPTIONALLY WELL*	*MANAGES APPROPRIATELY*	*MANAGES INCONSISTENTLY*	*MANAGES POORLY* — For example…
Involve learners in establishing appropriate level of comfort	Skillfully engages learners in group activities	Involves learners comfortably in group activities	Involves learners in a superficial or limited way	Makes little or no effort to involve learners
Manage … time available for course, group interaction/participation	Effectively adapts instruction to attention while maintaining the group's learning process	Adapts instruction to learners' needs, giving individual attention without seriously interrupting the group's learning process	Displays minimal evidence of Adapting instruction to meet Individual or group needs	Allows a few to dominate the group / Fails to link instruction to learners' needs
Resolve behavior problems	Manages time and activities exceedingly well, ensuring learners' progress toward the stated objectives	Manages time and group activities well, facilitating learners' progress toward the stated goals	Manages time and group poorly / Interactions inconsistently adequately at times, inadequately at other times / Has some difficulty with classroom management (e.g., behavior problems)	Rushes instruction or is tediously slow throughout / Is clearly ineffective in classroom management (e.g., behavior problems)

VIDEOTAPE SCORING GUIDE
Part A -- ibstpi Competencies Assessed on Videotape (continued)

COMPETENCY — Skills assessed on the videotape	4 - OUTSTANDING — Performs all or most of the skills in a highly effective way / COMMUNICATES EXCEPTIONALLY WELL	3 - SUCCESSFUL — Performs all or most of the skills in an appropriate way / COMMUNICATES CLEARLY	2 - LIMITED — Performs all or most of the skills in a limited way / COMMUNICATES INADEQUATELY	1 - SERIOUSLY DEFICIENT — Performs all or most of the skills negatively, if at all / COMMUNICATES POORLY
V. Demonstrate Effective Communication Skills				For example …
Use appropriate verbal and nonverbal language	Has excellent language skills	Has good language skills	Has weak language skills	Lacks basic language skills
Adapt verbal and nonverbal messages to learners' needs	Uses body language and appropriate pauses to extend and enhance communication	Uses body language and appropriate pauses to communicate effectively	Uses body language/pauses in ways that occasionally interfere with communication	Uses body language/pauses that interfere with communication
Use frames of reference familiar to the learners	Effectively relates content to learners' experiences	Appropriately relates content to learners' experiences	Relates content to learners' experiences in a limited way	Fails to link content to learners' experiences
Determine whether learners understand messages	Is constantly aware of how well learners are comprehending	Is generally aware of how well learners are comprehending	Demonstrates limited awareness of how well learners are comprehending	Generally ignores the learners
				Makes inappropriate or offensive comments
VI. Demonstrate Effective Presentation Skills	DISPLAYS EXCELLENT PRESENTATION SKILLS	DISPLAYS COMPETENT PRESENTATION SKILLS	DISPLAYS INADEQUATE PRESENTATION SKILLS	DISPLAYS VERY POOR PRESENTATION SKILLS
Use… the voice effectively, eye contact effectively, gestures, silence, movement posture, space, props effectively	Speaks very clearly in a well-modulated voice, stimulating learner interest	Speaks clearly in a well-modulated voice that helps sustain learner interest	Speaks clearly, but the vocal quality, modulation, or pacing does not adequately help sustain learner interest	For example … Speaks in a voice that adversely affects learner understanding and interest
	Makes frequent eye contact with individual learners	Looks frequently at the class	Looks occasionally at the class (e.g., tied to notes)	Rarely looks at the learners
	Skillfully uses gestures, silence, movement, posture, space, props that support the learning environment	Adequately uses gestures, silence, movement, posture, space, props that support the learning environment	Occasionally uses gestures, silence, movement, posture, space, props that support the learning environment	Hinders the learning environment using inappropriate gestures, silence, movement, posture, space, props
Organize content effectively	Presents instruction in an engaging, coherent, well-organized sequence	Presents instruction in an organized, coherent sequence	Presents instruction in sequence, but is occasionally disorganized or confusing	Presents instruction in a disorganized way
Use anecdotes, stories, analogies, and humor effectively	May use props, humor, and stories that are particularly effective for the class	May use props, stories, etc., that are clearly appropriate for the class	May use props, stories, etc., that are only somewhat useful or relevant	Uses props, stories, etc. in an inappropriate or confusing way

VIDEOTAPE SCORING GUIDE

Part A – ibstpi Competencies Assessed on Videotape (continued)

COMPETENCY — Skills assessed on the videotape	4 – OUTSTANDING — Performs all or most of the skills in a highly effective way. DISPLAYS EXCELLENT QUESTIONING SKILLS	3 – SUCCESSFUL — Performs all or most of the skills in an appropriate way. DISPLAYS COMPETENT QUESTIONING SKILLS	2 – LIMITED — Performs all or most of the skills in a limited way. DISPLAYS LIMITED QUESTIONING SKILLS	1 – SERIOUSLY DEFICIENT — Performs all or most of the skills negatively, if at all. DISPLAYS POOR QUESTIONING SKILLS — For example…
VII. Demonstrate Effective Questioning Skills and Techniques				
Use appropriate question types/levels (e.g., open ended, application, directed, review)	Skillfully asks a variety of questions and implements various questioning techniques to build confidence and promote learning among all the learners	Asks a variety of relevant questions to engage learners and promote learning	Asks few questions	Fails to ask questions
			Asks generally trivial, undirected questions	Asks questions that are unclear or irrelevant
Direct questions appropriately	Skillfully monitors learners' comprehension by directing questions to all learners	Uses directed questions to monitor learners' comprehension		
Use active listening techniques	Listens carefully and attentively to learners	Listens carefully to learners	Does not appear to listen carefully to learners	Pays little or no attention to responses or comments from learners
Repeat, rephrase, restructure Questions	Effectively rephrases/repeats questions, as needed	Clearly rephrases/repeats questions, as needed	Rarely rephrases/repeats questions, when needed	
Provide opportunity/time for learners to state questions, comments, concerns, and respond to questions	Skillfully creates an environment that encourages learners to initiate questions, dialogues, and comments	Adequately creates an environment that encourages learners to initiate questions, dialogues, and comments	Allows questioning, but does not seem to encourage it	Seems to discourage learners from asking questions

COMPETENCY	4 – OUTSTANDING — RESPONDS EFFECTIVELY	3 – SUCCESSFUL — RESPONDS APPROPRIATELY	2 – LIMITED — IS SOMEWHAT RESPONSIVE	1 – SERIOUSLY DEFICIENT — RESPONDS INEFFECTIVELY — For example…
VIII. Respond Appropriately to Learners' Needs for Clarification or Feedback				
Identify learners with clarification and feedback needs	Creates an environment in which the learners confidently seek clarification when needed.	Encourages learners to ask questions when necessary.	Does little to identify those who need help	Gives little or no positive feedback
Determine when and how to respond	Skillfully identifies and effectively responds to learners cues that clarification or feedback is needed	Recognizes indicators that clarification/feedback is needed and responds appropriately	Gives non-specific superficial feedback, responds inappropriately, or rarely determines learners' satisfaction with responses given	Ignores learners' needs
Provide prompt, timely, and specific feedback	Helps learners clarify questions/requests for feedback, and consistently verifies satisfaction with responses given	Is aware of learners' needs, responds to learners' comments/questions, and determines learners' satisfaction with responses given	Does not always listen carefully, or does not always give relevant responses	Gives vague or confusing answers
	Always gives specific, helpful feedback	Consistently gives clear and helpful responses		Discourages learners from asking for help

VIDEOTAPE SCORING GUIDE
Part A – ibstpi Competencies Assessed on Videotape (continued)

COMPETENCY Skills assessed on the videotape	4 – OUTSTANDING Performs all or most of the skills in a highly effective way *MOTIVATES EFFECTIVELY*	3 – SUCCESSFUL Performs all or most of the skills in an appropriate way *MOTIVATES WELL*	2 – LIMITED Performs all or most of the skills in a limited way *MOTIVATES INCONSISTENTLY*	1 – SERIOUSLY DEFICIENT Performs all or most of the skills negatively, if at all *MAKES LITTLE OR NO EFFORT TO MOTIVATE*
IX. Provide Positive Reinforcement and Motivational Incentives				For example …
Match learning outcomes to learner and organizational needs and goals	Skillfully presents this training module's objectives and relates them to the needs of the learner and/or the organization	Clearly presents this training module's objectives and relates them to the needs of the learner and/or the organization	Presents this training module's objectives, but may not communicate their relevance to the needs of the learner and/or the organization	Fails to state this training module's objectives or convey the importance of what is being taught
Use introductory activities to develop learner motivation	Uses relevant, highly motivational activities or information to introduce new topics	Uses relevant, motivational activities or information to introduce new topics	Rarely motivates learners when introducing new topics	Glosses over problems or gives gratuitous praise
Plan/use feedback/reinforcement during instruction	Gives specific, positive feedback to build the learners' confidence	Gives positive feedback to build the learners' confidence	Gives limited positive feedback, usually of a general nature	Rarely gives positive feedback
X. Use Instructional Methods Appropriately	*INSTRUCTS EFFECTIVELY*	*INSTRUCTS ADEQUATELY*	*INSTRUCTS INCONSISTENTLY*	*USES INSTRUCTIONAL METHODS POORLY* For example…
Implement variety of standard instructional methods, (e.g., lecture, demonstration, group or individual activity, discussion)	Skillfully uses a variety of active and passive instructional methods that are highly appropriate for the class (both learners and content) to facilitate achievement of learning outcomes	Uses active and passive instructional methods that are appropriate for the class	Uses methods that are not consistently well suited for the class, (e.g., may lecture too long on a simple topic that is best learned by doing)	Uses only one instructional method (e.g., lecture only) throughout the module
Manage the group dynamics associated with each method	Skillfully encourages, initiates, and maintains a high level of participation among group members	Initiates and maintains an adequate level of participation among group members	Rarely or inconsistently initiates participation among group members	Makes no attempt to initiate group participation
Employ instructional techniques appropriate to methods and situation	Makes smooth transitions, seamlessly adjusting techniques as needed	Makes fairly smooth transitions, adjusting techniques as needed	Makes transitions/adjusts techniques infrequently or in an awkward or confusing way	Uses instructional techniques in ways that impede learning
	Makes relevant, highly effective connections across topics and summarizes key points at well-timed intervals	Makes relevant, clear connections across topics and summarizes appropriately	Makes minimal connections across topics	

VIDEOTAPE SCORING GUIDE
Part B – ibstpi Competencies Assessed Primarily in the Documentation Forms

COMPETENCY Skills assessed on the videotape	4 – OUTSTANDING Performs all or most of the skills in a highly effective way	3 – SUCCESSFUL Performs all or most of the skills in an appropriate way	2 – LIMITED Performs all or most of the skills in a limited way	1 – SERIOUSLY DEFICIENT Performs all or most of the skills negatively, if at all
XI. Use Media Effectively	*USES MEDIA EFFECTIVELY*	*USES MEDIA COMPETENTLY*	*USES MEDIA IN A LIMITED OR INCONSISTENT WAY*	*USES MEDIA POORLY IF AT ALL*
Use media and hardware appropriately. (Media include materials such as, software, printed manuals, flip charts, white boards, overheads, and handouts)	Effectively selects and uses various media to engage learners at well-timed points in learning process	Selects and uses appropriate media to help learners understand particular points	Uses media very little or in ways that do not engage learners or enhance learning	For example... Fails to use media
Troubleshoot minor hardware and other simple problems	Uses media skillfully and efficiently, moving smoothly from one medium to the next	Uses media and equipment well, moving competently from one medium to the next	Uses media/equipment poorly at times, (e.g., gives information that is difficult to see, talks too much to the board, does not show learners where to look)	Uses media and/or hardware in highly distracting ways that disrupt learning
Substitute, add, switch, or create media as required	Is well prepared with alternative activities or media that meet instructional objectives if technical difficulties arise	Handles technical difficulties with ease and has planned alternatives	Is unable to handle technical difficulties smoothly	Is unable to handle technical difficulties
XII. Evaluate Learner Performance	*EVALUATES SKILLFULLY*	*EVALUATES ADEQUATELY*	*EVALUATES INCONSISTENTLY*	*EVALUATES INAPPROPRIATELY, IF AT ALL*
Monitor learner progress during instruction, (e.g., tests, activity sheets, questionnaires, hands-on practice, lab exercises, question and answer discussions)	Effectively assesses learners' progress at well-timed points by using evaluation techniques that are appropriately linked to content and learners' needs	Assesses learners' progress at appropriate opportunities. Uses relevant evaluation techniques, (e.g., introduces a technical skill and then checks to see how well each person can apply it)	Assesses learners' progress inadequately, (e.g., rarely checks progress, monitors only some of the learners, or uses somewhat inappropriate evaluation techniques)	For example... Does not monitor progress
	Effectively evaluates learners' attainment of module objectives, (e.g., interactive discussion that ties module objectives to learners' immediate attainment)	Adequately evaluates learners' attainment of module objectives, (e.g., interactive discussion that ties module objectives to learners' immediate attainment)	Does little to evaluate learners' attainment of module objectives	Asks irrelevant questions
	Monitors individual learners in a supportive way			Makes learners feel unsuccessful

VIDEOTAPE SCORING GUIDE
Part B – ibstpi Competencies Assessed Primarily in the Documentation Forms (continued)

COMPETENCY	4 - OUTSTANDING	3 - SUCCESSFUL	2 - LIMITED	1 - SERIOUSLY DEFICIENT
Skills assessed on the videotape and in the documentation	Performs all or most of the skills in a highly effective way	Performs all or most of the skills in an appropriate way	Performs all or most of the skills in a limited way	Performs all or most of the skills negatively, if at all
I. Analyze Course Materials and Learner Information	The documentation shows that the instructor:	The documentation shows that the instructor:	The documentation shows that the instructor:	The documentation shows that the instructor:
Review materials and audience information and identify areas where adjustments may be needed	has collected and thoughtfully analyzed course-relevant Information about the learners	has collected course-relevant information about the learners	has collected little relevant information about the learners	gives no relevant information about the learners in relation to the course
Make appropriate adjustments to learning materials when needed	has given a clear, well-reasoned explanation of why course adjustments are or are not needed	has explained clearly why course adjustments are or are not needed	has not explained clearly why adjustments are or are not needed	describes adjustments that are clearly inappropriate for the learners or the course
Note: The videotape may (but need not) show instruction being adjusted				Note: If the videotape seriously contradicts information in the documentation, a score of 1 may result
XII. Evaluate Delivery of Instruction	The documentation:	The documentation:	The documentation:	The documentation:
Evaluate the instructional design, as modified during delivery	gives an insightful reflection on how this module did or did not fulfill the instructor's objectives	clearly explains how this module did or did not meet the instructor's objectives	gives little account of how objectives were or were not met and is not contradicted by evidence in the videotape	gives no account of how the module met the instructor's objectives
Evaluate the instructor's performance as it relates to the instructional design and learning objectives	is clearly supported by evidence in the videotape	is supported by evidence in the videotape	gives an extensive account of how objectives were met, but is somewhat contradicted by evidence in the videotape	is seriously contradicted by evidence in the videotape

SCORE REPORTS AND INTERPRETATION

A score report will be provided immediately to all test takers who take the computer-based test. Those submitting a videotape for the performance assessment will be notified of their pass/fail status in the score reports mailed from The Chauncey Group as soon as final scores are received from the scoring judges. A score report also will be provided to all test takers who retake either assessment.

Computer-Based Exam

Each candidate should have some degree of familiarity with the subject matter of each question on the computer-based test. Each question is scored separately, and only correct responses contribute to a candidate's final score. Candidates should choose the best answer for each question. Only one answer choice can be marked for each question. No candidate is expected to obtain a perfect score.

Final scores on the CTT computer-based test are determined by converting the number of questions answered correctly to a scale that ranges from 0 to 1,000. The minimum passing score of 760, which corresponds to the minimum level of achievement that represents mastery, was decided by a panel of judges following the CTT Beta test. The computer-based CTT test forms are equated so that candidates' final scores are comparable across different forms of the CTT examination. Equating means that candidates will not be penalized or at an advantage if the test form they take is harder or easier than a form administered to other candidates.

Performance-Based Exam

The final score on the CTT performance-based examination is computed by totalling the final competency ratings. Each of the 12 competency areas will be rated. The ratings for each competency will be given on a four-point scale, in which a 1 indicates seriously deficient performance and a 4 indicates outstanding performance.

A score of 1 (Seriously Deficient) on any of the 12 competencies being assessed on the videotape or on the documentation will cause an automatic failure for the performance examination.

To pass the performance assessment, two criteria must be met: (1) an averaged total score of at least 36 points must be attained; and (2) a minimum of a 2 must be attained in each individual competency area. As with the computer-based test, the minimum passing score for the performance assessment was set by a panel of judges following the CTT Beta Test. Candidates must pass both assessments to receive CTT certification.

Candidates who fail one or both assessments will receive their final score, the minimum passing score, and diagnostic indicators based on the ibstpi competencies. Using this information, candidates will be able to determine their areas of relative strength and weakness based on the ibstpi competencies. Those who fail either assessment may design their study accordingly and retake that assessment.

COMMENTS OR QUESTIONS

Candidates with comments or questions about test center facilities and/or supervision, examination content, or any other matter related to the examination program should complete the exit evaluation questionnaire on the computer at the test center and/or write to The Chauncey Group at the following address:

Certified Technical Trainer Program
The Chauncey Group International
664 Rosedale Road
Princeton, New Jersey 08540 - 2218

All correspondence must include the candidate's name and address. If the questions or comments concern an examination already taken, the correspondence should include the name of the examination, the date of the examination, the location of the test center, and the candidate's social security number. The Chauncey Group will investigate each complaint and reply within a reasonable length of time. Inquiries about scores and procedures for retesting may also be directed to the above address.

PERFORMANCE VIDEOTAPE CHECKLIST
FOR QUALITY CONTROL

Before mailing the CTT Performance Videotape, please use the Quality Control Measures checklist below. Remember that this is a certification examination and requires serious planning and preparation. The videotape submission should be a demonstration of candidates' instructional practices presented in a 20-minute instructional module. All candidates are strongly advised to review their videotaped performance and critically assess it as thoroughly as they possibly can.

❏ Use a new, never-before-recorded videotape cassette for videotaping the instructional performance.
❏ Videotape several 20-minute instructional modules and select the one that provides the most effective demonstration of the instructional practices.
❏ Candidates should view the videotaped performance chosen as the performance assessment submission before mailing it for official scoring. Using the Videotape Scoring Guide, score the performance. As the videotape is viewed, ask the following questions:

1. Are the required ibstpi competencies clearly evident both audibly and visibly on the videotape?
2. Are the required ibstpi competencies clearly evident in the Videotape Documentation Form?
3. Did you analyze course materials and learner information? How?
4. Did you establish and maintain instructor credibility? How?
5. Did you manage the learning environment? How?
6. Did you demonstrate effective communication skills? How?
7. Did you demonstrate effective presentation skills? How?
8. Did you demonstrate effective questioning skills and techniques? How?
9. Did you respond appropriately to learners' needs for clarification or feedback? How?
10. Did you provide positive reinforcement and motivational incentives? How?
11. Did you use instructional methods appropriately? How?
12. Did you use media effectively? How?
13. Did you evaluate learner performance? How?
14. Did you evaluate the delivery of instruction? How?
15. Does the selected module have a beginning, a middle, and an ending?
16. Are the objectives of the instructional module clearly stated?
17. Is the instruction module organized?
18. Are at least five (5) learners visible in the classroom?
19. Are the learners actively engaged in the lesson?
20. Is the sound quality clear and loud enough?
21. Is there interference on the videotape such as static, noise from cars, radios, or fans?
22. Is there no more than a maximum of one stop in the videotaped performance? (If a second stop has been used, is the documentation of the need clear and complete in the paperwork?)
23. Are any graphics used during the instruction legible?
24. Is the room lighting appropriate?
25. Is everything that you want the scoring judges to consider actually shown on the videotape?

❏ Ask someone else to view the videotape and assess it.
❏ Create at least one backup videotape of the submission. All videotaped submissions become the property of The Chauncey Group International and will not be returned to candidates.
❏ Make copies of all submitted documentation for record keeping purposes.

PERFORMANCE VIDEOTAPE CHECKLIST FOR PERFORMANCE ASSESSMENT SUBMISSION MATERIALS

Before mailing the CTT Performance Videotape, please use the checklist below to ensure that all required items have been completed and submitted. The videotaped performance will not be scored if any item is missing. Failure to provide required items within the required timeframe will result in an automatic failure of the performance assessment and a forfeit of the fee. For convenience, candidates may copy the required forms directly from this handbook.

Did you remember to include?

❑ Videotape

❑ Videotape Performance Submission Form—Form A

❑ Videotape Release Form, signed by all persons shown in the videotape—Form B

❑ Videotape Documentation Form—Form C

❑ Color photo embossed by Prometric test center staff

❑ **Photocopy** of the score report issued to you at the Test Center upon completion of taking the computer-based test (Do not send the original)

❑ Check or money order made payable to The Chauncey Group International for $150.00 to cover examination fee, or

❑ Credit Card Authorization form to cover examination fee

THE CHAUNCEY GROUP INTERNATIONAL

VIDEO PERFORMANCE SUBMISSION
Form A

Certified Technical Trainer Program

Please complete and return this form with the videotape. Please complete these forms and enclose a check for $150.00 made payable to The Chauncey Group International.

Mail to:
Certified Technical Trainer Program
The Chauncey Group International
664 Rosedale Road
Princeton, NJ 08540

Name_____

Address_____

City/State/ZIP_____

Candidate ID or Social Security Number_____

Daytime phone #_____ E-mail _____

Please check the following and complete as applicable.

_____I have passed the computer portion of the examination.

Dates taken: CBT Center: Results:

_____   _____   _____

_____   _____   _____

_____   _____   _____

CANDIDATE INFORMATION QUESTIONNAIRE

Please answer each question by circling the number that most closely describes you or your practice setting or by writing in your answer, as appropriate. Please provide only one response for each question.

1. Which of the following best describes your current position?
   1 Trainer (training staff within an organization)
   2 Trainer (independent contractor)
   3 Instructional Designer
   4 Training Manager/Director

2. What is your specific job title? _____

3. At the present time, do you directly supervise other trainers?
   1 Yes
   2 No

4. What is the name and address of the company for which you work?
   Name of company: _____
   Address of company: _____

   City/State/Zip Code _____
                   City   State   Zip Code

5. Which of the following best describes your highest educational attainment?
   1 High school diploma
   2 Some college / Associates degree (Specify major:)
   3 Bachelors degree (Specify major:) _____
   4 Bachelors degree + some additional credit _____
   5 Masters degree (Specify major:) _____
   6 Masters degree + some additional credit
   7 Doctorate (Specify major:) _____

6. For how many years have you worked as a trainer? _____
                                               Years   Months

THE CHAUNCEY GROUP INTERNATIONAL

Videotape Release Form
Form B

Certified Technical Trainer Program

I hereby grant The Chauncey Group International permission to use for educational and informational purposes the videotape in which I appear as a participant in a class instructed by

_____ on _____.
(Name of the instructor)   (Date)

	Name (printed)	Signature
1.	_____	_____
2.	_____	_____
3.	_____	_____
4.	_____	_____
5.	_____	_____
6.	_____	_____
7.	_____	_____
8.	_____	_____
9.	_____	_____
10.	_____	_____
11.	_____	_____
12.	_____	_____
13.	_____	_____
14.	_____	_____
15.	_____	_____
16.	_____	_____
17.	_____	_____
18.	_____	_____
19.	_____	_____
20.	_____	_____

I hereby grant The Chauncey Group International permission to use for educational and research purposes the videotape in which I appear as a presenter. I verify that all who appear in the videotape have signed this release form.

_____ _____ _____
        (Printed name)   (Signature)   (Date)

THE CHAUNCEY GROUP INTERNATIONAL

Videotape Documentation Form
Form C

Certified Technical Trainer Program

Be sure to answer each question carefully since the scoring judges will review this form with the videotape. Type or print the answers in the space provided; scoring judges will not consider additional pages.

Name_____ Date_____

Candidate ID or Social Security Number_____

Street
Address_____

City/State/ZIP_____

Daytime Phone #_____ E-mail Address_____

General Information about the Presentation
1a. What is the subject of the instructional module?
_____
_____
_____

1b. Check the most appropriate category for the videotape content.

_____	**Business & Management Related Skills**	_____ **Scientific**
_____	**Career Development**	_____ **Software Related**
_____	**Customer Service**	_____ **Team Development**
_____	**Facilitation Services**	_____ **Technological (Non-Software)**
_____	**Human Resources**	_____ **Other** _____
_____	**Leadership**	
_____	**Marketing**	
_____	**Mechanical**	
_____	**Process and Quality Programs**	
_____	**Sales**	

THE CHAUNCEY GROUP INTERNATIONAL

Videotape Documentation Form C   **Page 2 of 3**

3. If this 20–minute segment is part of a longer course, how does it fit into the larger context of the training course? (The response to this question provides evidence related to Competency 1.)

_____
_____
_____
_____

<u>Planning</u>
4. What were your objectives for this module as stated in the videotaped performance? (The response to this question provides evidence related to Competency 1.)

_____
_____
_____
_____
_____
_____
_____

5. What did you do to prepare for training this particular group of learners for this specific taping session? If you adapted the material, explain how you adapted it and why. If you did not need to adapt it, explain why not. (The response to this question provides evidence related to Competency 1.)

_____
_____
_____
_____
_____
_____

6. If you have stopped the tape, indicate the reason for the stop. (See page 22 for the rules about stopping the tape.) Be sure to explain what activities occurred during the time the tape is stopped.

_____
_____
_____
_____
_____

THE CHAUNCEY GROUP INTERNATIONAL

Videotape Documentation Form C   **Page 3 of 3**

<u>**Reflection/Evaluation**</u>

7. To what extent does the videotape demonstrate how well you met your objectives for this module as it relates to **visible** evidence in the videotaped performance? (The response to this question provides evidence related to Competency 13.)

_____
_____
_____
_____
_____
_____
_____

8. How would you describe the success of this module? What activities worked well and why? What activities would you change and why? (The response to this question provides evidence related to Competency 13.)

_____
_____
_____
_____
_____
_____
_____

9. Please provide any additional information you think the scoring judges should know about your performance as it relates specifically to this instructional module, this group of learners, this specific performance, and this Videotape Documentation Form.

_____
_____
_____
_____
_____
_____
_____

The Chauncey Group International

664 Rosedale Road
Princeton, New Jersey 08540
Telephone: 1 (800) 258–4914 Fax: (609) 720–6550
E–mail: cttp@chauncey.com

CTT VIDEOTAPE
SUBMISSION
FORM

CREDIT CARD AUTHORIZATION

Name

Street Address

City, State

Country/Postal Code

Telephone   Area Code: (   )

I hereby authorize payment for the CTT video submission examination fee of $150.00 as indicated below:

❏ Visa   ❏ MasterCard   ❏ American Express   (Please check appropriate box.)

Credit Card Number: _____ Expiration Date _____/_____

                                                                                                  month/year

Cardholder's Signature _____

Please print Cardholder's Name: _____

❏ Please check box if different from above.

Videotapes cannot be processed without payment.

PLEASE MAIL THIS FORM WITH YOUR CTT VIDEOTAPE SUBMISSION

PREPARATION MATERIALS

ibstpi STANDARDS

Instructor Competencies: The Standards, Volume I

To help prepare for the CTT examination, candidates should be thoroughly familiar with the 14 competencies described in instructor competencies: *The Standards, Volume I*, also known as the *ibstpi Standards*. The *ibstpi Standards* were designed for trainers and provide an authoritative listing of competencies considered to be essential for effective training delivery. These standards provide a strong and credible base for developing certification assessments. *Ibstpi's* mission is to promote high standards of professional practice in the areas of training, performance, and instruction.

$17.95 per copy (plus shipping and handling)

Instructor Competencies: The Standards, Volume II

Volume I addresses four of the seven uses of the ibstpi Standards. Volume II addresses the remaining three uses making a unique contribution to their development of instructor skills. It allows more detail and precision in the development of evaluation instruments, in the design or selection of instructor training courses and programs, and in the development of job aids and other tools to assist instructors in carrying out their assignments. *Volume II* deals more extensively with the assessment of instructor competence against all 14 competencies. Three levels are defined: (a) Level One offers an overall assessment of instructor performance; (b) Level Two provides a detailed assessment of performance for use in evaluating specific aspects of an instructor's performance; and (c) Level Three provides a diagnostic analysis that assists in pinpointing specific skill and knowledge failures within individual competencies and performances. In addition, *Volume II* provides guidelines for constructing evaluation instruments and for providing feedback to instructors on their performance.

$25.95 per copy (plus shipping and handling)

CREATING A SUCCESSFUL VIDEOTAPE FOR THE CTT PERFORMANCE EXAMINATION

This is a videotaped (VHS only) presentation on how to prepare a successful videotape submission for the CTT performance-assessment examination. The tape illustrates the variety of ways trainers have successfully met the standards for certification. The examples shown were selected from successful submissions by trainers seeking certification and include commentary by a narrator describing the competency being demonstrated. The tape also includes several negative sequences to illustrate the kinds of techniques that have not helped trainers earn CTT certification.

$29.95 per copy (plus shipping and handling)

Call (800) 258-4914 to order.
Or use the order form on the reverse side.

The Chauncey Group International

664 Rosedale Road
Princeton, New Jersey 08540
Telephone: 1-800-258-4914 Fax: (609) 720-6550
E-mail: cttp@chauncey.com

**PREPARATION
MATERIALS
ORDER FORM**

Name _____

Street Address _____

City, State _____

Country, Postal Code _____

Telephone   Area Code (   )

DESCRIPTION	UNIT PRICE	TOTAL
Ibstpi Standards, Volume I, Instructor's Edition	$17.95 US	
Ibstpi Standards, Volume II, Training Manager's Edition	$25.95 US	
Creating a Successful Videotape- NTSC Format (US Format)	$29.95 US	
Creating a Successful Videotape- PAL Format (International Format)	$39.95 US	
Domestic Shipping & Handling	$5.00 <u>per item*</u> <u>$1.50 for each additional item</u>	
International Shipping & Handling	Varies	
Other options** ❒ UPS ❒ FEDEX	Varies	

***Only domestic shipping via US Mail is $5.00 per Item.
All other shipping requirements will be charged extra
to cover additional expense.**

****All orders require a 3-day processing prior to being
shipped**

6% Sales Tax **(NJ Residents Only)**	
TOTAL	

Payment methods: ❒ Check or money order made payable to **The Chauncey Group International.**
Please check appropriate box.   ❒ Visa   ❒ MasterCard   ❒ American Express

Credit Card Number: _____   Expiration Date: _____ / _____
                                                  mo.   yr.

Cardholder's Name (please print)
❒ Please check box if different from above

Cardholder's Signature

You may place your order by phone, fax, mail or e-mail. (See address and contact at the top of this form).

Orders cannot be processed without payment. Returns will not be accepted!

ANSWERS AND RATIONALES

Question 1

The correct answer is **"c"**.

Rationale: Option "c" involves the participants, giving them the opportunity to make the connection between the skill and its application, which contributes to motivation to learn the skill. Secondly participants can relate to the particulars of the situation and how the content applies. Options "a" and "d" put the instructor in the role of content application expert"—a dangerous position. Option "b" is somewhat condescending because it should be assumed that the learner has already tried to apply the content to the situation and cannot see the connection.

Question 2

The correct answer is **"a"**.

Rationale: Option "a" offers a learner-centered approach to a task that is often quickly covered by the instructor. It also permits the instructor to confirm that learning has occurred. Option "b" is incorrect because whether instructor bias occurs or not is not relevant to the goal. Options "c" and "d" are wrong because of the unlikely response. It should be noted that the instructor needs to guide the summary process but should not be concerned if minor points are included as well as major points. If the instructor manages the class effectively, control should not be lost.

Question 3

The correct answer is **"a"**.

Rationale: Option "a" relates to the guidelines about making eye contact that are similar to a one–on–one discussion. In Western cultures, direct eye contact gives the learner the feeling he or she is important and involved in the discussion. Option "b" is wrong because it excludes some members of the class. Option "c" and "d" are wrong because limiting eye contact or glancing around too frequently can give the learner feelings of being unimportant and/or disconnected from the process, neither of which puts the learner at ease.

Question 4

The correct answer is **"b"**.

Rationale: Option "b" has the greatest reliability that the ideas will be easily retrievable later in the lesson. It might also offer a way to get a learner involved in a way that might be less threatening than leading a discussion or some other direct activity. Option "a" is incorrect because it will take more time and will have less guidance from the facilitator. Option "c" is incorrect because using an overhead projector is more difficult to reference later on. Option "d" leaves the instructor with nothing to reference that is common to the entire group (learners all have their own lists, and all will be different).

FIVE-STEP PROCESS TO CERTIFICATION

1. Prepare for the two-part examination. Be sure to carefully read this *CTT Candidate Handbook of Information.* The examination is based on the competencies described in the *ibstpi Standards,* which can be ordered directly from The Chauncey Group at 800-258-4914, along with the videotape, *"Creating a Successful Videotape for the CTT Performance Assessment."* (See page 45.)

2. Register for the computer-based test by calling Prometric at 800-727-8490. (See page 12.) Or you may visit www.2test.com to register online.

   For on-line registration: 1. Select the certification from the drop-down menu and click "Go". 2. Enter your User Name and Password (PIN). If this is your first time registering for a test with Prometric, you will need to complete the new user form. 3. Click "Submit Login" to continue scheduling for your specific exam.

3. Take the computer-based test on the scheduled day. Remember to bring a recent color photograph and have it reviewed and embossed by Prometric test center staff. This embossed photo **must** accompany submission of the candidate's performance videotape.

4. Plan the performance videotape for an upcoming training session where you are delivering instruction. (See pages 19 to 23.)

5. Submit the completed performance videotape so The Chauncey Group receives it within **three months** of passing the computer-based test. If your videotape is not submitted within the required three-month period, your computer-based test score will no longer be valid. If extenuating circumstances prohibit you from meeting this time requirement, please e-mail your request for an extension to the CTT program at cttp@chauncey.com (providing complete candidate and testing information).

   Do not forget to enclose the following with your videotape submission:
   - the Prometric-embossed photo
   - a photocopy of the passing score report issued to you at the test center
   - the Videotape Submission Forms (pages 37, 39, and 40 to 42 of the candidate handbook)

   The Videotape Submission Forms are an essential part of the scoring process and successful completion of these forms will impact a candidate's final score.

   Upon successful completion of the CTT computer-based exam and performance assessment, candidates receive an official certificate, a lapel pin, and the CTT Logo mechanicals.

   If you have any questions, please contact the CTT Program staff at 800-258-4914, or e-mail us at cttp@chauncey.com.

Index

INDEX

ABOUT THE AUTHORS

Terrance Keys holds a Master's of Education degree from the University of Massachusetts at Amherst. Full time, Terrance is the Associate Director of Instructional Technologies at Monroe Community College. In this role, he oversees the Instructional Technologies department, which is responsible for all aspects of faculty and staff training, instructional design, distance learning support, instructional technologies support, the student computer learning center and general classroom support. Throughout his career, Terrance has taught in corporate, academic (high school and college,) and community environments. He has worked as an adjunct instructor at Monroe Community College in the Office and Computer Technology department for the last five years and currently holds the rank of Assistant Professor. The topics of instruction throughout his career have included computer applications, mathematics and swimming. Terrance has written numerous training documents for the college training program as well as computer training manuals used for corporate training programs. He has presented on a variety of training related topics at local, statewide and national conferences.

Andrew Zeff is Vice President of ZTAC, Inc. (Zeff Training And Consulting), a Microsoft Certified Technical Education Center. He is a Microsoft Certified Trainer, a Certified Technical Trainer, Certified Netware Instructor, and has over 12 years experience as a network engineer. He developed and teaches ZTAC's Train-the-Trainer Instructional Techniques Workshop throughout the United States and has taught Microsoft BackOffice courseware for 5 years. He is also a recognized CompTIA subject matter expert. Visit his web site at http://www.ztac.com.